Governing Virtual Wonderland

"Would you tell me, please, which way I ought to go from here?"
"That depends a good deal on where you want to get to," said the Cat.
"I don't much care where—" said Alice.
"Then it doesn't matter which way you go," said the Cat.
"—so long as I get SOMEWHERE," Alice added.
"Oh, you're sure to do that," said the Cat, "if you only walk long enough."

Alice in Wonderland, Lewis Carroll

Governing Virtual Wonderland

Power, Rules, and Rebellion in the Metaverse

Edited by

Mark Findlay

Distinguished Fellow, British Institute of International and Comparative Law, and Honorary Professorial Fellow, Law School, University of Edinburgh, UK

Noha Lea Halim

Doctoral Candidate, Department of Governance, Technical University of Munich, Germany

Sofie Schönborn

Doctoral Candidate, Department of Governance, Technical University of Munich, Germany

EE Edward Elgar PUBLISHING

Cheltenham, UK • Northampton, MA, USA

Published by

Edward Elgar Publishing Limited
The Lypiatts
15 Lansdown Road
Cheltenham
Glos GL50 2JA
UK

Edward Elgar Publishing, Inc.
William Pratt House
9 Dewey Court
Northampton
Massachusetts 01060
USA

Authorised representative in the EU for GPSR queries only: Easy Access System Europe – Mustamäe tee 50, 10621 Tallinn, Estonia, gpsr.requests@easproject.com

A catalogue record for this book is available from the British Library

Library of Congress Control Number: 2026934107

This book is available electronically in the **Elgar**online
Law subject collection
https://doi.org/10.4337/9781035362080

MIX
Paper | Supporting responsible forestry
FSC® C014540
www.fsc.org

ISBN 978 1 0353 6207 3 (cased)
ISBN 978 1 0353 6208 0 (eBook)
ISBN 978 1 0494 0299 4 (ePub)

Printed and bound in the UK by Short Run Press Ltd, Exeter EX2 7LW

Contents

List of contributors

Auxane Boch (she/her) is a cyberpsychologist and research associate at the Institute for Ethics in Artificial Intelligence (Technical University of Munich), where she spends her days thinking hard about the ethical and psychological impacts of technologies that talk back—such as social robots, video games, and the avatars we build to become ourselves. As an ambassador for Women in AI Germany and Women in Games, she's committed to digital futures where care, inclusion, and critical thinking are part of the main quest, not just side content. In her work with Bethany Thomas, she follows Alice through the looking-glass into a gaming adventure—first as a personal odyssey of immersion and identity, then as a deeper reflection on resistance, representation, and what it will take to build virtual worlds that don't just include us, but truly empower us all.

Ivan Daldoss combines an academic career in Legal Philosophy with a lasting passion for music. Trained in classical piano from 1991 to 2000, he later took up guitar and songwriting, studying jazz piano, composition, and arrangement with Maestro Stefano Raffaelli (2009–2018). His debut solo album, *Marte e Nettuno* (2015), fuses his Italian pop songs with jazz, Latin, and rock nuances. Graduating *cum laude* in Law (University of Trento, 2018), he earned an International Master's in Sociology of Law (IISL, 2019) and a PhD in Philosophy of Law (*cum laude*, Doctor Europaeus, Padua, 2023). Active as an editor, conference speaker, and author of numerous scholarly works, he became a Professor at the University of Granada in 2024, also serving abroad as a Visiting Professor. Alongside teaching Legal Theory and Human Rights, he continues his musical pursuits, most recently as pianist and arranger for Persefone's 2025 EP *Dancing Through the Seasons*.

Jonathan Fiene is an engineer and educator with a background in robotics, haptics, and mechatronics. After earning his PhD from Stanford University, he held academic positions at the University of Pennsylvania and the Max Planck Institute for Intelligent Systems. He has built scientific labs and startup teams and has experience ranging from high-precision control systems to wearable haptic devices. As the founder and CTO of Bergsonne Labs, he is leading the development of modular hardware systems that bring digital analytics closer to the physical world. Fiene's interest in the Metaverse is both practical and conceptual. He envisions it as a space where touch can counterbalance abstraction and reintroduce feedback, friction, and meaningful presence into virtual environments.

Mark Findlay thinks and writes about life experiences in a digital universe. His new book *Governing the Metaverse: Law, order and freedom in digital space* interrogates the choice between liberty and enclosure when we look to govern personhood in the virtual. As the junior in this editorial team, he has learned a great deal from the fresh ideas offered by our contributors, and hopes they start many conversations about empowerment and inclusion.

Noha Lea Halim is a doctoral candidate and research assistant at the Professorship for Governance, Public Policy & Innovative Technologies at the TUM School of Social Science and Technology. She was a visiting researcher and teaching fellow at Harvard Law School. Her research interests lie in AI governance and governance innovation. She is interested in how AI accelerates innovation in governance, innovation in regulatory approaches, institutional roles, and the conceptual foundations of how we govern technological systems. Noha's interest in virtual worlds is conceptual and exploratory. She is interested in the governance challenges posed by immersive technologies as a new technological frontier. For her, these environments (re-)pose questions around power, accountability, and personhood, inviting us to revisit past governance lessons through a new lens. She envisions virtual spaces as an incentive for us to renegotiate taken-for-granted concepts and reflect more deeply on the systems we inhabit, both immersive and offline.

Narges Keshavarz Bahadori holds two Bachelor's and two Master's degrees in law (International Trade and Economy and International and Comparative Law) from the University of Tehran and the University of Lausanne, conducted within two different legal jurisdictions: Iran and Switzerland. Passionate about future-facing technologies, she is currently undertaking her PhD research at the University of Lausanne on a controversial topic for which it is not an easy task to attribute a jurisdiction: Blockchains! More specifically, she is studying blockchain-based disputes and blockchain-based dispute resolution mechanisms. Selected as a contributor to this volume for her forward-thinking approach, Narges seeks to synthesize legal theories with real-world tech shifts and to make her own voice to be heard in the debates around law and the Metaverse.

Daniel Matter is a doctoral candidate at the Chair of Computational Social Science at the Technical University of Munich. He studied Mathematics, Computer Science, and Philosophy in Munich and Singapore, and now works at the intersection of machine learning and the social sciences. His research focuses on the analysis of large-scale data sets, with particular interests in complex networks, large language models, and the dynamics of democracy in the digital age. He is especially curious about how algorithmic infrastructures—recommender systems, generative models, and the invisible architectures of platforms—shape what we see, say, and believe. Lately, he has come to suspect that Foucault would have had a field day on TikTok. When not tracing the fault lines of digital power, he reads literary classics, scrolls through the algorithmic sublime, and wonders what kind of world we're training next.

Philipp Müller works at the intersection of digital governance, security, and technological change. He is VP Public at DriveLock SE and a fellow at the Technical University of Munich's think tank. His previous roles at Amazon Web Services, Gartner, and DXC Technology reflect his longstanding focus on the implementation of global technologies in complex political and organizational environments. With a background in philosophy and political science, as well as a doctorate from LMU Munich, he is particularly interested in the human experience of digital technologies. His interest in the Metaverse stems from his broader concerns about embodiment, trust, and the risks of disembodied design. At Bergsonne Labs, he explores how tactile interfaces can reconnect digital innovation with the human condition.

Sofie Schönborn is a doctoral candidate, Research Associate, and Lecturer at the Chair of Public Policy, Governance, and Innovative Technology at the Technical University of Munich (TUM). Her research sits at the intersection of digital governance and infrastructure studies, with a particular focus on how cloud computing and emerging technologies shape evolving debates on digital sovereignty. As initiator and co-lead of the Immersive Realities Group at TUM Think Tank, Sofie has built a space for exchange, experimentation, and shared curiosity, bringing together researchers, practitioners, and policy voices, many of whom are reflected in this volume. For her, immersive environments are not simply new technical frontiers, but living laboratories where questions of power, participation, and public value are constantly negotiated as digital and physical realities converge.

Somya Singh is an LL.M. candidate at the University of Lausanne and a *summa cum laude* law graduate of the Campus Law Centre, New Delhi. She views the frontier of law as a living, evolving organism, responsive to new challenges.

Her grasp of Indian, Swiss, and EU laws provides her with a bird's-eye view of global legal dynamics. It was this multifaceted grounding that compelled Somya to confront the Metaverse's legal frontier, an Alice in Wonderland-like dimension where age-old statutes falter and fresh doctrine must be forged at the speed of code, prompting the question: Can any statute drafted for brick-and-mortar realms withstand a world built on blockchain? Her chapter, 'Virtual Jurisdictions and Data Protection in Cross-Border Arbitration: A Comparative Analysis of India and Switzerland in the Age of the Metaverse', explores the Metaverse's tangled skein of data flows to safeguard individual dignity and re-envisage cross-border arbitration for this decentralised era with speed and sagacity.

Nikola Szirota (she/her) is a full-time raging feminist, MSc student, and science communicator from Vienna, Austria. Building on her education as a sociologist, socio-ecological economist, and political scientist, she navigates technologies between societal hopes and economic dependencies. With a soft approach to living together, she radically wants to implement empathy and consciousness for power dynamics. As a workshop moderator for finance education, she accompanies teenagers in their journey to grasp the complexities of the state they are living in. Next to that, her aspiration for a more equitable world for all influenced her to critically analyse the fictions of the Metaverse. In a time of technological futures built by the God complex of tech bros, she wants to join in with intersectional feminist perspectives.

Bethany Rhea Thomas (she/her) is a PhD researcher at Edge Hill University, where she explores the intersections of gender, identity, and gaming. As a lifelong gamer, Beth's academic journey began with a controller in hand and a critical lens on how gender unfolds in digital spaces. Her research focuses on unpacking gamer identity and the intersection with gender, exploring the construction of gamer identity for women gamers. As a Women in Games ambassador and a member of the BPS Cyberpsychology Committee, she is committed to amplifying underrepresented voices in digital spaces. Drawn to the Metaverse for its promise (and peril) as a site of identity exploration, she views these immersive spaces as modern mirrors and battlegrounds—capable of reflecting, distorting, or reimagining who we are.

Darius Torabi is a doctoral candidate and MEXT Scholar (Japanese Government) in the International Programs in Law at Kyushu University, where he explores the conceptual boundaries of traditional legal doctrines. Formerly a Research Associate at Freshfields and a Criminal Law Lecturer at EBS University, he now conducts empirical experiments to examine how humans attribute moral status and personhood to non-human entities. Specializing in criminal law, criminology, and legal philosophy, with legal education spanning Germany, Switzerland, and Japan, his research focuses on how legal frameworks can account for deviant behavior by agents that are neither human nor fully under human control—such as autonomous machines, virtual personas, or intelligent code. His interest in the metaverse arises from a deeper inquiry: as 'reality' increasingly unfolds across virtual stages, how can we confront the law's anthropocentric assumptions and rethink the architecture of justice for entities coded into being rather than born into life?

David Torabi is a doctoral candidate in the International Programs in Law at Kyushu University and a recipient of the Japanese Government (MEXT) Scholarship. He studied philosophy and law in Germany and is a member of the German–Japanese Lawyers' Association. David's doctoral research focuses on the evolving legal architectures of the metaverse. Drawn to Alice in Wonderland as both metaphor and method, he is intrigued by how virtual worlds unsettle the boundaries of our socio-legal fabric, offering a rare chance to reimagine law and governance beyond the constraints of the physical world. In parallel with his doctoral research, David is conducting empirical studies on human–robot interaction using augmented reality devices at the Institute for Advanced Study (Kyushu University). Before entering academia, he worked as a Graduate Research Associate at the global law firm Allen & Overy (now A&O Shearman).

Konstantinos Tsakiliotis is an attorney-at-law specializing in intellectual property and IT law with a focus on patent litigation. He studied Law at the Humboldt University in Berlin and Science & Technology Studies at the Technical University of Munich. He was drawn to the Metaverse phenomenon by a curiosity for the legal aftershocks of so-called *technological bubbles*—emerging phenomena like the Metaverse that oscillate between hype, speculative investment, and alternative governance models. It was during a seminar with Professor Mark Findlay at TUM that Konstantinos began critically examining the legal fiction of personhood in AI, the performativity of innovation systems, and the blurred frontier between law and code. For him, the Governance of the Metaverse is a case study in how normative systems endeavor to imagine, normalize, and sometimes hallucinate the (digital) future.

Acknowledgements

This journey would not have been the same without the support of the Immersive Realities Working Group at the TUM Think Tank. As both a resonance board and an incubator, the community played a vital role in shaping many of the ideas explored in this collection. Several contributors to this volume are proud members of this group.

We are especially grateful to the TUM Think Tank for providing the space, infrastructure, and spirit of interdisciplinary collaboration. As a platform for experimentation and exchange, particularly among early-career researchers, it has played a formative role in fostering the community vital to making this book come to life.

Finally, we want to extend our gratitude to our mentor, supervisor, and friend Urs Gasser, who created the space in which many of us first met, thought together, and began to imagine what this project could become.

1. Introduction

Noha Lea Halim and Sofie Schönborn

DOWN THE DIGITAL RABBIT HOLE

Just as Alice tumbled down a rabbit hole into the bewildering world of Wonderland, today's young voices are diving into the metaverse, a digital realm where reality bends and familiar rules are inverted. In this virtual landscape, identities shift, and physical laws do not have to apply, offering a new canvas for ideas, imaginations, and societal reordering.

> [W]hen the Rabbit actually took a watch out of its waistcoat-pocket, and looked at it, and then hurried on, Alice started to her feet, for it flashed across her mind that she had never before seen a rabbit with either a waistcoat-pocket, or a watch to take out of it, and burning with curiosity, she ran across the field after it, and fortunately was just in time to see it pop down a large rabbit-hole under the hedge. In another moment down went Alice after it, never once considering how in the world she was to get out again. The rabbit-hole went straight on like a tunnel for some way, and then dipped suddenly down, so suddenly that Alice had not a moment to think about stopping herself before she found herself falling down a very deep well.[1]

Guided by an insatiable curiosity akin to Alice's, many of us have embarked on explorations into the digital wonders of the metaverse. This book emerges from such explorations. It brings together contributions from young and novel perspectives engaging with the metaverse. Exploring virtual worlds from different motivations and angles, these contributions revolve around key ideas of *identity and representation*, *community and participation*, *power and platform design*, and *governance and futures*. Rather than prescribing answers, this volume can be considered food for thought, inviting readers to grapple with the fluidity of personhood and governance in virtual worlds.

As the contributions in this volume illustrate, even casual or playful engagements with virtual worlds can give rise to deeper reflections on who we are and how we relate to others in digital spaces. These reflections show us that new understandings of identity and representations of personhood can emerge from the most ordinary motivations for entering the metaverse, like gaming or connecting on specific platforms. Yet, these are not merely recreational outcomes that incidentally touch on selfhood, play and interaction often centre on experimenting with identity, navigating digital communities, and engaging in forms of self that may be less accessible in physical space. The technological gateways to these spaces are constatly evolving, and future devices likely will deepen the entangelement of realspace and virtual worlds. Future advancements may introduce even more immersive experiences, novel devices, or advanced technologies, further entwining the digital with the physical reality. For Alice, the rabbit hole marked the beginning of her journey. For today's metaverse explorers, the portal is technological. Both invite moments of confusion and instability, but also the possibility of experiences not previously imagined.

For many young people, who often spend substantial amounts of their time in virtual environments, navigating between real and virtual spaces has become routine. They are not typically the architects of these worlds in a technical sense. Instead, their usage patterns, social interactions, and cultural productions nonetheless shape how virtual spaces are experienced, inhabited, and imagined. Frequent transitions equip them to critically assess, discuss, and influence these emerging spaces. Furthermore, they embody traits reminiscent of Alice: a readiness to transcend physical confines, to challenge and redefine identities, and to actively engage in the unfolding narrative of new realms.

As technologies continue to develop and everyday life becomes increasingly mediated by digital platforms, what is at stake goes beyond technological infrastructure or interface. It touches on the kinds of realities being constructed, realities shaped not only by code, but by imagination, narrative, and the values embedded in the stories we tell about life in these virtual spaces. The metaverse is not just a technical project, but a cultural and societal one, where presence, power, and personhood are continually reimagined because it is a lived space. By living something, people continously infer new meaning. For instance, challenging conventional understandings of property in the digital world (as was the case in Wonderland) also challenges traditional notions of ownership, possession, and wealth. Alternative stories about how we live, work, and value our existence might prompt us to imagine a new social order wherein virtual properties comprising data and images, not bricks and mortar, can be infinitely replicated and utilised without the constraints of physical scarcity.

This ongoing transformation lets us envision how new digital worlds can reshape our social and market arrangements. They make unprecedented possibilities available to us and generate the need for innovative forms of governance to ensure a safe and liberating form of social ordering.

These reimaged realities are the beginning of this collection, not with governance as a predefined concern, but with stories. Stories told by *young contributors* navigating the metaverse not as policymakers or technologists, but as participants and observers of emerging worlds. Their reflections focus on how identity is shaped, how presence is felt, and how personhood is performed when the lines between physical and digital blur. Yet inevitably, these questions lead to others: who decides what is possible, acceptable, or fair in these evolving spaces?

The complexities young people describe from lived experience call governance into being; it does not arrive preformed. Their experiences surface implicit architectures of power, design choices that govern without being named, and values encoded in platforms that shape their digital selves. Through the Alice in Wonderland metaphor, and critical engagement with digital life, young contributors claim agency over the narratives, structures, and systems shaping their virtual worlds. Drawing on Alice's journey, governance in the metaverse is seen as a dynamic, often contested, space of negotiation where meaning, authority, and identity are constantly redefined by those who dare to speak sense amid the nonsense.

Governance here is not an endpoint but a horizon; it is a way of asking what kinds of rules, relationships, and responsibilities are emerging, and how they might be reimagined. Taking young voices seriously means recognising them not only as subjects of governance, but as contributors to its redesign. In worlds that are still unfolding, their perspectives may offer the clearest view of what governance ought to be.

Virtual worlds discussed in this book are technologically constructed; however, the key focus lies on their being socially inhabited. Across the contributions in this collection, virtual worlds are perceived as environments charged with meaning, shaped by contributors' expectations, interactions, and shared norms. What causes them to be perceived as "worlds" is, of course, technical sophistication – but even more so, engagement, the presence of others and the sense of continuity and meaning that become attached to it. Many contributors continuously return to this idea. Often, virtual experiences might start out as technical products or platforms but ultimately turn into social spaces with their own customs, power dynamics, and informal rules. They are understood as becoming virtual worlds because they are lived and living spaces. Virtual worlds can shape people's social and personal realities and this, in turn, shapes later discussions of property, risk, and participation. Treating the metaverse as a social reality in this book means taking its implications seriously, and doing so also in the offline worlds; for example, those originating from its design and use. The metaverse does not exist completely separately from the physical world, and vice versa.

A similar perspective is embedded in this selection on personhood. Personhood is not simply taken from the offline world but reimagined. In this book, contributors engage with questions around how digital environments might complicate traditional understandings of individuality, identity, and self. In virtual worlds, it might not only be about understanding oneself, but about the possibilities for who you could become. Avatars, usernames, and profiles are seen as more than just expressions but as experiments in personhood, tools for testing boundaries, and instruments of recognition and belonging.

Personhood in virtual worlds is understood not to dissolve the self but to multiply expressions of it. Further, it can be a way to challenge traditional legal and philosophical understandings through reimagination. Some contributors take up the idea that young users move fluently between different identities, personas, and communities online, and adapt not because they want all worlds to look alike but because they seek change in personhood and the opportunities that come with it. This adaptability points to a different kind of personhood: one that is relational, performative, and situated in context. This reflects a broader theme, a more fluid and participatory understanding of how personhood might be seen. Recognising this is not only a conceptual point in this collection but also has implications for the way in which questions of rights, recognition, and governance in the metaverse were approached. This understanding of personhood sets one of the core topics of the book, which draws on metaphor to navigate the complexities of identity, governance, and digital life. In what follows, the Alice in Wonderland metaphor becomes both a narrative device and a conceptual lens through which these young voices explore and reimagine life in the metaverse.

IMAGINING THE METAVERSE

Like "Alice in Wonderland", this collection is a multi-dimensional metaphor. In essence, we introduce key imaginings about the metaverse from *young thinkers* who have a broad and lived experience of many digital universes, and for whom the transit between realspace and virtual social spaces is as regular as it is seamless. What binds these contributions are concerns for how identity and personhood will be negotiated in the metaverse and the place of innovative governance forms for ensuring safe and liberating social ordering.

> Alice took up the fan and gloves, and, as the hall was very hot, she kept fanning herself all the time she went on talking: 'Dear, dear! How queer everything is to-day! And yesterday things went on just as usual. I wonder if I've been changed in the night? Let me think: was I the same when I got up this morning? I almost think I can remember feeling a little different. But if I'm not the same, the next question is, Who in the world am I? Ah, that's the great puzzle!'[2]

This early moment of self-reflection in Wonderland captures a recurring concern across metaverse experiences: the discrepancy between continuity and change, and the difficulty of anchoring identity when social and spatial coordinates are in flux.

Alice's adventures in Wonderland have many meanings, including the essential search for identity as she shakes off the old and struggles with the new. We chose this dreamscape as our driving metaphor for exploring governance in the metaverse because it reveals the vast possibilities, challenges, and conundrums that await those who travel down the rabbit hole and into a digital universe. The metaphor is not just a narrative ornament but a conceptual device. It frames the metaverse as an environment of interpretive instability where identity, power, and logic are in flux, and invites us to consider what forms of governance could meaningfully operate within such conditions.

> Down, down, down. Would the fall never come to an end! 'I wonder how many miles I've fallen by this time?' she said aloud. 'I must be getting somewhere near the center of the earth. Let me see: that would be four thousand miles down, I think—' (for, you see, Alice had learnt several things of this sort in her lessons in the schoolroom, and though this was not a very good opportunity for showing off her knowledge, as there was no one to listen to her, still it was good practice to say it over) '—yes, that's about the right distance—but then I wonder what Latitude or Longitude I've got to?' (Alice had no idea what Latitude was, or Longitude either, but thought they were nice grand words to say.)[3]

The story is about much more than the often nightmarish encounters of a young mind in a realm of topsy-turvy fantasy. Analogous to lived experiences in the metaverse, Alice's adventures bring her up against profound questions about the adequacy of transplanting realspace thinking into novel social spaces and unfamiliar encounters in virtual environments. Logic, with which we are familiar, may not hold in a digital universe, and the expectations around valuing social engagement may be new and transforming. In such settings, governance projects require engaging not only with new languages but also with alternative paradigms for communicating essential human arrangements. Governance of Wonderland is an exercise in ordering lived experiences without conventional boundaries or accepted definitions.

> 'What sort of people live about here?'
>
> 'In that direction,' the Cat said, waving its right paw round, 'lives a Hatter: and in that direction,' waving the other paw, 'lives a March Hare. Visit either you like: they're both mad.'
>
> 'But I don't want to go among mad people,' Alice remarked.
>
> 'Oh, you can't help that,' said the Cat: 'we're all mad here. I'm mad. You're mad.'
>
> 'How do you know I'm mad?' said Alice.
>
> 'You must be,' said the Cat, 'or you wouldn't have come here.'

> Alice didn't think that proved it at all; however, she went on, 'And how do you know that you're mad?'
>
> 'To begin with,' said the Cat, 'a dog's not mad. You grant that?'
>
> 'I suppose so,' said Alice.
>
> 'Well, then,' the Cat went on, 'you see, a dog growls when it's angry, and wags its tail when it's pleased. Now I growl when I'm pleased, and wag my tail when I'm angry. Therefore I'm mad.'
>
> 'I call it purring, not growling,' said Alice.[4]

This iconic exchange illustrates the difficulty of applying rational expectations or stable categories to systems in which logic is inverted and norms are not shared, a key challenge for governance in internationally connected digital spaces. The questions arise of how to reimagine, who reimagines, and what is reimagined. Connecting these conjectures to thoughts on governance, agency becomes a central but contested theme.

Alice's Adventures in Wonderland is about Alice's agency and personhood constantly being challenged and reshaped. However, Alice is the centre of Wonderland, and as such, it should never be forgotten that the virtual depends on the imagination and interpretation of humans. Users in today's digital environments navigate systems built and governed by others. Agency here is real, but it is constrained by platform design and data economies.

Wonderland is occurring in Alice's head – in her imagination – and as such, she is her own agent and the creator of the domain in which her personhood is in flux. Throughout her journey, she encounters situations where her choices seem bizarre or illogical, and yet, she must navigate these to move forward. To understand agency in the metaverse, then, is to consider both the interpretive creativity of the user and the structural power of the systems they traverse.

Alice's decisions, from following the White Rabbit to taking (or disputing) advice from various characters, highlight her ability to act as her own person despite environments of uncertainty. This speaks not to total autonomy, but to the forms of situated judgement and moral experimentation that governance must learn to accommodate in fluid digital spaces.

This reflects a unique form of agency that is shaped by the rules of a nonsensical world. Alice is impacted by Wonderland, but also shapes its vitality. In this, we glimpse a paradox of agency that is not resolved but explored in the contributions to follow: how personhood is constructed not outside governance, but through experiences of instability, negotiation, and often contradiction. These reflections point to the importance of governance approaches that are not only technically functional but epistemically open and able to accommodate uncertainty, dissent, and multiple ways of knowing. It is precisely this kind of grounded, exploratory perspective that young voices in this collection bring to the table, offering insights from lived digital experience.

YOUNG VOICES

Why highlight *young voices* when thinking about identity, experience, and governance in the metaverse? The rationale is not demographic, but epistemic. These contributions emerge from individuals who bring fresh, unencumbered perspectives shaped by deep immersion in digital environments, many of which are insufficiently recognised by more established and compromised interpretations. In focusing on *voices*, we are encouraging a conversation between these thinkers and their audience, perhaps of a similar demographic, speaking about issues that they see as relevant in the formulation of virtual identities and communities, and seeking out safe and trusted spaces in which to share life experiences. In this way, the Alice metaphor is a platform from which to generate and reflect on dialogue in the same way that Alice so often stood outside herself and wondered.

In established systems of knowledge production, voice is often tied to experience understood in conventional terms, publication records, institutional roles, or disciplinary status. In the context of emerging technologies and digital life-worlds, such measures can obscure other forms of expertise. *Young voices*, as understood here, are defined less by age and more by attitude: openness to new questions, proximity to lived digital experience, and the capacity to unsettle inherited norms.

This collection emphasizes contributions that are "young" in this sense. They are marked not by naivety but by a willingness to see differently, to resist the premature closure of categories, and to reimagine core governance concepts such as identity, representation, and participation. In digital environments where personhood is fluid, rules are experimental, and social norms evolve rapidly, these voices offer insights grounded in everyday practice, often before those practices are formally recognised or theorised.

Legal and policy frameworks often rely on fixed definitions of personhood, capacity, and legitimacy when engaging with governance questions. This collection intentionally gives space to contributors whose thinking reflects direct engagement with digital spaces, without first passing through the filters of disciplinary convention, and seeks to inspire by taking a closer look at "young" perspectives.

The notion of "young" is both relative and absolute. When referring to a person as being young, this is measured against calendar years (absolute insofar as a particular calendar is accepted) and relative if someone is viewed as younger than another (in terms of years). To be young is a state of existence. However, saying you act "young", have a young appearance, a young demeanour, or a young way of thinking may not be dependent on calendar years. Young is a matter of context, perception, and appreciation. One can say they feel young without this being reflected in calendar years. Others can view a person's actions and ways of behaving or thinking as young, independent of the attitude of the person concerned or objective determinants of age or ageing.

Similarly, the value of young ideas and voices is not constrained by the length of experience or academic history but by their ability to inspire, innovate, and illuminate new perspectives – to engage with non-established thinking that is new in that it has not been frustrated through grounded conventions.

This is a collection of contributions that represent not only the voices of young scholars deeply immersed in the metaverse as a lived experience, but also the curation of these different perspectives principally by young editors steeped in fresh understandings of the digital world, its innovative governance, and the importance of ensuring the integrity of personhood. The contributions commenced as individual research endeavours focusing on particular areas of interest when considering the metaverse, governance, and personhood. They have developed with the benefit of mutual critique and collective guidance. What follows represents an interdisciplinary exercise with contributors and editors grounded in a variety of fields within the social and natural sciences. Located in a university environment committed to stimulating engagement between technology and society, the thinking evidenced in this collaboration has a unique joined-up quality as it interrogates the metaverse and productive possibilities for its governance. Law, psychology, sociology, computer science, and many aspects of frontier technology feature in the disciplines that inform the contributions and binding commentary.

Instead of overthinking what it means to be young or how youth should be valued, we should focus on the added value that young voices bring to this exercise and effort of empowerment. Too often, this demographic is muzzled in shaping governance frameworks. Yet they are not just a disempowered group that needs to be heard for the sake of equity; they often understand the object of governance as a lived experience and social reality better than many of those currently influencing it. Further, these are the generations who will live longer in the virtual world and, as such, should be offered prime positions when it comes to determining the future of their digital existence. Along with being heard, they need to be provided with creative space to talk with others who have similar interests and concerns. This collection has consciously offered contributors control and confidence when it comes to positioning their thinking in a collaborative exploration that examines governance and personhood in the virtual. The editorial process was oriented around support, not standardisation, thereby trying to enable contributors to position themselves confidently within the governance debates that most affect their lived digital realities.

The editors, through their application of metaphor methodology to govern this introductory reflection and give consistency to their commentaries (which link the contributors' thematic intentions), add a novel dimension to understanding a digital universe beyond market imperatives or technological jargon. Editorial conversations thread the contributors' voices into thematic sections, drawing out the patterns, tensions, and provocations that hold this collection together. This collection also ends with a glossary-style section, not to present fixed definitions, but to offer interpretive lenses for understanding how the contributors view and make sense of the metaverse. These additional elements are intended to encourage you, the reader, to reflect on concepts, metaphors, and ideas that shape virtual experiences.

We employ Alice in Wonderland and its panoply of crazy characters and their confronting counterintuitions to parody the journeys of young people in present-day explorations of the virtual. In this role, the editors do more than offer selective insights into the contributions and bind their central themes. The Alice metaphor takes the reader on a new Wonderland journey that rediscovers the Cheshire Cat, the Mad Hatter, and the Caterpillar's oracles – all relocated in a digital universe. The stories are similar, the messages universal, but the understandings to be drawn from these have an immediacy and vitality that frontier technology and hopes for future life experiences make so relevant when seeking social ordering in the metaverse that satisfies the expectations of the young. Having woven this metaphor throughout the introductory reflection, we now turn to articulate its function more explicitly as a metaphorical framework that underpins the entire collection.

METAPHOR METHODOLOGY

This volume adopts Alice in Wonderland as a metaphorical framework, one that supports a deeper inquiry into how personhood, agency, and governance are being reshaped within emerging digital environments. By drawing on Alice's journey through Wonderland, the collection provides a shared symbolic structure through which contributors can reflect on their own experiences navigating virtual spaces. The metaphor serves as a conceptual anchor that is accessible, imaginative, and open-ended, and capable of holding together complex ideas about identity, control, logic, and system design.

The playful yet profound nature of Alice's story provides a rich backdrop for discussing the real-world implications and opportunities of living and interacting in digital spaces, encouraging a deeper engagement with the critical themes proposed in the contributions. The decision to use Wonderland as a metaphor is grounded in the understanding that metaphors do not merely illustrate experience; they structure it.

For the metaphor methodology, we adapt Lakoff and Johnson's idea, which uses metaphor to help give a direction, a context, and a frame to the readers.[5] These frames aid in our thought and language process, giving us conceptual reference points to start forming explanations. In this respect, metaphors do more than mirroring life. They give grounding for how personal interpretations and shared meanings can be related to established popular wisdom, and from there, obtain a more vivid impact. Whether it was as bedtime reading or through more developed imaginative interrogation, both Alice and Wonderland provide the journeys and characters that can act as comparative referents when endeavouring to explain the formative envisaging of humans and technology in virtual space. The metaphor draws attention to questions of agency and imagination. Alice is not solely a part of Wonderland but also becomes an active actor. This might be similar to emerging technologies of which people become users but also shapers, through the way they interact with them. Their actions offer insight because they are situated within the dynamics they are deploying.

The metaphor links to the state of consciousness that is present both in the book and in the metaverse. It reflects the moment of disorientation between real-world environments and digital space. This phase is characterised by the brief time it takes to understand "where you are". It is a moment in which we immerse ourselves into the virtual or offline world – but that brief moment in transit, the "in between"; the space that seems to be neither/nor, *this* is where we might turn towards the Alice metaphor. It represents a "hard to grasp" state of consciousness that is neither fully awake nor asleep, neither entirely virtual nor completely offline. In this space, Alice navigates a world where traditional meanings are inverted, and her perception of power is constantly open to renegotiation. The importance of power dynamics in the Alice stories is translated into the contributions to follow, where different windows into the metaverse look at who has power and who has not in ways that offer freedom or propose enclosure.

At the same time, the metaphor makes space for a critique of platform power and technological dependency. Falling down the rabbit hole can not only signify exploration, but also capture a loss of autonomy through addictive design, surveillance architectures, or opaque systems of control. But just as Alice eventually reclaims her narrative, contributors reflect on the forms of agency that persist even within constraining environments. These include creative use, critical refusal, and the building of alternative communities and imaginaries, acts that carry governance implications beyond formal rules.

In this way, Wonderland becomes a field of experimentation, not just confusion. It allows us to consider governance not as a fixed set of tools, but as a process of meaning-making, institutional design, and participatory sense-making. The metaphor thus gives space to both possible critiques of current governance regimes and calls for inclusive innovation, especially in imagining what governance could look like when shaped by those most deeply embedded in digital cultures.

The editorial choice to use metaphor as a method is also a governance gesture in itself. It reflects an effort to open interpretive space, allowing contributors to speak from their own conceptual ground, rather than fitting their insights into pre-established academic or policy templates.

SO SAID ALICE: "IT'S NO USE TO GO BACK TO YESTERDAY, BECAUSE I WAS A DIFFERENT PERSON THEN"

This introduction, in common with what will follow, is not in the usual format. We haven't set out to summarise or even foreshadow what the young voices will say. To do so would contradict any genuine commitment to *giving voice* and, along with that, autonomy in how these contributions should be received. In saying this, we, as editors, need to make clear the nature and scope of our intervention. While curating this collection, of course, we have been active in encouraging and even at times cajoling the evolution of the voices and how they interconnect. As you will see, we have also drawn out from the different contributions a range of themes that we interweave into a binding commentary, not intended to take precedence over the voices but rather to emphasise that despite their differences in style, subject matter, and vibe, there are prevailing and at times common concerns and interests that colour how these disparate voices envisage a good life in the virtual.

In drawing this brief reflection to a close, we are comfortable with Dolata and Schwabe's research[6] that conceives the metaverse as the product of social construction, and whether the "social" employs technology to create the digital universe does not identify the transcendental space beyond indicating how it can be entered and maintained. They hold that as a collective sense-making process, the metaverse is like any other social space that employs the makings of humans to create a dynamic social experience – thus it is a space more than a thing or a place that can be owned or marketed.

This book is also an exercise in collective sense-making. We hope that it opens up more questions than it resolves. In enabling voices to speak freely and in their chosen styles and languages, it is intended that some tremendously complex and challenging considerations about the world of the future are presented in an accessible, entertaining, and provocative manner that leaves the reader ready to spread the conversation and have their own voice heard.

As we delve deeper into these digital wonders through the perspectives of young thinkers, it becomes imperative to consider how their imaginations and experiences will inform our collective approach to organising and governing our future in the metaverse. This journey transcends mere risk-minimising of technological innovation; it involves designing spaces and modes of governance that resonate with the values and aspirations of a new generation.

We invite you, the reader, to join us and the contributors of this collection in our quest to explore, question, imagine, and rethink the meaning of ideas and concepts and how these might change in a transition to the metaverse – and back to the real world – with a curious and open mind.

NOTES

1. Lewis Carroll. *Alice's Adventures in Wonderland.* Project Gutenberg. Accessed March 9, 2026. https://www.gutenberg.org/files/11/11-h/11-h.htm
2. Lewis Carroll. *Alice's Adventures in Wonderland.* Project Gutenberg. Accessed March 9, 2026. https://www.gutenberg.org/files/11/11-h/11-h.htm
3. Lewis Carroll, *Alice's Adventures in Wonderland*, illus. John Tenniel (Chicago: VolumeOne Publishing, 1998; BookVirtual Digital Edition, v.1.2, November 2000), Chapter 2.
4. Lewis Carroll, *Alice's Adventures in Wonderland*, illus. John Tenniel (Chicago: VolumeOne Publishing, 1998; BookVirtual Digital Edition, v.1.2, November 2000), Chapter 6.
5. George Lakoff and Mark Johnson, *Metaphors We Live By* (Chicago: University of Chicago Press, 1980).
6. Mateusz Dolata and Gerhard Schwabe, "What is the Metaverse and who Seeks to define it? Mapping the site of social construction", *Journal of Information Technology* 38, no. 3 (2023): 239–266.

PART I

Down the digital rabbithole: identity, representation and gender – who am I, who are we?

Introduction to Part I

Noha Lea Halim and Sofie Schönborn

Alice, as many of us do, found herself falling, lost in an unknown Wonderland. Wonderland came naturally; it was a space filled with phenomena unknown to Alice and viewed from a place of curiosity but also confusion, fear, and ultimately joy. Each world and each space around us allows us to become different versions of ourselves. Identity has facets, and these facets can manifest as stronger or more subtle, depending on the environments that surround us, the people with whom we interact, and the ways in which these make us feel empowered, scared, happy, etc. Identity is dynamic. It emerges over time. The way an environment perceives you today might be different from what it would perceive and mirror of you in five years, because you and the environment change. An environment can provide the mirror to the way we might be in these moments.

To Alice, these dimensions of identity mirrored her curiosity. They showed her that she wanted to dive deeper, that she was fascinated by these worlds and ultimately lost and found herself in them. Our authors might have similar ways of approaching Wonderland, driven by curiosity and a will for exploration. Wonderland, as a concept known to most of us, has promised ways to reimagine and question what we take as a status quo. Wonderland existed detached from the world as Alice knew it. But what if that might not be the same for virtual realities? Maybe it is not so much the virtual realities and emerging technologies that create the excitement, but the opportunity they offer as an outlet to think about identity, representation and gender. Perhaps what draws us in is the possibility of becoming new versions of ourselves, of becoming immersed in spaces where we can be seen and interpreted differently by others, and where we can explore the many facets our identities hold. Maybe it is an exploration of a way in which we can learn more about ourselves. And perhaps it also becomes a way to feel that there might be a form of accountability and action that we can take to work on the things we might not view as just from "realspace", such as gender representation. All this can happen with reimagining identity. We take these reflections from one world to another. If we travel to another part of the world tomorrow and meet people that show a different side of us and, thereby, take us closer to knowing ourselves, maybe this is what our authors aspire to be able to take from the virtual.

Our contributors suggest that we might be seeking ways out of power dynamics in virtual worlds. But what if it is about reshaping, reimagining the power dynamics we want? Maybe virtual worlds should not be "an escape" from what we want to abolish, reject, and no longer carry with us but instead a way to think about what could be? This could once again have a spillover effect into realspace. Other authors have engaged with the analogy of the mirror, as mirrors can reflect and transform.

Our contributors are interested in looking behind present imaginings and projecting future experiences. We continuously observe new and emerging technologies, but is it necessary to ask what is novel about how they make us think? What is new about the opportunities they entail and what challenges they might pose, which we have not seen before? Maybe avatars in this sense don't simply reflect our intended images, but rather the metaverse itself could develop into a realm for imagining what could actually become.

What do we still dream of, or demand, from the future of games and immersive spaces? And what might these aspirations teach us about what to demand in realspace?

This section explores what it means to enter a world where identity can be reimagined. The contributions reflect on how personhood is assembled and negotiated in spaces where norms are reimagined, and roles are fluid. The rabbit hole becomes a passage into thought experimentation, where who we are and can become is shaped as much by possibility as by the power of imagination.

Source: Generated using DALL-E, building on the original illustrations from *Alice's Adventures in Wonderland*, drawn by John Tenniel, https://www.alice-in-wonderland.net/resources/pictures/alices-adventures-in-wonderland/

Figure I.1 Alice exploring Wonderland and herself

2. Alice meets herself and others: understanding the relevance of diverse representation, identification, and immersive experience in the Metaverse

Bethany Rhea Thomas and Auxane Boch

INTRODUCTION

Growing up in the same era as the introduction of smartphones, social media, and the rapid advancement of the digital gaming revolution means that I, Bethany, have never really known what life is like "offline". In fact, for me, there is no distinction between an online or offline world, as both reflect, shape, and are intrinsically intertwined with each other. My early experiences as a woman playing video games played a key role in shaping my later research interests, and I quickly fell down the rabbit hole (*excuse the pun*) of video game research. This interest, coupled with my boiling passion for gender equality (*I'd like to think of myself as a Jo, maybe an Amy, rather than a Beth, if the reader permits a nod to other classic literature with iconic women leading the story*), pushed my interest towards diversity, identity, and representation in technology. I think a lot about how we are represented in digital media and the perpetuation of stereotypes and pigeonholes placed around identities. I think a lot about aspects of my own identity, the intersection between these, and my experiences and relationships with both privilege and oppression. Most of all, I think about how technology offers us so much opportunity for real change, but so often falls short.

Building on this, I, Auxane, can attach myself to the sentiment expressed here by Beth. Reflecting on how technology can shape us, our choices, our behaviours, and how we see and interact with each other has been at the heart of my reflection for a long time, to the point of making it my job. It's not really about the good or bad, but rather the how, and what are we going to do about it, and with it…

Because of this, when prompted with this Metaverse metaphor of Alice in Wonderland, our intersecting interests and strong values for inclusion led us to reflect on identity in the Metaverse – wanting to understand how this is constructed, shaped, performed, and explored. But, more importantly, we want to reflect on whether the possibilities and opportunities for constructing identity in the Metaverse are truly diverse and representative, allowing all users to feel they can explore what it means to be a "person" in these immersive virtual spaces. Finally, we want to understand how identities, rights, and responsibilities translate, or transform, within the Metaverse.

The Metaverse is quickly following in the footsteps of digital gaming in terms of growth and access; because of this, we find ourselves wondering if the former will do what the latter still struggles to achieve – to challenge the hegemony and stereotypes of society. While writing this chapter, we seem to be reaching the crux of an ongoing media and culture war and at the centre of this is equality, diversity, and inclusion, so to echo Alice, considering these authors' perspectives – "*'tis love, 'tis love, that makes the world go round!*" Much like games, we believe the Metaverse offers us a fluid, boundary-breaking immersive environment where users can shape their experiences and identities, often in ways that challenge or reinforce existing societal norms. At its core, the Metaverse holds the promise of greater inclusivity, but it also raises critical questions about diversity and representation in virtual spaces. As the next generation steps into the continuously blurring online–offline world, it is vital that environments like the Metaverse are used as more than a mirror, reflecting the constraints of a user's physical and social world back to them. A guiding principle in the construction and governance of identity in the Metaverse is transcending real-world limitations, accommodating diverse needs, and fostering inclusive participation in these environments.[1] We very much agree with the sentiment of these authors, and emphasise the key role of immersive digital spaces in challenging our norms and expectations.

Alice in Wonderland offers many metaphors for understanding the Metaverse and is particularly helpful for communicating the impact, opportunities, and importance of making these spaces rich in diversity and representation. For example, themes in the original text, like Alice's self-discovery, growth, exploration (and questioning) of self and identity, inspire our retelling of this tale, focusing on identity exploration and immersive experiences in metaverse environments – a virtual looking glass for self-discovery and play. Additionally, although Alice is a leading character, what makes Wonderland *Wonderland* are its inhabitants. Because what would Wonderland be without the Mad Hatter, the White Rabbit, the Cheshire Cat, or the Queen of Hearts? The presence of her peculiar and fascinating friends, different from herself, is an important part of Alice's story. Wonderland became a place for her to escape from the constraints of her everyday life, the expectations of her societal "role", and her social circle.

All this being said, in our chapter, we use the Alice in Wonderland metaphor to emphasise the importance of diversity, representation, and identity in the Metaverse and the impact on exploration and immersive experiences. We specifically consider the idea of the Metaverse as a virtual looking glass, or a "mirror", and we outline how mirrors can be simple reflections … or something much more interesting and transformational. Our story follows our version of Alice as a proxy of a user entering the Metaverse for the first time, but Alice is also our vehicle – showing our own experiences and concerns when exploring diverse representation, identification, and immersive experiences in the Metaverse. In our story, we begin with Alice "seeing herself", where we focus on the role of avatars, playing with the expression and representation of her identity in these virtual spaces; then our Alice "meets others" as we highlight the impact of representation, creating diverse and inclusive stories and spaces in the Metaverse wonderland. Hopefully, through our re-told tale, we will give you the keys to know the "what", so you get to decide what you will do about it …

LOOKING IN THE METAVERSE MIRROR: ALICE SEES HERSELF

> "Who in the world am I? Ah, that's the great puzzle."
>
> Alice, from Alice's Adventures in Wonderland[2]

Where better to begin than at the beginning? And so that's where we join Alice, who has decided to journey into the Metaverse, but she can't simply tumble down the rabbit hole in this story. First, she must look into the metaverse mirror and see (or design) her virtual self… her avatar…

So, we're going to see Alice create her avatar… but, what is an "avatar"?

Well, avatars are users' mirrors to the metaverse – acting as a reflection and visual representation of users in these digital environments. Because of this, avatars play a central role in user experience as they are the primary medium through which users are represented and interact with both the metaverse and each other.[3] Avatars provide users with a sense of identity in these virtual spaces through self-presentation and self-representation,[4] and offer a way to engage with others in these environments. Consequently, avatars play an important role in forming social connections and communities as they reflect our own selves in the given environment and our chosen behaviours. We draw from our expertise in gaming here, where avatars play a very similar role in the exploration of identity for video game players – and also present very similar challenges to avatars in the Metaverse, in that they are often significantly restricted and a poor representation for users who do not fit hegemonic identities (e.g., male, white).

An avatar in Metaverse environments is often positioned as a "blank slate" for users to design and change however they want to represent themselves in these environments – and a closer design often leads to better immersion, as we will discuss later. But we question again here, are avatars really ever truly "blank" slates? The avatar design mechanics can vary by environment and context, but they are often designed to allow users a level of customisation and personal expression through their digital representations. Avatar designs can range from a series of pre-designed models with opportunities for slight modifications to blank canvases offering extensive and exhaustive customisation. Think here of picking a built character in *Borderlands* or spending hours deciding on every skin mark and slope of the face in the *Sims 4* or *Skyrim.* Research tells us how the ability to customise can enhance users' emotional investment in the virtual world, making users feel more connected to their virtual persona.[5] Users may be able to modify their avatars' appearance, voice, body shape, facial features, hair, and clothing, making each avatar unique. In some instances, users can even use their avatars to convey a wide range of human emotions in these spaces, making social interactions feel more authentic and engaging. Personalised avatars and the level of immersion facilitate users' sense of presence, agency, and body ownership, which are essential for the Metaverse to be a compelling and continuous space for users to return to.[6] As we consider the power and potential of avatar customisation, we must also reflect on how these so-called "blank slates" are shaped by design choices, cultural assumptions, and technological limits. This reminds us that true self-representation in the Metaverse is never entirely neutral and not truly autonomous (as Alice is structured by systems she doesn't control), but despite this, it is something we must continually negotiate and advocate for together.

We offer a point of reflection here for readers who may be stakeholders connected to the Metaverse – *do your avatar mechanics allow you to truly facilitate a user's experience of personhood and immersion in your virtual space?*

But we know avatars can be so much more than virtual characters we use as placeholders for our physical bodies in these spaces. In fact, how we design our avatars can impact how we perform and interact in these environments. We can use underpinnings from psychology to explain this – the Proteus Effect outlined the phenomenon where users' behaviour conforms to the characteristics of their avatars[7] and demonstrates how virtual representations can influence real-world behaviours. For example, people with more authoritative-looking avatars, such as those who are taller or more muscular, may tend to behave more assertively. Similarly, avatars with stereotypically attractive features might encourage more sociable or extroverted behaviour. This highlights that identity in immersive virtual worlds is not simply reflective but can be transformative, influencing how people interact with others and how they perceive themselves. Users' agency in avatar creation is also crucial in shaping their virtual interactions. Yet, we question whether these immersive environments do offer this agency for their users, and if not – why not? Particularly when this agency plays such an important role in their experiences in these spaces.

So, now we know what an avatar is, we wonder what this means for identity in the Metaverse. Why does this even matter?

Well, we believe it is imperative that avatar design mechanics in the Metaverse, whether pre-designed or fully customisable, include wide-ranging and diverse design options for users to create virtual versions of themselves. For us, this statement stems predominantly from our personal values, but for stakeholders creating these spaces, we strongly suggest considering the research and impact of this because a user's perceived similarity with their avatar increases their user satisfaction. After all, research outlines how avatars act as an extension of users' physical identity[8] and how a user's similarity with their avatar impacts their self-disclosure, which is important for relationship building.[9] Therefore, avatars impact not only the user's immersive experience but also their social connection with others in the metaverse.

In digital game contexts, we see time and time again a significant failure of diversity and representation in protagonists and avatars. This means that despite the profound potential of games as places for identity play and exploration, they only mirror the societal constraints of users. For example, many games (such as *Stardew Valley*) only offer players a male or female avatar body, which impacts gendered dialogue in the games. This has a real-world impact on players and can lead to the misgendering of the players themselves. We think the Metaverse has a chance to do better and break these boundaries, so users do not encounter these barriers of expression and authenticity in these environments.

But how could the Metaverse break this cycle? And begin to break the mirror?

Firstly, diverse design mechanics are key to unlocking avatar realism, which is crucial for user experience. Both user–avatar relationships and the user's intention to use the avatar are increased by avatar realism.[10] Furthermore, research highlights how users' identification with their avatars plays an important role in fostering their self-efficacy.[11] As such, if avatar design mechanics are limited and do not offer a wide and diverse range of physical traits, users will be unable to fully represent their physical identity. This will negatively impact their relationship-building, identification, immersive experience, and exploration in the Metaverse. Focusing on representation, diversity, and inclusion in these spaces is not simply a tick-box but can significantly impact a user's experience in these spaces – and why create these immersive environments, with opportunities to shift reality, just to limit users to the same world they face every day?

Expression and formation of digital identities through tools such as avatars could impact and shape users' real-world social interactions, perceptions, and psychological states. For example, for users with social anxiety, avatars provide a buffer between their real-world identity and the virtual social space. This separation may buffer any fear of judgement and could increase users' social confidence. For example, due to the digital connection between a user's body and their avatar, they are a more engaging and embodying approach to exploring and affirming aspects of identity, encouraging users to make these changes in their physical world.[12] Research illustrates how our digital representations can not only mediate social experiences in virtual environments but also catalyse meaningful personal growth and identity exploration beyond the screen. For these reasons, we strongly advocate for diverse, inclusive, and boundary-breaking opportunities and representations within the Metaverse. There is so much room for positive impact in a social climate where inclusion is being repealed daily.

Beyond realism, avatars also offer possibilities to be designed in ways so that users can transcend the limitations of their physical world, allowing them to represent themselves in ways that may not be possible in real life due to physical, geographical, or societal constraints. Avatars do not have to be limited to representations of users but can be extensions of the self. Ultimately, there needs to be better inclusion embedded within existing metaverse structures, but now we wonder… Is the Metaverse only capable of a better reflection of demographic representation? What if the Metaverse can do more and create a space for a more radical redefinition of digital citizenship and community?

THROUGH THE LOOKING-GLASS: ALICE IS REIMAGINED

> "I can't explain myself, I'm afraid, sir," said Alice, "because I am not myself you see."
>
> Alice's Adventures in Wonderland[13]

When first designing her avatar in the Metaverse, Alice focused on re-creating her physical identity: her golden hair, her pale skin, and her sky-blue dress. But soon, she began to wonder, in this virtual world of endless possibilities, if this meant that Alice could explore the possibilities of who she truly felt herself to be.

Metaverse worlds can be built on an architecture of agency, and they provide users with the opportunity to explore the multifaceted dimensions of identity, where the boundaries of selfhood are permeable, and identity becomes a malleable construct for them to explore.[14] This means they have the opportunity to empower users, presenting them with opportunities to explore new identities, choices, experiences, and social dynamics.

If the avatar mechanics in the Metaverse are dynamic and diverse, users' expression and exploration of their identities can be shaped by how they choose to present themselves. Unlike the fixed nature of physical identities, in these virtual spaces, users can create, explore, and perform different aspects of themselves through their avatars.[15] In these virtual worlds, through our avatars, we have the chance to make choices that are different from those we may make in our offline or physical world. These identities can reflect aspects of the self that are either close to or far removed from the user's real-world identity. We believe there is a profound potential for users to engage in an immersive social reality experience where aspects of their self are salient, which they may be unable to explore in their physical reality (e.g., trans or gender-diverse users affirming their gender identity in the Metaverse, where they may feel unsafe to do so in their physical world).

Users in virtual spaces can construct avatars that reflect either their ideal selves[16] or fantasy personas, allowing for greater flexibility in their self-representation. Avatar customisation empowers users to experiment with their identities, and these virtual identities are often extensions of real-world traits, values, or goals.[17] Similarly, avatars allow individuals to engage in identity play, where users can safely explore different facets of their personality and identity.[18] For example, in video game contexts, avatars offer the opportunity for players to engage with self-representation, exploration, and affirmation of their gender identity more accurately than in their physical spaces.[19] Through this freedom of expression and exploration, we gain new ways to understand ourselves, try out different ways of being, and potentially carry these insights back into our offline lives.

Avatar customisation in digital gaming environments, not dissimilar from those in the Metaverse, offers users (i) a low-stakes environment for identity exploration; (ii) the internal and external validation of gender identity and transition goals; (iii) a chance to achieve their appearance goals; and ultimately (iv) increasing immersion and escapism in these contexts, such as for trans and gender diverse users.[20] The opportunities offered through avatar customisation in the Metaverse can have a significant benefit for all users, but especially for users who feel they cannot express or explore their identity safely in the physical world. Subsequently, we know avatar design mechanics must be flexible and rooted in diversity, ensuring users can engage with this exploration to facilitate their immersive experiences.

Avatars serve as more than mere digital stand-ins; they are extensions of users' identities that transcend the user's physical constraints. They reflect not only the users' conscious choices made during their creation, but also deeper, often unintended aspects of identity play and exploration. In these immersive social environments, users can reimagine and renegotiate their facets of self. Avatars invite users to engage in identity construction and meaning-making, revealing the transformative potential of virtual, immersive environments for identity exploration. However, there are significant ongoing challenges for us all to consider more closely, as not all virtual and augmented worlds design environments or avatars that provide diversity, inclusion, and representation for every user.

> *Alice had wandered deep into the mirrored room, where more pre-designed avatar outlines fluttered like butterflies, each one carefully crafted by the hands of its creator. But soon, she noticed something strange. These avatars, so many of them, looked eerily similar. The women were all impossibly slim with flowing gold hair, while there was no build with broad shoulders, or powerful fists. "Why does each one look the same, why can't I be another version of me?" Alice wondered aloud, tugging at the edges of her blue pixelated petticoat. A passing cat, grinning wide with pearly white teeth, appeared in a shimmer of code, "Because, dear Alice," it purred, "here, you can be anything... so long as it fits inside a tidy little box." Alice frowned, sensing the silent pressure behind the choices made, the narrowing of who could truly feel seen in this strange, fragmented world. There were no avatars with different skin, no bodies that defied perfect symmetry, and no expressions that dared to break free from the mirror's boundaries.*

In the 2010 film adaptation of Carroll's story, we see Alice's world of the late 1800s when women and Alice were expected to marry to fulfil their familial duty and societal role of wife, mother, and property. Many digital spaces, including those of social virtual realities, perpetuate similar gender-based stereotypes, with hyper-sexualised female avatar designs serving as prime examples of this issue. This is a significant issue as women users' experiences of harassment in these digital environments have impacts in their real world.[21] As women, of all the issues we see concerning representation in virtual spaces, we are particularly personally attached to the role, representation, and narrative assigned to women and femininity within the Metaverse.

But the gender-based stereotypes embedded and reinforced within and by these digital environments are in no way the only issues we see. Digital environments, such as video games and virtual and augmented reality spaces, face ongoing challenges concerning their (lack of) representation of women, the LGBTQ+ and Black, Asian, and Minority Ethnic (BAME) communities, and their frequent portrayal in stereotypical roles. When we look back to avatars, the design of avatars across virtual spaces is geared towards white, male, or Western-centric aesthetics – limiting the customisation options for users from different racial or cultural backgrounds. This significant restriction can alienate users who feel their identities are not authentically reflected or represented.

For example, research suggested that users who could choose an avatar with their own skin tone had a higher performance of prosocial behaviours and higher social presence compared to those who couldn't choose their skin tone in a virtual environment.[22] Therefore, if avatar customisation across the Metaverse realities does not include a wide range of design options, such as those in the BAME community, this will negatively impact the potential for positive social interactions and immersive experiences of the underrepresented individuals.

"Who am I? Who can I be?" the mirror reflects back at Alice, a cascade of virtual faces and forms she could wear, each imbued with a fragment of her potential self. Here, as in Wonderland, choice is endless. Yet, with each choice, Alice feels the pull of something greater – a desire for connection, understanding, and a world that embraces more than just one story.

In the Metaverse, the boundaries of identity can be as fluid as the users' imaginations, offering a landscape rich in possibilities for self-expression and exploration. Yet, this journey of self-discovery rests upon a critical foundation: the values embedded in each virtual space and the diversity in representation that these worlds offer. Without the inclusion of varied cultural and moral dimensions, the Metaverse risks becoming a reflection of societal limitations, a virtual "looking glass" that excludes rather than embraces. Just as Alice encountered curious, varied characters who expanded her sense of the world, users in the Metaverse should find an environment that honours and reflects a spectrum of identities and experiences, fostering a space for cultural exchange and moral growth.

Social play in the Metaverse adds a layer of communal identity construction, as interactions with others allow users to explore roles and personas in a shared virtual context. Through social play, users not only discover different aspects of their personalities but also engage in moral learning, developing empathy and ethical decision-making through collaborative experiences.[23] This interactional space makes the Metaverse more than a playground for individual identity – it becomes a social laboratory where users collectively shape the values, behaviours, and narratives that reflect a new, inclusive virtual culture.

Cultural representation within the Metaverse is more than a collection of avatars or aesthetic diversity – it forms the core of meaningful social interactions, helping users feel seen and valued. Studies indicate that when avatars can accurately represent users' cultural backgrounds, users feel more connected and validated in their virtual identities, enhancing social interactions and reducing alienation.[24] When users see representations that echo their own experiences or engage with avatars that reflect the diversity of the broader world, the Metaverse transforms into a platform for cross-cultural understanding and empathy. Such variety allows users to explore facets of their identity that may be underrepresented or even marginalised in the physical world, offering them a freedom and visibility that extends beyond their offline experiences.[25] It is important that when these spaces are created, we prioritise authentic cultural representation, ensuring that the Metaverse becomes a place where all users feel recognised.

This "freedom", however, must be met with moral consideration.

Virtual worlds without ethical frameworks can reproduce real-world inequalities or foster environments where discrimination and exclusion persist, disrupting the potential for identity exploration and growth. Pluriculturally adapted ethical structures within the metaverse are essential for ensuring inclusivity and respectful interactions, creating spaces where users feel safe to express themselves fully. Without this moral foundation, the experience of the Metaverse can turn into something disempowering, mirroring the social exclusions found in traditional settings.[26] Instead, spaces that uphold moral guidelines, grounded in equality and inclusivity, support the creative freedoms of all users, allowing them to navigate identity exploration without fear of judgement or hostility.[27] As we continue to build and participate in these digital environments, we must collectively commit to shaping ethical frameworks that prioritise inclusion so that the Metaverse becomes a space where everyone can thrive, connect, and grow.

However, users are not, and cannot be, wholly responsible for governing these power structures present within the Metaverse...

> *Alice was almost ready to step into the boundless landscapes of the Metaverse, but as the digital realm shimmered into focus, a thunderous voice cut through the air. A Queen draped in crimson robes, pixelating with regal authority, appeared. "No further, Alice! This domain is mine to command!"*

Governance in the Metaverse (i.e., the establishment and enforcement of rules, norms, and systems that shape user behaviour and interactions) plays an important role here, and there are power dynamics relevant to avatar creation that can impact a user's social interactions in these spaces. For example, platforms may impose limitations on avatar design, such as approved body types, clothing options, or even skin tones. These restrictions would limit self-expression and identity representation. Users with avatars that deviate from dominant norms may face prejudice, mirroring real-world social biases. This could lead to ostracism, microaggressions, or harassment. Platforms with centralised control may impose top-down rules about avatar design and behaviour. This could prevent harm (e.g., banning inappropriate avatars) but might also limit freedom of expression.

Algorithms driving avatar-creation tools could reflect inherent biases in training data, favouring certain aesthetics, genders, or races over others. This could lead to unequal representation and reinforce stereotypes. Alternatively, in decentralised or minimally governed Metaverses, users might police each other's avatars, questioning the authenticity of individuals to embody certain identities. For example, a user wearing a culturally significant avatar might face accusations of cultural appropriation, potentially leading to exclusion or harassment. In user-led governance models, the majority might impose norms that marginalise minority groups. As we continue to build and participate in digital spaces, we must be aware of how both algorithms and community dynamics shape inclusion.

Other important factors can create barriers to representation through avatars in the Metaverse. For example, premium customisation options might require payment, creating economic divides. Users with greater financial resources may have more freedom to create avatars that align with their identities, while others are left with generic options. The appearance of an avatar may influence social status and interactions. Users with highly customised or visually appealing avatars may be perceived as more influential or authoritative; in particular, users with high-end design items might be treated preferentially, reinforcing hierarchies. Those deciding which cultural elements are included in avatar options wield power over whose identities are represented or commodified. A platform might include certain hairstyles or clothing only as purchasable add-ons, capitalising on cultural diversity rather than celebrating it. For reflection for those who play a role in shaping these virtual worlds, do you consider who has access to self-representation? It is crucial that we challenge systems that turn identity into a commodity so that all users can express themselves fully and authentically.

In this mirror-like Metaverse, Alice wonders aloud, "If I can be anyone, then who must I be to reflect the best of myself?" Here, as in all worlds, the journey is one of balance – between freedom and responsibility, self-expression and empathy, fantasy and the cultural and moral realities that guide us.

Now Alice has created her avatar, exploring the many mirrors through which she can change how she looks and maybe even who she is, it is time for Alice (and us) to go beyond the looking glass. As Alice ventures further into the Metaverse, she'll soon encounter a host of other curious characters. In the next section of this chapter, we discuss the importance of diversity of others in the Metaverse, the impact on its inhabitants (users), and what it means for representation and inclusivity in these advancing, virtual, fantastical spaces.

A WONDERLAND OF EXPLORATION, DIVERSITY, AND REPRESENTATION: ALICE MEETS OTHERS

> "If I had a world of my own, everything would be nonsense. Nothing would be what it is, because everything would be what it isn't. And contrary wise, what is, it wouldn't be. And what it wouldn't be, it would. You see?"
>
> Alice's Adventures in Wonderland[28]

Alice wandered past the looking glass and through the pixels, soon stumbling upon an unusual fork in the road. To her left was a virtual world in shades of black and white, where everyone she saw looked remarkably like her – same size, same shape, same expressions. It was a world of familiarity, but it looked strangely hollow, as if something vital was missing. To her right, just past a broken bridge, was a place bursting with colour. In the distance, she saw vibrant and diverse stories and characters filling the landscape, each unique and dazzling in its own way. Intrigued, Alice hesitated, torn between the comfort of sameness and the allure of a world where differences are celebrated and the air buzzed with the promise of discovery.

If Alice is able to create herself, why should she care about others?

When digital environments lack a wide and diverse representation of people, stories, and experiences, a multitude of social, cultural, and psychological problems follow. These include the perpetuation of stereotypes and bias, feelings of alienation, and cultural and identity erasure.

Stereotypical representations of marginalised groups in virtual immersive environments perpetuate harmful biases. Research has demonstrated that repetitive exposure to such representations influences users' perceptions of those groups in the real world. Video game research highlights how Black and Latinx characters are often depicted according to stereotypical and harmful characteristics and roles (e.g., being violent), whereas women are hypersexualised or portrayed as weak and dependent.[29] When we engage with immersive worlds, we must critically reflect on the narratives they promote and advocate for more authentic, respectful portrayals that challenge, rather than reinforce, real-world biases.

So why does this matter?

The lack of diversity or negative portrayals in virtual environments can have profound psychological impacts on users from underrepresented communities. For example, the reinforcement of negative stereotypes (i.e., stereotype threats) towards individuals' identities can impact their performance.[30] Additionally, research informs us how these problems can lead to diminished self-esteem, as users may internalise negative portrayals or feel that their identity is not valued.[31] Finally, virtual spaces that cater primarily to dominant groups (e.g., white, male, cisgender users) create a sense of exclusion for people from marginalised backgrounds. LGBTQ+ players, for example, often report feeling unwelcome or harassed in digital gaming communities that lack diverse representation or fail to address hostile behaviour.[32] As we navigate and help shape these virtual spaces, we must recognise the importance of inclusive representation and actively work to create environments where all users can see themselves reflected, respected, and empowered.

When the portrayals of groups and individuals reinforce negative stereotypes, they not only impact the user but also contribute to broader societal biases. For example, representations in our media are closely linked to the formation of implicit biases, where repeated exposure to stereotypes can lead individuals to form these stereotyped associations themselves.[33] This can translate into discriminatory attitudes and behaviours, meaning if Metaverse worlds perpetuate these issues, then their users may become targets of, or perpetrators of, discrimination.

The lack of diversity and inclusion in these spaces can facilitate the toxic behaviours of users. When homogenous groups dominate these spaces, they often become breeding grounds for harassment, discrimination, and hostility towards users. When virtual spaces fail to implement strong policies on inclusion and diversity, discriminatory behaviours become normalised. This cultivates an environment where users from marginalised backgrounds are constantly subjected to microaggressions and hostility.[34] Finally, the absence of diversity in these spaces can reinforce ingroup–outgroup dynamics, where users feel a stronger connection to their own group and view their outgroups with suspicion or hostility.[35] In such virtual environments, stereotypes are more likely to be reinforced, leading to social division rather than cohesion and interaction.

> *Alice, tired of the sameness that surrounded her, twirled her teacup in frustration. "Why," she wondered aloud, "is everything here so dreadfully alike?" The flowers all whispered in identical tones, and even the clouds seemed to march in single file across a dull sky. Irritated, Alice declared, "I shall find a place where colours dance and cultures collide, where every face tells a different story!" And with that, she set off towards the broken bridge, determined to find a corner of this digital realm where the stories untold could finally take shape.*

Immersive virtual reality environments like the Metaverse present opportunities for embodied perspective-taking, which can reduce users' negative attitudes and stereotypical beliefs about a group.[36] Virtual reality environments have the potential to increase empathy by allowing users to interact with diverse perspectives.[37] This perspective-taking enables users to "step into someone else's shoes" with significant benefits. For instance, embodying avatars of different racial, ethnic, gender, or socio-economic backgrounds decreases implicit biases, fosters inclusive attitudes, and increases emotional empathy and a greater understanding of the challenges faced by marginalised groups.[38] This means Metaverse spaces can be powerful tools to help combat stereotypes and reduce prejudice.

However, when these virtual spaces are homogeneous or rely on stereotypical portrayals of groups and cultures, they fail to facilitate meaningful cross-cultural exchanges and interactions between users. This lack of exposure to diverse perspectives can lead to reduced empathy and understanding of marginalised groups. Additionally, the possibility for anonymity when engaging in social interactions in the Metaverse may reduce sensitivity or empathy for others in general.[39] This proposed impact is rooted in the digital nature of social interactions, suggesting this may impact sensitivity and empathy for others. This is evidenced by the report of experiences of crime and abuse towards avatars' metaverse spaces with no challenge or interjection from other users. Considering these reports, it is imperative for immersive virtual environments to create safe opportunities for perspective-taking, promote cross-cultural user interactions, and design spaces where diverse cultures are represented and are designed in a way that discourages hostility between their inhabitants. Additionally, strict regulations for inappropriate behaviour in these spaces are imposed and regulated by the organisations that create them.

Looking at specific types of populations, LGBTQ+ representation in virtual environments is critical for ensuring these are safe and inclusive spaces. We see digital media following one of two paths: either perpetuating stereotypes and facilitating hostility and stigma or challenging these and fostering acceptance. When media representations show the latter – for example, when virtual environments allow users to create avatars that reflect diverse gender identities and sexual orientations – they empower individuals to express their authentic selves and find communities of support.

Authentic portrayals of individuals in these groups have various benefits, as they can counteract the negative effects of stereotype-laden content[40] and affirm and empower users' identities, positively impacting their well-being.[41] Additionally, virtual environments serve as safe spaces for LGBTQ+ youth to form supportive networks, reduce feelings of isolation, and provide emotional support.[42] Finally, authentic LGBTQ+ media representation plays a significant role in improving public attitudes towards the LGBTQ+ community.[43]

The immersive social reality environments in the Metaverse offer opportunities for LGBTQ+ individuals to see themselves represented and validate their identities in a way that their physical world is unable to or does not.

> *"How curious," thought Alice as she watched the avatars parade across the digital field, each as perfect and polished as a porcelain doll. Every figure moved with an identical ease, their bodies untouched by age or difference. "But where," Alice wondered, "are the shapes and forms that tell other stories? The lines of life lived*

in unique ways, the bodies that carry a different strength?" And with a determined glint in her eye, Alice set out to discover a world where every ability could shine.

In the Metaverse, diversity of identity should extend beyond culture and gender to encompass the rich, varied spectrum of physical and cognitive abilities. Yet, much like Alice's encounter with the uniform avatars, too often, virtual worlds portray a narrow definition of what bodies and abilities "should" look like. When avatars fail to represent the full range of human experience, such as wheelchairs, prosthetic limbs, or unique modes of movement, the Metaverse becomes an echo of real-world exclusions rather than an inclusive space of limitless self-expression. Authentic representations of ability are essential for fostering a virtual world that truly embodies diversity, granting every user the chance to see themselves reflected in a way that honours their lived experience. In this part, we discuss disability relating to physical impairment and differences.

Traditional media and entertainment have long portrayed people with disabilities in restrictive, stereotypical roles, framing them as pitiable or sinister.[44] Such narratives reinforce a single story that limits the perception of those with disabilities, framing them either as inspirational for merely existing or as tragic figures. This bias becomes problematic when translated into virtual spaces, where limited avatar options for people with disabilities restrict the ability of users to accurately and proudly reflect their physical identities. By expanding avatar options to include diverse abilities, the Metaverse can offer users with disabilities a powerful opportunity to see themselves represented in ways that celebrate, rather than diminish, their experiences.

Representation matters in the Metaverse, not only for self-identity but also for shaping social interactions. When virtual spaces include accurate, diverse avatars, they become mirrors that empower users, instilling a sense of belonging and visibility.[45] For users with disabilities, the ability to design avatars that authentically reflect their unique forms and abilities can affirm their identities and challenge the stereotypes prevalent in everyday society.[46] Furthermore, studies indicate that users who encounter realistic representations of others (in this case, Black people) in virtual spaces experience increased empathy and understanding, breaking down biases and fostering more inclusive social environments.[47] This effect could extend to disability.

In this virtual wonderland, the possibilities for self-expression thus extend beyond simple replication of real-world identities. Users with disabilities might choose to explore alternate, augmented versions of themselves, whether through bionic avatars or avatars with enhanced mobility. Research shows that bionic representations can be transformative, enabling users with disabilities to experience new forms of agency and mobility.[48] However, if presented in a stereotypical "superhuman" context, these options risk reinforcing the notion that people with disabilities must be "fixed" or enhanced to be valuable. Therefore, the Metaverse must carefully balance empowerment with authenticity, allowing users to explore their identities in ways that honour their reality and aspirations without enforcing ableist norms.

As Alice ventured deeper into this strange and boundless realm, she found herself in a place that pulsed with life and possibility, unlike anything she had known. Here, across shimmering fields of pixelated light, she glimpsed figures dressed in the colours and customs of lands far and wide, voices with accents that painted pictures of distant places. Each corner seemed to reveal a new story, a glimpse of a world rich with history and tradition, vibrant and alive. She increasingly understood that everywhere she looked was a new language, food, pattern... She was now encountering people from different cultures...

As exemplified and discussed already, Metaverse spaces must be rooted in representing and including diverse groups and cultures to promote users' belonging in these immersive experiences. However, the responsibility for diversity should not be placed on the users' choices through physical representation (e.g., avatar skin colour). Additionally, this should not be included merely for the sake of achieving "diversity" without creating meaningful depth or authentic stories. The appropriate and adequate representation of diverse groups and cultures is the responsibility of designers, and they should be integrated into Metaverse environments. For example, immersive virtual reality environments are useful digital spaces for cultural heritage with a wide range of applications. In these spaces, users' immersive experiences are meaningful, and users can benefit from the exploration and appreciation of cultures and their histories through storytelling.[49]

Representing a wide range of cultures in virtual reality environments not only mirrors the real world but can foster cultural exchange and inclusivity. There are various benefits to metaverse environments, including varied cultural narratives and identities, which help users feel seen and respected. Digital media and platforms where cultural norms and practices are accurately represented help prevent the perpetuation of cultural stereotypes and promote respect for different traditions and worldviews.[50] We believe a diverse metaverse encourages users to explore and appreciate a range of cultural experiences, contributing to greater mutual understanding.

As Alice tumbled down this rabbit hole, she encountered a world that defied her expectations – a place where the new, different, exciting, and familiar thrived, and diverse cultures and communities were celebrated.

When virtual reality environments reflect the diversity of the real world, they serve as sites for cultural innovation. When different traditions, narratives, and identities intersect, users benefit from diverse storytelling and richer content.[51] Diverse and inclusive virtual environments help establish positive norms for behaviours in digital spaces, which may have ripple effects on how society views and treats marginalised groups. When online communities are founded on inclusion and diversity, such as promoting respectful dialogue and reprimanding hate speech, they can reduce discriminatory behaviours and create a more supportive environment for all users.[52] These norms can spill over into real-life interactions, fostering more inclusive behaviours beyond these virtual worlds.

Much like Alice's journey through Wonderland, the Metaverse offers a boundless realm of possibilities, but it, too, must avoid falling into the trap of becoming a narrow reflection of our physical reality. Instead, Metaverse worlds need to embrace the rich diversity of their users, ensuring that everyone, regardless of their background or identity, finds representation in this digital wonderland. As these immersive realities integrate into our everyday lives, they must also reflect the vast spectrum of human experience, allowing each user to explore and belong.

SHATTERING THE LOOKING GLASS: ALICE'S AND THE AUTHORS' CONCLUDING THOUGHTS

> "I know who I was when I got up this morning, but I think I must have been changed several times since then."
>
> Alice, from Alice's Adventures in Wonderland[53]

Surrounded by a room of mirrors, there is only Alice to see. She is confined to a single reflection... her own experiences are all she knows. But when she shatters the mirror, she sees the shimmering edges and a thousand reflections of herself. In each fractured piece, she discovers a new and different version of Alice, with new ideas and experiences. Breaking free from her constraints, Alice finds parts of herself she hadn't seen before. Now the looking glass is broken, Alice sees new wonderful worlds and people from different places, each with thoughts and feelings diverse from her own; she learns their stories and struggles. Shattering the mirror of narrow representation, and through the creation of inclusive spaces, Alice encounters a vibrant world of belonging...

We have explored how the virtual worlds of the Metaverse hold profound opportunities for identity exploration, affirmation, construction, presentation, and social connection. When these spaces are rich in diversity and representation, then users benefit from rich and meaningful immersive experiences. The Metaverse reflects the complex and evolving landscape where digital realms can both mirror and redefine our social world, our understanding of community and self-expression. As these environments slot into part of many people's everyday lives, beginning in turn to play an integral role in our social interactions, the need for diversity, inclusion, and representation in these spaces becomes ever more critical. The Metaverse offers opportunities and challenges in shaping culture and fostering empathy across diverse communities. By embracing and embedding diversity in these worlds, we can cultivate a more inclusive future where individuals can authentically express themselves while engaging meaningfully with others.

Diverse representation in these spaces empowers users from marginalised groups by ensuring they feel seen and heard through experiences, environments, and opportunities that celebrate a variety of identities, representations, and stories. But, to drive the design of a good Metaverse, which is rooted in inclusion and diversity, guidelines of good practice and regulations must be informed by further research and experts in the field.[54] As we navigate these evolving virtual and augmented realities within the Metaverse, it is imperative to ensure that they foster a sense of belonging and empowerment for all users – transcending our physical limitations to create an interconnected and inclusive online and "offline" world.

Personhood and identity in the Metaverse are deeply intertwined with how individuals express and experience themselves in virtual environments. These immersive environments can allow users to explore different facets of their identity, offering opportunities for self-expression that may be limited in the physical world, maybe giving them a safe space allowing them to feel whole as persons. However, for this exploration to be meaningful, it must be rooted in diversity, representation, and inclusion. When digital spaces reflect a broad spectrum of identities, cultures, and experiences, users feel seen, valued, and empowered. Conversely, the lack of representation or the reinforcement of harmful stereotypes can marginalise users and undermine their sense of personhood. Therefore, fostering inclusive environments in the Metaverse is essential for enabling all individuals to navigate, express, and affirm their identities without fear of exclusion or erasure.

We conclude our chapter with some final questions for both our future selves and our readers, as Alice's story may have finished here, but our story is not really over. Is Alice's choice in the Metaverse Wonderland truly autonomous, or is it illusory, and structured by systems she does not control? Is Alice really free to explore, or only choosing within preset scripts?

NOTES

1. Yang, L., Xu, Y. and Hui, P. (2025), 'Metaverse Identity: Core Principles and Critical Challenges'. *Telecommunications Policy*, 49(3), 102906. https://doi.org/10.1016/j.telpol.2025.102906

2. Carroll, L. (1865), *Alice's Adventures in Wonderland*, London: Macmillan & Co.
3. Hennig-Thurau, T., Aliman, D.N., Herting, A.M., Cziehso, G.P., Linder, M. and Kübler, R.V. (2023), 'Social interactions in the metaverse: Framework, initial evidence, and research roadmap', *Journal of the Academy of Marketing Science*, 51(4), 889–913. https://doi.org/10.1007/s11747-022-00908-0
4. Miao, F., Kozlenkova, I.V., Wang, H., Xie, T. and Palmatier, R.W. (2022), 'An emerging theory of avatar marketing', *Journal of Marketing*, 86(1), 67–90. https://doi.org/10.1177/0022242921996646
5. Ducheneaut, N., Wen, M.H., Yee, N. and Wadley, G. (2009, April), 'Body and mind: A study of avatar personalization in three virtual worlds', in *Proceedings of the SIGCHI Conference on Human Factors in Computing Systems*, pp. 1151–1160. Boston, MA: CHI.
6. Waltemate, T., Gall, D., Roth, D., Botsch, M. and Latoschik, M.E. (2018), 'The impact of avatar personalization and immersion on virtual body ownership, presence, and emotional response', *IEEE Transactions on Visualization and Computer Graphics*, 24(4), 1643–1652.
7. Yee, N. and Bailenson, J. (2007), 'The Proteus Effect: The effect of transformed self-representation on behaviour', *Human Communication Research*, 33(3), 271–290. https://doi.org/10.1111/j.1468-2958.2007.00299.x
8. Barta, S., Ibáñez-Sánchez, S., Orús, C. and Flavián, C. (2024), 'Avatar creation in the metaverse: A focus on event expectations', *Computers in Human Behaviour*, 156, 108192. https://doi.org/10.1016/j.chb.2024.108192
9. Hooi, R. and Cho, H. (2014), 'Avatar-driven self-disclosure: The virtual me is the actual me', *Computers in Human Behaviour*, 39, 20–28. https://doi.org/10.1016/j.chb.2014.06.019
10. Kim, D.Y., Lee, H.K. and Chung, K. (2023), 'Avatar-mediated experience in the metaverse: The impact of avatar realism on user-avatar relationship', *Journal of Retailing and Consumer Services*, 73, 103382. https://doi.org/10.1016/j.jretconser.2023.103382
11. Kim, C., Lee, S.G. and Kang, M. (2012), 'I became an attractive person in the virtual world: Users' identification with virtual communities and avatars', *Computers in Human Behaviour*, 28(5), 1663–1669. https://doi.org/10.1016/j.chb.2012.04.004
12. Freeman, G., Zamanifard, S., Maloney, D. and Adkins, A. (2020, April), 'My body, my avatar: How people perceive their avatars in social virtual reality', in *Extended Abstracts of the 2020 CHI Conference on Human Factors in Computing Systems*, pp. 1–8. New York, NY: Association for Computing Machinery. https://doi.org/10.1145/3334480.3382923
13. Carroll, L. (1865), *Alice's Adventures in Wonderland*, London: Macmillan.
14. Ünlüoğlu, D.Ü. (2023), 'Is history repeating itself? #WOMANINMETAVERSE', *Adıyaman Üniversitesi Sosyal Bilimler Enstitüsü Dergisi*, 16(45), 324–352. https://doi.org/10.14520/adyusbd.1355736
15. Mancini, T. and Sibilla, F. (2017), 'Offline personality and avatar customisation: Discrepancy profiles and avatar identification in a sample of MMORPG

players', *Computers in Human Behaviour*, 69, 275–283. https://doi.org/10.1016/j.chb.2016.12.031
16. Wonica, P. (2014), 'Exploring the Idealised Self: Avatars as a Vessel for Adolescent Identity Exploration and Growth', in J.E. McDougall, S. Nichols, and L. Thomas (eds), *Engaging with Videogames: Play, Theory and Practice*, Leiden: Brill, pp. 27–36.
17. Vasalou, A., Joinson, A., Bänziger, T., Goldie, P. and Pitt, J. (2008), 'Avatars in social media: Balancing accuracy, playfulness and embodied messages', *International Journal of Human–Computer Studies*, 66(11), 801–811. https://doi.org/10.1016/j.ijhcs.2008.08.002
18. Kafai, Y.B., Fields, D.A. and Cook, M.S. (2010), 'Your second selves: Avatar designs and identity play', *Games and Culture*, 1(5), 23. https://doi.org/10.1177/1555412009351260
19. McKenna, J.L., Wang, Y.C., Williams, C.R., McGregor, K. and Boskey, E.R. (2022), '"You can't be deadnamed in a video game": Transgender and gender diverse adolescents' use of video game avatar creation for gender-affirmation and exploration', *Journal of LGBT Youth*, 1–21. https://doi.org/10.1080/19361653.2022.2144583
20. McKenna, J.L., Wang, Y.C., Williams, C.R., McGregor, K. and Boskey, E.R. (2022), '"You can't be deadnamed in a video game": Transgender and gender diverse adolescents' use of video game avatar creation for gender-affirmation and exploration', *Journal of LGBT Youth*, 1–21. https://doi.org/10.1080/19361653.2022.2144583
21. Schulenberg, K., Freeman, G., Li, L. and Barwulor, C. (2023), '"Creepy Towards My Avatar Body, Creepy Towards My Body": How Women Experience and Manage Harassment Risks in Social Virtual Reality', *Proceedings of the ACM on Human–Computer Interaction*, 7(CSCW2), 1–29.
22. Herrera, F. and Bailenson, J.N. (2021), 'Virtual reality perspective-taking at scale: Effect of avatar representation, choice, and head movement on prosocial behaviours', *New Media & Society*, 23(8), 2189–2209. https://doi.org/10.1177/1461444821993121
23. Gabriels, K., Poels, K. and Braeckman, J. (2014), 'Morality and involvement in social virtual worlds: The intensity of moral emotions in response to virtual versus real life cheating', *New Media & Society*, 16, 451–469. https://doi.org/10.1177/1461444813487957
24. Howarth, C. (2002), 'Identity in whose eyes?: The role of representations in identity construction', *Journal for the Theory of Social Behaviour*, 32, 145–162. https://doi.org/10.1111/1468-5914.00181
25. Bibri, S. (2022), 'The social shaping of the metaverse as an alternative to the imaginaries of data-driven smart cities: A study in science, technology, and society', *Smart Cities*, 5(3), 832–874. https://doi.org/10.3390/smartcities5030043
26. Zhang, Q. (2022), 'Rule of the metaverse', *Metaverse*, 3(1). https://www.researchgate.net/publication/365073113_Rule_of_the_Metaverse

27. Mao, X., Li, X., Lu, W. and Li, Y. (2023), 'Metaverse: Deconstruction and differentiation of identity under the new media environment', *Advances in Social Sciences Research Journal*, 10(3), 229–236. https://doi.org/10.14738/assrj.103.14265
28. Carroll, L. (1865), *Alice's Adventures in Wonderland*, London: Macmillan.
29. Burgess, M.C.R., Dill, K.E., Stermer, S.P., Burgess, S.R. and Brown, B.P. (2011), 'Playing with prejudice: The prevalence and consequences of racial stereotypes in video games', *Media Psychology*, 14(3), 289–311. https://doi.org/10.1080/15213269.2011.596467
30. Steele, C.M. and Aronson, J. (1995), 'Stereotype threat and the intellectual test performance of African Americans', *Journal of Personality and Social Psychology*, 69(5), 797–811. https://doi.org/10.1037/0022-3514.69.5.797
31. Behm-Morawitz, E. and Mastro, D. (2009), 'The effects of the sexualization of female video game characters on gender stereotyping and female self-concept', *Sex Roles: A Journal of Research*, 61(11–12), 808–823. https://doi.org/10.1007/s11199-009-9683-8
32. Shaw, A. (2014), *Gaming at the Edge: Sexuality and Gender at the Margins of Gamer Culture*, Minneapolis, MN: University of Minnesota Press.
33. Greenwald, A.G. and Banaji, M.R. (1995), 'Implicit social cognition: Attitudes, self-esteem, and stereotypes', *Psychological Review*, 102(1), 4–27. https://doi.org/10.1037/0033-295X.102.1.4
34. Gray, K.L. (2012), 'Intersecting oppressions and online communities: Examining the experiences of women of color in Xbox Live', *Information, Communication & Society*, 15(3), 411–428. https://doi.org/10.1080/1369118X.2011.642401
35. Tajfel, H. and Turner, J.C. (1986), 'The Social Identity Theory of Intergroup Behaviour', in S. Worchel and W.G. Austin (eds), *Psychology of Intergroup Relations*, Chicago, IL: Hall Publishers, pp. 7–24.
36. Yee, N. and Bailenson, J. (2006, August 24), 'Walk a mile in digital shoes: The impact of embodied perspective-taking on the reduction of negative stereotyping in immersive virtual environments', paper presented at PRESENCE 2006: The 9th Annual International Workshop on Presence, Cleveland, OH.
37. Slater, M., Spanlang, B., Sanchez-Vives, M.V. and Blanke, O. (2010), 'First person experience of body transfer in virtual reality', *PloS One*, 5(5), e10564. https://doi.org/10.1371/journal.pone.0010564
38. Banakou, D., Hanumanthu, P.D. and Slater, M. (2016), 'Virtual embodiment of white people in a black virtual body leads to a sustained reduction in their implicit racial bias', *Frontiers in Human Neuroscience*, 10, 226766. https://doi.org/10.3389/fnhum.2016.00601
39. Dwivedi, Y.K., Kshetri, N., Hughes, L., Rana, N.P., Baabdullah, A.M., Kar, A.K. et al. (2023), 'Exploring the darkverse: A multi-perspective analysis of the negative societal impacts of the metaverse', *Information Systems Frontiers*, 25(5), 2071–2114. https://doi.org/10.1007/s10796-023-10400-x

40. Behm-Morawitz, E. (2014), 'Examining the intersection of race and gender in video game advertising', *Journal of Marketing Communications*, 23(3), 220–239. https://doi.org/10.1080/13527266.2014.914562
41. Craig, S.L., McInroy, L., McCready, L.T. and Alaggia, R. (2015), 'Media: A catalyst for resilience in lesbian, gay, bisexual, transgender, and queer youth', *Journal of LGBT Youth*, 12(3), 254–275. https://doi.org/10.1080/19361653.2015.1040193
42. DeHaan, S., Kuper, L.E., Magee, J.C., Bigelow, L. and Mustanski, B.S. (2013), 'The interplay between online and offline explorations of identity, relationships, and sex: A mixed-methods study with LGBT youth', *Journal of Sex Research*, 50(5), 421–434. https://doi.org/10.1080/00224499.2012.661489
43. GLAAD (2020), *Where we are on TV Report*, Gay and Lesbian Alliance Against Defamation. https://glaad.org/whereweareontv19/
44. Black, R. and Pretes, L. (2007), 'Victims and victors: Representation of physical disability on the silver screen', *Research and Practice for Persons with Severe Disabilities*, 32, 66–83. https://doi.org/10.2511/rpsd.32.1.66
45. Koss, M. (2015), 'Diversity in contemporary picturebooks: A content analysis', *Journal of Children's Literature*, 41, 32–42.
46. Seigneur, J. and Choukou, M. (2022), 'How should metaverse augment humans with disabilities?', *13th Augmented Human International Conference*. https://doi.org/10.1145/3532525.3532534
47. Banakou, D., Hanumanthu, P.D. and Slater, M. (2016), 'Virtual embodiment of white people in a black virtual body leads to a sustained reduction in their implicit racial bias', *Frontiers in Human Neuroscience*, 10, 226766. https://doi.org/10.3389/fnhum.2016.00601
48. Meyer, B. and Asbrock, F. (2018), 'Disabled or cyborg? How bionics affect stereotypes toward people with physical disabilities', *Frontiers in Psychology*, 9. https://doi.org/10.3389/fpsyg.2018.02251
49. Zhang, X., Yang, D., Yow, C.H., Huang, L., Wu, X., Huang, X. et al. (2022), 'Metaverse for cultural heritages', *Electronics*, 11(22), 3730. https://doi.org/10.3390/electronics11223730
50. Nakamura, L. (2009), *Digitizing Race: Visual Cultures of the Internet*, Minneapolis, MN: University of Minnesota Press.
51. Nakamura, L. (2009), *Digitizing Race: Visual Cultures of the Internet*, Minneapolis, MN: University of Minnesota Press.
52. Fox, J. and Tang, W.Y. (2014), 'Sexism in online video games: The role of conformity to masculine norms and social dominance orientation', *Computers in Human Behaviour*, 33, 314–320. https://doi.org/10.1016/j.chb.2013.07.014
53. Carroll, L. (1865), *Alice's Adventures in Wonderland*, London: Macmillan.
54. Zallio, M. and Clarkson, P.J. (2022), 'Designing the metaverse: A study on inclusion, diversity, equity, accessibility and safety for digital immersive environments', *Telematics and Informatics*, 75, 101909. https://doi.org/10.1016/j.tele.2022.101909

3. Alice between gendered violence and empowerment: implications for a feminist metaverse

Nikola Szirota

The first characteristic we notice about Alice is that she is a young woman. It does not matter if she identifies as such, but Alice does not enter Wonderland isolated from gender dynamics. Even though Alice imagines Wonderland as an escape from daily life, she soon notices its ambivalence. Wonderland is a place of creativity, madness and fun, but it is full of unexpected danger. This chapter takes us on a journey along the cracks of the metaverse: it analyzes its promises, uncovers its traps, and suggests ways out of power dynamics within this virtual world. Moreover, it draws parallels between women's[1] experiences in online gaming spaces and Alice's escape from Wonderland. Finally, it introduces the notion that personhood in the virtual cannot be genderless but is composed of affirmative identity categories.

I first learned of virtual violence in a seminar about online hate. A workshop moderator played a video in which a female gamer summarized numerous incidents of verbal abuse and assault in online games. The creator's series, "OMG a girl", comprises 40 videos documenting various cases of online harassment she experienced.[2] Male gamers' comments were violent, vulgar and attacked female co-players simply because of their gender. I was shocked, but not because I had never experienced harassment. Somehow, I had expected that people would adopt different behavior when they became a fictional character in a space dedicated to fantasy.

The metaverse promises a revolutionary social space detached from current physical and societal constraints. The imagination of a "blank" or even neutral social space raises hopes for a new society independent of current sociopolitical power relations.

As we will find out through our journey, I aim to show that online spaces are not disconnected worlds from our offline lives but reproduce their power dynamics. My story of video games, embodiment and feminist platform governance tries to question an illusionary emancipatory imagination of the metaverse.

Based on research on harassment in virtual spaces, I illustrate how online actions resemble the crossing of physical boundaries. Then, this chapter moves on to conceptualize Virtual Reality (VR) spaces as platforms, building on Gorwa.[3] It discusses adequate governance to guarantee metaverse users' safety regardless of their gender. It combines theoretical gaps in the theory of early cyberfeminism with various feminist lenses on three modes of governance. This chapter serves as a place to brainstorm forms of governance enabling personhood that includes an empowered notion of gender. It argues that collaborations based on similar gendered experiences hold the potential to change hierarchical structures that typically enforce gender discrimination. Overall, this piece aims to contribute to the discussion of feminist platform governance for a future virtual economy.

THE METAVERSE OF CYBERFEMINISM: A GENDER-FREE UTOPIA?

When Alice first enters Wonderland, she finds a world far removed from her own. In the 1951 movie adaptation of the novel Alice's Adventures in Wonderland, Alice recognizes anthropomorphic creatures she had previously only imagined. Her Wonderland changes shapes and paths and leads her to adventures of a completely new dimension. It seems like her existence as a little girl from England does not matter anymore. Can the metaverse take social life to a new level, independent of gender, race or class? Could individuals of marginalized groups create their own empowering version of the metaverse, just like Alice did with Wonderland?

Broadly, "metaverse" refers to a digital society in which people participate through their digital identities.[4] Hence the metaverse is co-created by people, machines and artificial intelligence.[5] Virtual reality takes place on digital infrastructure and services provided by commercial entities.[6] A rather new development suggests that the metaverse can be envisioned as a collaborative social space. When I first heard about the metaverse, I imagined a site in which people escape from their "real" life. I hoped that personhood would gain a new meaning, detached from identity categories I sometimes felt reduced to as a young woman. I was excited to imagine a social space that could uncover my "raw" identity, independent of preconceptions people have because of my gender, age or cultural background. Initially, literature research showed me that feminists of the 1990s have previously shared similar hopes. "Cyberfeminism" is a feminist movement that discusses the emancipatory potential of cyberspace. It gained popularity after Donna Haraway's publication of the "Cyborg manifesto".[7] The "cyborg" served as a feminist imagination envisioning a post-gender identity transcendent of the virtual and the real.[8] The political aim of cyberfeminism was equal access to various identities. It was built on a genderless approach replacing male domination. Moreover, cyberfeminism developed a transformative commitment to changing cyberspace towards gender equality. It rests on the assumption that the internet and digital sphere are inherently shaped by patriarchal and exploitative ideals and represent a male space.[9] Cyberfeminist strategies include online activism influencing social policy, technological empowerment and transcendence of technological power structures, as well as the critique of surveillance culture.[10]

While disembodied, gender non-conforming personhood might be the goal of a genderless utopia, scholars such as Brophy[11] suggest that the eradication of social categories could deny the situated experiences of individuals. Indeed, cyberfeminism stumbles over a central concept of feminist theory: embodiment. Embodiment entails physical experiences of subjective identity. It is ground for political inclusion or exclusion, as Threadcraft[12] writes. Feminists encountered embodiment with ambivalence: should it be embraced or transcended, as in a genderless cyberfeminist future?

In the 2010 movie adaptation by Tim Burton, Alice immerses herself in the adventures of Wonderland. To her, Wonderland is not real, and she cannot be harmed by the tyrannical Red Queen's army. If nothing is real, is anything possible? And if anything is possible, should we leave behind categories that have made up our identity?

Against hopes for a new disembodied future, there are arguments against leaving the gendered body behind. Overcoming embodiment might end up in neglecting real-life political issues in favor of technological solutionism.[13] Feminist theory faced the dilemma of aiming for a gender-free space versus establishing digital female personhood. My summary shows that theoretical groundwork for gender in the metaverse has existed since the 1990s. Next, I want to explore the reality of women in cyberspace.

VIOLENCE IN TODAY'S GENDERED VIRTUAL SPACES

Alice returns to a world in which agents already have a preconception of who she is. The Hatter welcomes her back, and her companions are surprised that Alice does not take on the role they have predicted. She has a dedicated place in Wonderland but is confused by its meaning. This predisposition equals the stereotyping of female players in online games, as they cannot escape from other gamers' preconceptions.

Recently, incidents of harassment against women in online spaces have come to the attention of academics, policy makers and global organizations, such as the United Nations.[14] Increasing political attention indicates that virtual actions are received similarly to offline issues.

This is because immersive gaming technologies allow for reality-like gaming experiences. Schulenberg et al. describe the current state of VR games as "Social VR",[15] allowing for real-time and embodied interaction "similar to face-to-face communication".[16] Technological tools are designed on a spectrum of VR, Augmented Reality (AR), and Extended Reality (XR).[17] This leads players to experience virtual worlds in a hyper-realistic way, which entails realistic experiences of assault and discrimination for gamers read as women.

Multiplayer real-time virtual worlds promote an enhanced perception of online reality through virtual and augmented reality technologies. They deliver live transmissions of audio signals by other players. This sensory experience leads not only to a reality that is perceived as real, but also to gendering processes within it. As Muhammad Ashraf[18] points out, voice transmissions in online games give away identity signals that are hard to mask. Additionally, the visual design of avatars hints at the gender of fellow gamers. Hence, the potential for gendered abusive behavior in the metaverse is connected to an immediate act of gendering among users.

Also in Wonderland, gender is omnipresent. Even though Wonderland is mostly inhabited by animals, many characters possess male gender attributes. Alice, however, remains a character read as a female human, even though she could have adapted and turned into an animal character. Alice's example illustrates how we continue to take our real-life identity with us to the virtual, even though we might not be aware of it.

Cyber-based violence towards women has been discussed since the first incident of a rape in cyberspace in 1993.[19] For today's virtual realities, two publications summarize virtual abuse and its implications. Schulenberg et al.[20] illustrate cases when women online were discriminated solely based on their voice or the design of their avatar. All their over-30 study participants reported having been a victim of sexual harassment in social VR. Likewise, Muhammad Ashraf[21] summarizes visual physical attacks by gamers against female characters during gameplay, as well as threats through audio live chats.

These studies highlight three factors through which the metaverse enforces discriminatory experiences: immersion, active presence and embodiment.[22,23] Live audiovisual tools not only reinforce but require active online participation. The tools strengthen the immersive sensory experience, so that embodiment of an avatar plays a crucial role in social virtual reality. From interviews, the authors recount that gamers' avatar bodies and their own physical experience felt entwined. The illusion of the ownership of the avatar's body leads to the perception of the intrusion into one's own personal space. Schulenberg et al. report on the so-called "phantom sense" – cases where some women "can feel so embodied in their VR avatars that they feel a 'phantom' sense of touch on their physical bodies when their avatar bodies are touched".[24]

According to Muhammad Ashraf,[25] debates around the real or virtual nature of sexual violence in cyberspaces and consequently rules about participation in virtual worlds have not yet been resolved. The transition between virtual and real boundaries could become even more blurred in the future of social VR. Ashraf highlights current plans to develop haptic vests as physical gaming garments. They would allow an extended sensory gaming experience by transmitting physical sensations of what is done to one's avatar – and risk transferring virtual assaults to the physical level. As Jonathan Fiene and Philipp Müller's chapter highlights, haptics could become an important feature of the metaverse.

Consequently, current literature links virtual and physical reality. Even though the virtual offers possibilities for gender-free expressions, established notions of gender find their way back into it. This connection is reinforced when women belonging to other marginalized, for example racialized, groups are affected by even more discrimination online. Moreover, scholars report cases of the collection of personal data of fellow female gamers among male VR participants.[26] The link between data collection of anonymized avatars highlights complex gender dynamics that cannot be regarded as isolated from the society they are happening in. Moreover, they are amplified by platform structures that facilitate harmful communication patterns and reinforce embodied experiences of gendered violence. It seems like a disembodied virtual experience outside of gendered norms becomes less realistic as immersive technologies become more and more so. Even if avatars of female players reflect a different body from their own, technology facilitates gendering according to established socio-physical categories like voice. Consequently, technology constructs a gendered virtual space. In Brophy's[27] words, by accessing the virtual world, people performatively cross a threshold into a form of intra-agency, where self-representation is enacted through a bodily experience.

What can we learn from the stories of female gamers? Technological infrastructure or affordances create an environment in which users immerse themselves. They dive into their own Wonderland, experiencing social interaction and even harassment. Gameplay technology and social interaction create internal consistency over the virtual. On the other side, phenomena like the phantom sense create an externally lived experience of the virtual. As Woods[28] highlights, online game spaces become fluid. Since experiences are tied to one's avatar as online personhood, they transcend the game space. Avatar actions feel real.

Video games as early stages of the metaverse exemplify how power is reproduced in digital spaces. My elaborations on the technological infrastructure of online games do not even touch on the commodification of female personhood. In game designs, womanhood is over-simplified. Female characters are hyper-sexualized in their visual appearances through the design of oversized breasts and bottoms.[29] The category of "female" tends to be limited to physical traits according to the beauty standard. Moreover, female characters are often given the role of a helpless damsel in distress or appear as the reward for game tasks. Like in advertising, the image of womanhood is often reduced to a few core tasks associated with romantic or sexual relationships or the home. Conversely, manhood is multifaceted. Game design thus transcends the real space and reproduces its power dynamics. The same can be said for Alice's experience in Wonderland. The design of the movie adaptation in 2010 equips Alice with tailored and extravagant outfits during her time in Wonderland, even though they do not contribute to her adventurous quest. Only when she fights the creature "the Jabberwock" and takes on a stereotypically male role does she wear armor.

Having gathered insights into women's experience of VR abuse, a disembodied exploration of the metaverse far away from intersectional power dimensions seems truly utopian. Today's applications of the metaverse prove that the transition into a virtual social space cannot leave behind central aspects of gender, as they are rooted in the existing social relations.

A FEMINIST PERSPECTIVE ON GOVERNING VIRTUAL SPACES AS PLATFORMS

The example of social VR as a site of gendered violence proves how gender is enforced through sensorial embodiment practices. Virtual spaces occupy the position of social spaces in which societal power structures are enforced into violent experiences. Hence, turning online spaces with discriminatory potential into sites of empowerment and free digital personhood requires suitable forms of governance.

This chapter relates "governance" to more than authority exercised by the state. Other actors like non-governmental organizations (NGOs) and companies shape the processes and relations within systems of governance towards governing networks.[30] Civil society has gained momentum in feminist theory, though it itself is a thoroughly gendered and racialized space. Governance thus assumes characteristics of fluid processes and interactions instead of persistent state steering.

However, governing virtual sites requires conceptualizing them as political spaces. At first, VR sites seem like a place for imagination, but I want to highlight that we should not fall into a trap of conceptualizing virtual spaces as detached from power dynamics. Online games and their faraway fantasy locations might appear as if they create worlds entirely different from our own, but they only serve to entertain the individual user.

In accordance with the famous feminist quote that "the private is political", I want to highlight that the most private and individual spaces are shaped by politicized ideas of dominance. This is why we need an approach that conceptualizes games as more than entertainment. The lens of political economy offers answers: by analyzing economic ownership and power structures, virtual spaces like gaming VR are framed as more than social sites and products. VR gaming sites present not only popular products but also companies with their corporate strategies. They mediate their users' behavior through technological tools in line with their business interests.

Political economy literature has researched digital products and networks as *platforms*, a perspective this chapter builds on. Platforms are services provided by technology companies, as well as by the corporate actors themselves.[31] By framing VR games and modern metaverses as platforms, the monetary aspirations behind products gain importance. Virtual reality worlds as current metaverses merge social worlds, entertainment products, and businesses. Behind these different purposes are also different interest groups. Gorwa ascribes civic labor as an attribute of platform governance: users and programmers, as well as governments, show interest in virtual worlds.[32] Therefore, Gorwa's definition of platform governance as a complex network of rule and norm setting within an online community can be applied to virtual worlds.

Governance may be defined by three modes: self-governance, external governance and co-governance.[33] In order to get a feeling for possible feminist intervention into violent cyberspaces, an analysis of power structures within these three platform governance modes is necessary. Furthermore, I want to present governance modes in their fluidity. Governance should therefore not only function to punish violators but work on more basic levels.

Self-governance

The first governance mode leaves regulatory mechanisms to the platform providers themselves. Self-governance allocates the platform companies with authority in creating sets of rules within their own company policies through technical tools or transparency efforts.[34] As Egliston et al.[35] report, most industry representatives favor self-governance. Nonetheless, it relieves them of liability towards civil interest groups or public actors. A feminist critique of self-governing platforms by Schneider[36] argues that companies understand measures of self-governance as governing users. Platforms frame users as responsible for potential harm, thus evading structural change of technical infrastructures that enforce discriminatory behavior. The author views technology companies as reinforcing patriarchal structures of top-down control, in which users take the role of passive customers acclimating to the regulatory systems of service providers.[37] Users therefore cannot shape governance mechanisms.

Current offers of content moderation on VR platforms illustrate the limits of self-governance. As part of their inquiry into assault experiences, Muhammad Ashraf and Schulenberg et al. asked female players about their typical reactions to online violence. They conclude that reporting back to platform providers is made difficult by the demand for proof of assaults via videos or written statements – which in fast-paced social VR is hard to document. Live content moderation cannot keep up with the number of assaults.[38, 39] Other measures include actively disabling abusive, but also all other remaining, avatars. Reporting or blocking transgressors is an active, yet not preventive measure and leaves the responsibilities with the people who have been negatively affected. Further counteractions are active ignorance, withdrawal or direct private confrontation.[40] I can only imagine how tiring it must be to feel responsible for a culprit's actions. Our society has managed to shift the responsibility of avoiding violence towards women, as we can see in victim blaming when women get raped, hurt or even murdered. Somehow, men as the agents of violence are still rarely targeted in public campaigns against violence. For example, prevention measures in public policy are underfunded. We can recognize an incomplete image of male personhood: an identity of an aggressor does not fit the image of personality that we have for men. While women are usually identified as victims, political measures cannot yet unite the reality of men as aggressors with measures against violence. Personhood comes with responsibility, but it seems our society has assigned responsibility to the genders differently. Consequently, modes of platform governance are directly connected to the meaning of personhood.

This digression into the micro-level of current metaverse dynamics on gendered personhood suggests that, like content moderation on social media, the responsibility for governing a digitized social sphere depends on platform providers and their technological infrastructure.[41] Their governance is steered by profit interests and not yet aligned with guidelines for a wider public good. Moreover, providers can establish rules independent from each other and fail to offer a generally safe user experience.

Alice faces similar challenges. Her constant shape-shifting and change in size can be seen as a metaphor of how she and VR users adapt to external consequences, not knowing of other ways. Even though Alice has agency in Wonderland, she accepts the means offered by her surroundings. Her inconsistent and unpredictable change in size through cakes marked by "Eat me" illustrates the way platform infrastructure regulates user experience.

The way that users find their safe spaces within virtual worlds can be interpreted as platform adaptation. Just like Alice, users try to adapt to the platform in the best way possible by forming alliances or using reporting mechanisms. Yet, the potential for harm is not reduced by adaptation mechanisms.

External Governance

Public governance can work as a response to the lack of universal standards for platform companies. Government initiatives hold a variety of binding legislative and jurisdictional measures. Nonetheless, a broad scope for national measures as well as international cooperation requires coordination among public interest groups, money and time resources. As Egliston et al. elaborate, some countries question the efficacy of domestic regulations in dealing with multinational firms.[42]

This might be the reason for transnational endeavors primarily focused on commercialization, market participation and content moderation.[43] However, states like Germany, with its "Netz DG" German Network Enforcement Law, and Australia, with a principle-led governance approach, stand out through their sovereign efforts on platform governance.[44]

Not much research touches on explicit feminist notes of external platform governance. Still, insights into government intervention on social media platforms from the Global South provide valuable insights into feminist struggle with state regulation. Suarez Estrada highlights how legal governmental initiatives can relieve platforms from responsibility by making them simply adhere to orders.[45] However, the author sees a threat to politically involved feminist activists and women. By declaring the virtual space to be an interest of the state, we risk opening paths for censorship and data privacy infringement. Instruments of state regulation thus carry the potential of politically disciplining citizens. Therefore, Suarez Estrada recommends that states offer public policies that provide protection, counseling and psychological support against digital violence.[46]

Returning to Wonderland, we find that the Red Queen is known for ruling violently. As soon as members of the court deviate from her expected behavior, she calls for their execution. The reasons for her "Off with their heads!" command are incomprehensible. Any citizen, regardless of their capacity to understand her orders, could become targeted. Supervising cyberspace presents a challenge, as the safety of individuals needs to be secured. Nevertheless, determining the seriousness of a crime requires an elaborated legal basis to prevent randomness. Moreover, as in Wonderland, the infrastructure of cyberspace complicates the tracing of personhood connected to cyber identities. Alice's companion, the Cheshire Cat, has found a way to manipulate its surrounding space, as it can dis- and reappear. This way, it evades the Red Queen. The Cheshire Cat in Wonderland shows us how cyber identities and their actions happen in dimensions that are insufficiently legally traceable. Therefore, total supervision of all cyberspace would require surveillance mechanisms even the Red Queen would dream of, and risks becoming totalitarian.

Co-governance

Co-governance assigns responsibility across involved interest groups. As Gorwa notes, co-governance models "seek to provide some values of democratic accountability without making extreme changes to the status quo."[47] Co-governance draws on extensive user participation in policy decisions. From a feminist standpoint, users, collaborations, NGOs and activists are crucial stakeholders. In contrast to self-governance, co-governance acknowledges all agents as democratic actors and thus offers a fuller picture of personhood.

NGOs can freely choose their field of action and build activist networks, connecting individuals. Gorwa points out that collectively organized protests or walkouts by unions hold the potential to steer company actions from the inside.[48] They can challenge individual parts of the system and act as an important counterpart, based on bottom-up momentum. This way, the personhood of users is not limited to victims but extends to interest groups in political negotiations.

The extension of user agency corresponds with the cyberfeminist approach to actively create safe and equal online spaces. Even though Schneider is not explicitly cyberfeminist, the author favors transforming platforms into so-called *governable spaces*.[49] This implies users having the agency to create their own separate spaces in the digital realm. Building on the feminist conception of selves as embedded in networks of relations, Schneider highlights collective moments. Participatory mechanisms like board meetings, elections and petitions involve users in decision-making processes. Hence, they are not subject to top-down platform control. Still, democratic processes alone do not guarantee the safety and inclusion of all users. In our social VR worlds, would players gendered as female receive the democratic means they deserve when their virtual environment is dominated by men? Virtual spaces hold the potential for discriminatory group behavior if most members engage in it, as the example of online gaming shows. Consequently, a user-centric approach requires digital infrastructure for equal participation to guarantee safe online behavior.

A counter-draft to hierarchical online spaces could promote self-organized online spaces for victimized users, as they hold potential for empowerment. Yet, they preclude access to resources, networks and programming skills not everyone affected by cyber violence can gain. The question remains whether we aim to implement safety in isolated spaces alongside or within virtual sites. Still, the future of emancipatory virtual spaces will present a fruitful research field for feminist scholarship.

In 1951's movie adaptation of *Wonderland*, as well as the original novel, Alice flees the Queen of Hearts at the last minute. She becomes aware that the world surrounding her is a dream and decides to wake up. This conscious process of waking up can be interpreted in two ways: either Alice flees from the Queen's danger, gives up, and never comes back; or her exit from Wonderland is also an emancipatory act, through which she leaves an unjust world behind and continues to dream of a more equal one.

Scholarship summarizes governance drafts of cooperation between multiple actors. Egliston et al. refer to the "triangle" of tech governance,[50] which consists of dyadic and triadic models of co-governance between state agencies, NGOs and tech companies. Such a collaboration could enhance "multiple governance",[51] which Suarez Estrada envisions as public policy informed by human rights and gender aspects that also holds platform companies accountable. Even though Gorwa describes co-governance models as unlikely in the near term (but still fruitful for a just digital economy), employable tools for the platform economy already exist.[52]

The setting of standards for platform providers could be informed by female gamer initiatives and nudge firms into accountability for their game design. Governments could position themselves as intermediaries between citizen interests and multinational companies. With governments sticking to recognizing all individuals as political stakeholders based on international law, states can manage to acknowledge personhood in official ways that platforms are currently evading. Through public funding, studies and campaigns can bring multiple stakeholders together. One example is the Gender in Play project funded by the Finnish Ministry of Justice, which brought together researchers with game developers for research about gender-based violence in online games.[53]

After all, platforms offer the infrastructure and affordances for collective action. Player collectives could assemble outside of the virtual and feed back into the development of a fair digital space. Such processes of feedback reassert personhood of VR users, as their right to speak up solidifies their existence in the digital. The 2010 movie adaptation of Alice's journey through Wonderland sketches Alice as an active character, who listens to her companions and fights the monster of the "Jabberwocky". As the story progresses, Alice's character becomes more and more recognized because of her efforts to fight the Red Queen. By forming an alliance with the White Queen, Alice contributes to changing the injustice she experienced in Wonderland.

GENDER AND PERSONHOOD IN THE METAVERSE

What can we learn from Alice's adventures in Wonderland, and how can we connect it to gendered personhood in the metaverse?

The digital sphere today, whether it pertains to our smartphones or takes place in virtual reality, works through gamification of the social. For example, dating apps create a competition for the best partners and thrive on new matches as rewards. Online marketing is based on data analyses of users and targets their screentime. Alice's journey through Wonderland is also shaped by game-like experiences. Whether she must eat or drink the correct amount to finally be the right size, or whether she is forced to play croquet with the Queen of Hearts, in Wonderland, Alice is lost in an abundance of madness, and her boundaries are crossed multiple times – to the extent of possible execution. She keeps looking for rules that could help clarify her own role in Wonderland, but she is mostly left in the dark. This irrational and bewildering mistreatment corresponds to the abuse female players experience in social VR games. Alice's constant act of eating refers to the "eat and be eaten" attitude of Wonderland and applies to online game environments.

In fact, we can observe Alice's human identity as a disruptive factor in Wonderland, which consists of animals and fictitious characters. Alice's reactions, emotions and irritability make her vulnerable to her mad surroundings. Her embodied experiences are thus portrayed as a barrier. Pearson[54] (2024) highlights the embodiment of female players as a disruption factor to the male-dominated gaming world. Male players are seen as the default identity, steering gaming through rationale. However, female players are reduced to their avatar's or technologically mediated vocal characteristics and perceived as a mismatch. Pearson draws the parallel of gaming identities to legal personhood by stating that the default legal person is still perceived as white and male, and female or otherwise marginalized identities represent deviations from it. Hence, she argues that law also reproduces the binary of embodiment (a female or marginalized trait) vs. reason (associated with the default and male identity).[55]

Notwithstanding, legal personhood and virtual online experience are inseparably intertwined with bodily experiences. Moreover, virtual actions transcend to the offline worlds and will be further mediated through haptic technology. As Pearson states, online games and metaverses necessitate the existence of avatars as embodied identities.[56] As we have seen at the beginning of our story, they are inherently gendered by design. Because gendering processes are deeply rooted in our society, they are transferred to the virtual. This does not mean that gender cannot be used in an empowering momentum. But we need to acknowledge that current virtual worlds are inherently biased towards gender. From what scholarship has gathered about digital violence in social networks, people in the metaverse will also harass others based on race, religion and cultural background. This outlook is quite pessimistic. We learned from cyberfeminist discussions that reshaping personhood into a cyborg risks eliminating crucial identity categories. I also gathered proof that even though users might conceal their identity, other people in the virtual world will expose and in turn commit digital violence. The manipulation of victims' identity is made difficult. In turn, culprits of digital violence profit from the intransparency of their avatars and evade facing consequences. These power relations resemble legal personhood in real life, especially when it comes to gendered violence and sexual assault.

"Personhood" is a category that is differently styled depending on who it applies to. As my comparison with victim blaming showed, responsibility for abuse is often ascribed to female victims. VR platforms are currently not created with technological tools that prevent assaults, and culprits can easily evade consequences. Pearson theorizes that "personhood" means a neutral entity but implicitly is sketched to apply to men only. This is why VR spaces nowadays are limited to a few mechanisms to limit violence, of which most must be taken up by victims. I conclude that the supposed neutrality of personhood neglects harassment and violence, which is the reason for limited preventive measures. Moreover, platforms perceive personhood as a passive attribute of their users, which is why they favor self-governance. Yet, users are not at all passive. This shows when male online gamers become culprits and exert violent abuse on others, so that the whole gaming experience transforms for e.g. female users. The absence of activity and a neutral perception of personhood leads to men not facing consequences for their violent behavior online. This is why I end my chapter with a call for action towards establishing multifaceted notions of personhood. In real or virtual life, personhood is gendered. As long as we ignore this, we shift responsibility for assaults from aggressors to victims. Therefore, I call for an explicitly gendered concept of personhood, as it should adequately encompass identities and experiences of all genders. But identities are not only gendered – they are queer, young and old, disabled, BIPOC, and much more. Just like our offline world does not accommodate a variety of personhood – look at the discrimination of trans people by law or the barriers that disabled people face in their daily and working life – the virtual is not yet accessible for users whose identities deviate slightly from what platforms have coded as "normal". Consequently, we need a multifaceted approach to personhood.

Because of the transcendence of identity from the offline world into the virtual, I assume that future users of the metaverse will not discard their offline identity when they log in online. I conclude that personhood can be empowered and maybe even be detached from real life – but only in a way that recognizes the variety in experiences that shape one's identity.

At the end of my story, I do not want to leave you with a pessimistic outlook on life in the metaverse.

Alice decided to shape Wonderland by either fighting its evils or leaving it altogether. Indeed, the virtual feature of the metaverse suggests that it can be malleable, and co-governance models suggest that representative groups have the potential to call for a change in digital environments. Pearson argues that we need to reconfigure legal personhood in favor of non-male identities, and I urge personhood to be prepared in the metaverse for the embodied experiences of various users.

The metaverse at some point will be used by a variety of people, which means they could all co-create the virtual worlds they use. Pearson highlights that fan narratives of online games hold an empowering momentum. Counter-narratives to established stereotypes will thus play a crucial role in the creation of a just metaverse. As a final section, I introduce feminist imperatives influenced by an activist framework for feminist digital justice.

OUTLOOK: IMPLICATIONS FOR A (CYBER) FEMINIST METAVERSE

At the end of Alice in Wonderland, our main character wakes up from her trip. She might ask herself: was this even real?

This is a question people who are read as female might have wondered when they left the virtual world after having experienced acts of violence by fellow online gamers. My story proved gender plays a significant role in cyberspace. I empathize with early cyberfeminist wishes for a cyborg identity, as a world in which societal categories play no part serves as a seductive escape. But the end of my chapter indicates that we need to revise the cyberfeminist narrative into a story that acknowledges diverse personhood and the platform mechanisms enabling and constraining it. Still, cyberfeminist notions of changing technological infrastructure remain highly relevant. Indeed, together with political economic and feminist notions from the Global South, they end up expanding accountability to platform providers and policy makers.

As we drew parallels between platforms and the metaverse, we became aware of its ownership structures. The metaverse is not a neutrally designed space, as virtual worlds are created with a particular design, infrastructure and goal. Video games are built on gamifying competition, which ends up with profit for their creators and violent experiences for some of their users. Technological infrastructure and game design reproduce stereotypes and promote violence. Moreover, the tendency of corporations to move to a monopoly position and the paternalistic structures of platforms present key factors in today's data economy.

An initiative by a collaboration between the research and activist networks DEVELOPMENT ALTERNATIVES WITH WOMEN FOR A NEW ERA (DAWN) and IT FOR CHANGE from the Global South has launched the so-called "Declaration of Feminist Digital Justice".[57] Its counter-narrative of a just virtual world is characterized by a non-market logic building on participation and collective action towards collaborative spaces. These spaces would be governed globally, but publicly accessible to scrutiny. A publicly funded communication infrastructure could lead cyberfeminist identities to thrive.

The state can therefore be involved but not dominant in creating equally accessible cyberspaces. NGOs and citizen initiatives could use their representation and collective momentum to participate in the creation of just platform structures. The more people who have access to designing the metaverse, the more it can adjust to differing needs. Gender as an identity category might become less important in the faraway future of the metaverse, but this requires active co-creation of virtual spaces between platform founders and users.

Alice herself was never afraid to share her opinion and mastered the adventures of Wonderland even in times of confusion and insecurity. My story should therefore not portray users affected by online discrimination as victims but points out the ways in which they can collaborate. As the Declaration of Feminist Digital Justice[58] shows, users of all kinds are joining together to create better conditions for a just metaverse. Various gaming collectives have evolved out of Facebook groups for gamers to network and have established relationships with platform providers and funding organizations. In a short online search, I could find collectives like Black Girl Gamers,[59] Qweerty Gamers[60] and Femme Gaming.[61] Stakeholders are already organizing in favor of their representation, and I assume would be ready for shaping a metaverse built on equality.

In the end of the 2010 movie, Alice goes back to the real world. In Wonderland, she gained confidence through fighting for her beliefs and ending the reign of the tyrannical Red Queen. Back in her real life, she is not afraid to act against what others have determined for her. Alice returns empowered and makes her own decisions. In an ideal metaverse, all users would feel empowered by virtual experiences. Until then, we have a long way to go. In the story I just told, I disenchanted the narrative of a metaverse without power relations. If Alice had known what awaited her in Wonderland and whom to ask for advice, she might have navigated her path more easily. My story could not cover all aspects of intersectional feminist theory and included only snippets of political economy. Still, it could hopefully give Alice a little direction for her next visit to Wonderland.

NOTES

1. The terms "woman" and "female" describe anyone who identifies as such. This chapter will also address gendering as an external process by others onto people who do not necessarily identify as women but face sexist harassment.
2. Spawntaneous, "What Girl Gamers REALLY Have To Deal With", OMG a Girl Series, episode 1, April 19, 2018, 7 min., 59 sec., https://www.youtube.com/watch?v=jL0aVqVslSE.
3. Robert Gorwa, "What Is Platform Governance?" *Information, Communication & Society* 22, no. 6 (2019), https://doi.org/10.1080/1369118X.2019.1573914.

4. Li Qian, "A Study on Gender Politics of Feminist Narration in Metaverse Context", in *Frontiers in Artificial Intelligence and Applications*, ed. Lakhmi C. Jain, Valentina Emilia Balas, Qun Wu and Fuqian Shi (IOS Press, 2023), 628.
5. Qian, "Gender Politics", 628.
6. Gorwa, "Platform Governance", 3.
7. Donna Haraway, *Simians, Cyborgs and Women: The Reinvention of Nature* (Routledge, 1991).
8. Haraway, *Simians, Cyborgs and Women*, 149–50.
9. Gözde Ersöz, Gökmen Kantar and Meltem İnce Yenilmez, *Reconstructing Feminism through Cyberfeminism* (BRILL, 2024), 13.
10. Ersöz, Kantar and Yenilmez, *Reconstructing Feminism*, 208.
11. Jessica E. Brophy, "Developing a Corporeal Cyberfeminism: Beyond Cyberutopia", *New Media & Society* 12, no. 6 (September 2010): 933. https://doi.org/10.1177/1461444809350901.
12. Shatema Threadcraft, "Embodiment", in *The Oxford Handbook of Feminist Theory*, ed. Lisa Disch and Mary Hawkesworth, Vol. 1 (Oxford University Press, 2015).
13. Brophy, "Beyond Cyberutopia", 931–32.
14. "Video Games and Violence Against Women and Girls: A Double-Edged Sword in the Digital Age", United Nations Western Europe, last modified December 8, 2023, https://unric.org/en/video-games-and-violence-against-women-and-girls/.
15. "Social VR is one type of VR system that allows multiple users to join a collaborative virtual environment and communicate with each other, usually by means of visual and audio cues." Definition by Jie Li and Pablo Cesar, "Chapter 22 – Social Virtual Reality (VR) Applications and User Experiences", in *Immersive Video Technologies*, ed. Giuseppe Valenzise, Martin Alain, Emin Zerman and Cagri Ozcinar (Academic Press, 2023), 609.
16. Kelsea Schulenberg, Guo Freeman, Lingyuan Li and Catherine Barwulor, "'Creepy Towards My Avatar Body, Creepy Towards My Body': How Women Experience and Manage Harassment Risks in Social Virtual Reality", *Proceedings of the ACM Human–Computer Interaction* 7, no. CSCW2, 236 (October 2023): 5. https://doi.org/10.1145/3610027.
17. Ben Egliston, Marcus Carter and Kate Euphemia Clark, "Who Will Govern the Metaverse? Examining Governance Initiatives for Extended Reality (XR) Technologies", *New Media & Society* 27, no. 6 (2024): 3361–3381, 3364. https://doi.org/10.1177/14614448231226172.
18. Merrin Muhammad Ashraf, "Gender-Based Abuse on the Metaverse: The New Internet Is Being Coded on a Toxic Palimpsest", Merrin Muhammad Ashraf, *Bot Populi* (blog), last modified January 23, 2023, https://botpopuli.net/?post_type=post&p=6887.
19. Richard MacKinnon, "Virtual Rape", *Journal of Computer-Mediated Communication* 2, no. 4 (1 March 1997), https://doi.org/10.1111/j.1083-6101.1997.tb00200.x.

20. Schulenberg, Freeman, Li and Barwulor, "'Creepy Towards My Avatar Body, Creepy Towards My Body'", 22.
21. Muhammad Ashraf, "Gender-Based Abuse on the Metaverse".
22. Muhammad Ashraf, "Gender-Based Abuse on the Metaverse".
23. Schulenberg, Freeman, Li and Barwulor, "'Creepy Towards My Avatar Body, Creepy Towards My Body'", 9.
24. Schulenberg, Freeman, Li and Barwulor, "'Creepy Towards My Avatar Body, Creepy Towards My Body'", 15.
25. Muhammad Ashraf, "Gender-Based Abuse on the Metaverse".
26. Schulenberg, Freeman, Li and Barwulor, "'Creepy Towards My Avatar Body, Creepy Towards My Body'", 9–15.
27. Brophy, "Beyond Cyberutopia", 938–39.
28. Orlando Woods, "Feminist Geographies of Online Gaming", *Digital Geography and Society* 2 (2021): 100015. https://doi.org/10.1016/j.diggeo.2021.100015.
29. Woods, "Feminist Geographies of Online Gaming", 3.
30. Ki-young Shin, "Governance", in *The Oxford Handbook of Feminist Theory*, ed. Lisa Disch and Mary Hawkesworth, Vol. 1 (Oxford University Press, 2015): 304–325. https://doi.org/10.1093/oxfordhb/9780199328581.013.16.
31. Gorwa, "Platform Governance", 4.
32. Gorwa, "Platform Governance", 9.
33. Gorwa, "Platform Governance", 12.
34. Gorwa, "Platform Governance", 13.
35. Egliston, Carter and Clark, "Who Will Govern the Metaverse?", 8.
36. Nathan Schneider, "Governable Spaces: A Feminist Agenda for Platform Policy", *Internet Policy Review* 11, no. 1 (2022): 5. https://doi.org/10.14763/2022.1.1628.
37. Schneider, "Governable Spaces", 3.
38. Muhammad Ashraf, "Gender-Based Abuse on the Metaverse".
39. Schulenberg, Freeman, Li and Barwulor, "'Creepy Towards My Avatar Body, Creepy Towards My Body'", 15–17.
40. Schulenberg, Freeman, Li and Barwulor, "'Creepy Towards My Avatar Body, Creepy Towards My Body'", 15–17.
41. Caroline Haythornthwaite, "Moderation, Networks, and Anti-Social Behavior Online", *Social Media + Society* 9, no. 3 (2023): 6. https://doi.org/10.1177/20563051231196874.
42. Egliston, Carter and Clark, "Who Will Govern the Metaverse?", 7.
43. Tambiama Madiega, Polona Car, Maria Niestad and Louise Van de Pol, "Metaverse: Opportunities, Risks and Policy Implications. Briefing", European Parliamentary Research Service, 3–7, last modified 24 June 2022. https://www.europarl.europa.eu/RegData/etudes/BRIE/2022/733557/EPRS_BRI(2022)733557_EN.pdf.
44. Gorwa, "Platform Governance", 3.

45. Marcela Suarez Estrada, "Feminist Struggles against Criminalization of Digital Violence: Lessons for Internet Governance from the Global South", *Policy & Internet* 14, no. 2 (2022): 419. https://doi.org/10.1002/poi3.277.
46. Suarez Estrada, "Feminist Struggles", 420.
47. Gorwa, "Platform Governance", 15.
48. Gorwa, "Platform Governance", 12.
49. Schneider, "Governable Spaces", 6.
50. Egliston, Carter and Clark, "Who Will Govern the Metaverse?", 3.
51. Suarez Estrada, "Feminist Struggles", 420.
52. Gorwa, "Platform Governance", 16.
53. Taina Myöhänen, "Gender-Based Violence in Games: Game Developers' Perspectives", *We in Games Finland*, last modified June 22, 2022. https://weingames.fi/gender-based-violence-in-games-game-developers-perspectives/.
54. Ashley Pearson, "The Parallel Lives of Legal Persons and Video Game Avatars", in *The Routledge Handbook of Cultural Legal Studies*, ed. Karen Crawley, Thomas Giddens and Timothy D Peters, 1st ed. (Routledge, 2024), 228.
55. Pearson, "The Parallel Lives", 230.
56. Pearson, "The Parallel Lives", 225.
57. "The Declaration of Feminist Digital Justice", Working Group on Feminist Digital Justice 2023, last modified 2025, https://feministdigitaljustice.net/.
58. "The Declaration of Feminist Digital Justice", Working Group on Feminist Digital Justice 2023.
59. "Black Girl Gamers: Home", Black Girl Gamers, accessed June 10, 2025, https://www.theblackgirlgamers.com.
60. "Qweerty Gamers", Qweerty Gamers, accessed June 10, 2025, https://www.qweertygamers.org.
61. "Femme Gaming | About Us", *Femme Gaming*, accessed June 10, 2025, https://femmegaming.gg/about-us/.

4. Wonderland rebooted: Alice's gaming odyssey in the Metaverse

Auxane Boch and Bethany Rhea Thomas

INTRODUCTION

> "I am not crazy, my reality is just different from yours"
>
> Cheshire Cat, Alice's Adventures in Wonderland[1]

Hello, readers: here are Auxane and Beth. Before we take you to Alice's Odyssey, we'd like to tell you about our own Odyssey.

I, Auxane, became a gamer very early on, though at the time I didn't know that was what I was becoming. At first, I enjoyed simple digital games with my parents (*Pacman* and arcade games), sharing laughs around the screen and building those early bonds through pixels and play. Then came LAN parties with my brother, *Duke Nukem* and *Counter-Strike*. Those sessions weren't just about winning; they were about connection. In fact, I think that time, huddled over clunky keyboards and CRT monitors, was when our relationship was at its best. We learned how to work together, compete (sometimes) fairly, and laugh at the chaos of it all. Those games gave us a language when we didn't have many others. As I got older, I was drawn towards more complex games – enigma-based adventures and investigation narratives that challenged my mind. I devoured titles that asked me to think beyond surface-level actions to piece together stories from fragmented clues. These games didn't just teach me how to solve puzzles; they taught me empathy. I began to understand that different characters (and people) could have vastly different motivations. What I perceived as a bad action might come from a place of love, fear, or necessity. These digital investigations mirrored human complexity and quietly shaped how I saw the world.

Then came the *Assassin's Creed* series when I was about 9 or 10 – particularly the Ezio saga – and I fell in love with learning history through gameplay. Those games gave me a curiosity I didn't know I had. When I visited Florence at 23, it felt oddly familiar, as if I already knew the layout, the architecture, and the political tensions. Games, I realised, could be cultural education wrapped in adrenaline and beauty. *Warcraft I* and *II*, *StarCraft*, and *Diablo* pulled me into the world of strategy. I loved the planning, the multitasking, and the project management (even if I wouldn't have called it that at the time). It's funny how that stuck, because those are skills I still use every single day. *The Sims* sparked a fascination with architecture and interior design. Then came more narrative games that challenged my views of the world in general, from *Heavy Rain* and its incarnation of a parent looking for their child to *Life is Strange* and realising that big topics such as climate change and bullying have a real-life impact. French studios made us think!

That deep connection between play, learning, and empathy eventually led me to become a cyberpsychologist. It felt like the most natural next step – studying how technology and digital environments shape our minds, behaviours, and relationships. But even within that field, I found myself pulled towards one focus: game psychology. I knew, instinctively and through experience, that games were more than just entertainment. They were powerful tools for education, empathy, and critical thinking. Games put us in someone else's shoes, sometimes quite literally, and ask us to make decisions, face consequences, and understand perspectives different from our own. Whether it's navigating moral dilemmas, managing complex systems, or seeing the world through the eyes of a character nothing like ourselves, games give us space to reflect and grow. I believed then, and still believe now, that if we want to build a more compassionate and thoughtful world, games are one of the best places to start. Games have given me so much. They've helped me reflect on myself, understand others, and view the world through entirely new lenses. They stretch our minds and make us think critically, often without us even realising it. Games aren't a distraction from learning – they're one of its oldest and most powerful forms. From pretend play in childhood to expansive digital quests in adulthood, games have always been tools for discovery.

That's why I believe games must be part of any serious conversation about our future. They're not childish. They're not trivial. They are some of the most sophisticated tools we have for thinking, feeling, and growing. And as we step further into immersive technologies and the Metaverse, we have to recognise the power of play, not just as entertainment, but as a force for transformation.

Like Auxane, I (Beth) was a gamer before I knew what a gamer was, although I still question what a gamer truly is. I do not have an answer, but I do know this: I remember stealing my sister's first console, becoming hyper-fixated when I finally got my own, and hiding it under my pillow every school night to keep playing until the late hours of the evening, as often as I could. Games have been a part of my life for over 22 years, something I have been quietly passionate about for a long time, and as I have found my voice in studying games and gamers, I've become louder about my interest, my belonging in the space, and more importantly – my anger. I'm angry that, as an industry, games continuously seem to take one step forward and three steps back. It isn't good enough anymore, and games know it. We know that games have such a tremendous potential to make a profound impact on players, in so many ways, from cognitive skills to perspective-taking and empathy-building, to well-being, to social support, to identity exploration and affirmation… games could do it all. And yet they fall flat, almost every time. In Alice's story, we also show the "dark side of games", not because we believe games are bad – in fact, quite the opposite: we show this side because we love games, and we want much more for them, and for players.

And speaking of origins… we (Beth and Auxane) actually met on one site, the one we won't name because its current owner seems to believe free speech includes Nazi gestures, apartheid sympathising, and anti-trans rants. Spoiler: it doesn't. But back on the 8th of July, 2022, that site gave us a single spark – a shared interest in games, gamers, EDI, wild project ideas, and the ongoing crime of calling everything "British" when it's very much Scottish or Welsh or Northern Irish (respect the regions, folks). From that spark came years of support, late-night DMs, very academic meltdowns, PhD commiserations (they're almost done, we promise), and a beautiful friendship that turned into collaboration. Writing these chapters together didn't just come from shared research; it came from shared values, shared laughter, and shared rage. When we talk about the Metaverse here, we mean the future of immersive, connected, interactive worlds. This work, both this chapter and the one on Alice meeting herself, is rooted in friendship, feminist resistance, ethical reflection, digital joy, and the belief that the world can be better… especially if we build it ourselves. Let's begin.

LEVEL 1: THE ENTRANCE TO WONDERLAND

> "Begin at the beginning," the King said gravely, "and go on till you come to the end: then stop."
>
> Alice's Adventures in Wonderland[2]

Alice, yawning and blurry-eyed from her adventures in Wonderland, stumbled upon a mysterious link in a forum she'd never seen before. She had heard from the Hatter, who was oh so mad about the new updates for "WonderGround", the latest in metaverse gaming, when a new notification blinked in the corner of her vision: "Try the White Rabbit Experience?" The text was simple and unassuming, but as soon as Alice hovered over the link, her VR headset buzzed with anticipation. Playing games? Really? Alice felt torn. Part of her felt as though games were a childish diversion, and after all, she'd never seen herself as a "gamer". Sure, she'd dabbled at croquet with the Queen of

Hearts and played the occasional round of Pogs, but joining a real game in the metaverse, and maybe even a team? It felt like an intimidating leap, a step she was unsure how to take.

"Press Start … Press Start … Press Start," the text flashed. Alice pondered for a moment; she realised this was one experience she had yet to try, one that her friends there had talked about often. And so, without thinking twice, she clicked.

In a swirl of light and colour, Alice found herself spiralling downward, deeper and deeper, as if gravity had decided to invert itself and she was plummeting towards… somewhere else. She wasn't sure if she was falling, flying, or something in between, but she knew for certain… she was ready to play.

Alice, now fully within the White Rabbit Experience, steps into a reimagined Wonderland. It is digital. It is detailed. And yet, it is unlike any simulation she has entered before. The space feels real, not in its fidelity to the physical world, but in the way it holds her. The landscape is absurd: floating teacups drift past surreal forests, and card soldiers march upside down. But her body responds as though this reality matters. This is what we call immersion. Technically, immersion refers to the objective capacity of the system to deliver a multisensory environment. It's about input fidelity – how well the VR setup can stimulate the senses through visuals, sound, touch, and even spatial presence.[3,4] In Wonderland, this is achieved through spatial audio cues, haptic feedback synced to Alice's interactions, and high-resolution rendering of impossible-yet-convincing virtual terrains.

But immersion alone is not enough. Alice is not just reacting to stimuli; she's feeling herself in the world. That's presence, the perceptual illusion of non-mediation, or what has been called the sensation of "being there".[5] Presence is subjective and deeply tied to how the user internalises the experience, arising when the sensory information is sufficient to trigger reflexive, automatic responses.[6] In Alice's case, presence creeps up on her slowly. At first, she notices her hands moving with surprising intentionality. She begins responding to shadows, turning towards sounds that no speaker in her room could be emitting. Her perceptual system has accepted Wonderland as a working reality, even if her logical mind still knows she is wearing a headset. This dual state is central to the Metaverse experience: to be physically grounded and digitally immersed; to know but still believe.

The deeper Alice ventures, the more her cognitive system struggles to reconcile conflicting truths. Wonderland feels real, her body says so, but her conscious awareness still clings to the knowledge that this is a simulation. This tension creates what researchers refer to as cognitive dissonance; this phenomenon has been explored as a form of reality testing.[7] The mind toggles between acceptance and rejection of the virtual world. For Alice, this manifests in moments of doubt, as when she tries to remember where the walls of her room should be or questions whether the wind brushing past her cheek was imagined. VR presence results from a perceptual-cognitive delay: sensory systems react reflexively to immersive stimuli, while cognitive systems lag, evaluating and questioning the inputs.[8] This delay can intensify the immersive experience but can also lead to confusion or disorientation. Alice catches herself flinching when a cat jumps from a tree. She leans away from cliffs and crouches when branches sweep overhead. These aren't roleplay gestures – they're embodied reactions. The immersion is working. But the cost is a sense of slipping into confusion, wonder, and a world that resists the usual rules of perception. VR does not just speak to the eyes. It speaks to the heart, to the skin, to the nervous system.

Alice finds herself sweating slightly as she runs towards a floating chessboard. Her pulse quickens. Her shoulders tighten at the sight of the Queen of Hearts. Physiologically, her body is responding to threats. Not imagined, but perceived. Immersive VR environments activate the autonomic nervous system in ways analogous to physical-world stressors.[9] Heart rate variability, skin conductance, and cortisol levels can shift in response to virtual cues. In other words, the illusion doesn't stay on the screen – it invades the body. The implications here are powerful. VR can offer embodied experiences that transcend passive observation. This is transformative for users like Alice, who may have previously felt disconnected from their avatars or digital personas. The body becomes a site of virtual participation.

Alice approaches a door. It's absurdly tall and made of keys. As she reaches out, her controller emits a pulse – a vibration timed perfectly with her movement. It's a small gesture, but it anchors her. This is haptic feedback, the technology of touch in virtual spaces – tactile realism enhances spatial awareness and emotional involvement.[10] In Wonderland, the vibrations simulate texture, resistance, and even temperature. They ground the visual illusion in the physical. And that matters. Because as Alice touches more of Wonderland, she becomes more of it. The tactile becomes the real.

But not all is pleasant. After several intense sequences, leaping across checkerboard ravines, evading flamingo riders, Alice begins to feel a creeping discomfort. Her vision blurs slightly. Her stomach churns. Cybersickness, a common side effect of VR, is caused by sensory conflict between the visual and vestibular systems.[11] Her eyes register motion; her inner ear does not. The result is nausea, disorientation, and a growing desire to rip off the headset. And yet, she persists. She spots a glimmering mushroom. Atop it sits a familiar bottle: "Drink Me." She almost rolls her eyes. But her stomach clenches again. Her body demands a solution. She drinks.

As Alice sips, the world subtly adjusts. The edges of her vision darken during movement, a technique known as vignetting – this significantly reduces visual overload and motion sickness.[12] She turns her head to follow a darting rabbit, and the motion is smooth this time. The system has activated asynchronous time warp, a technique that adjusts the VR display to real-time head movement.[13] Meanwhile, her footsteps now sync with pulses in her controller. These haptic cues provide a rhythm that her brain can trust. Aligning visual and tactile feedback can reduce dissonance and stabilise the user's spatial orientation.[14] Finally, the system introduces structured breaks – gentle pauses in gameplay that let her rest. A gradual exposure and pacing are recommended to reduce the cumulative effects of cybersickness.[15] Together, these techniques don't break immersion – they protect it.

By the end of Level 1, Alice has crossed not one but many thresholds. From observer to participant. From presence to embodiment. From curiosity to confidence. Her journey reminds us that VR is not just visual – it is visceral. It moves through the skin, through the heartbeat, through the dissonance of knowing and still believing. Immersion is not merely about simulation fidelity; it is about sensory harmony. And presence is not merely about being tricked… it's about choosing to believe.

And belief in the Metaverse can be a radical act.

Alice keeps going and runs into friends who are playing games; they tell her to join. She feels a bit overwhelmed by the idea, but after all, why not?! She's not a gamer, but a bit of fun never killed anyone (as long as the queen with a penchant for beheading doesn't show up in the background!).

LEVEL 2: ALICE JOINS THE GAME

> "That's a great deal to make one word mean."
>
> Alice, Through the Looking-Glass, and What Alice Found There[16]

"Hm, a gamer?" Alice pondered aloud, gazing into the dazzling, animated worlds beyond the glowing gameboard. "I suppose anyone might be a gamer – but would 'anyone' include me?" Her hesitation came swiftly, carrying echoes from old stories whispered in her ear … gaming was a world for someone else, someone male, competitive, and solitary.[17,18] The images she'd seen, the voices she'd overheard, suggested a space not designed with her in mind. Yet her curiosity tugged gently at the edges of her uncertainty. With one last glance backwards, she stepped forward, whispering, "Perhaps I'll belong if I dare to try."

At first, Alice played without a plan or purpose. She chased digital rabbits across neon landscapes, laughed when defeated by a goose in pixelated croquet, and danced beneath showers of virtual fireworks. Each moment felt light, spontaneous, and deeply freeing – much to her surprise. This playfulness ignited feelings of autonomy, connection, and competence; elements fundamental to psychological well-being.[19] Games weren't merely contests or distractions; they became gentle invitations to explore and enjoy, a space for joyful presence rather than mere performance. Alice felt herself breathe easier, finding comfort similar to players who had sought solace in games like *Animal Crossing: New Horizons* during chaotic times such as the COVID-19 pandemic.[20] In play, Alice discovered more than enjoyment – she found peace.

But soon, the games began presenting her with sharper challenges. Alice's hands trembled slightly as she raced against time, deciphering puzzles that grew more complex with every level. One moment, she constructed fragile bridges with limited resources; the next, she rerouted electronic circuits moments before explosions lit her goggles. Though intense, these challenges became a source of pride. She realised she wasn't merely playing games but actively honing skills: logic, problem-solving, and swift decision-making abilities transferable beyond digital realms.[21,22,23] Her reflexes sharpened, confidence soared, and creative thinking blossomed. When Alice delved into narrative adventures like *Detroit: Become Human* or puzzles like those in *Portal 2*, she noticed growth in her memory, attention, and capacity to learn.[24] Each digital victory wasn't simply entertainment – it was genuine self-development.

Soon, the worlds she visited were not solitary adventures but vibrant hubs of cooperation and friendship. Initially hesitant, Alice cautiously joined collaborative quests. Quickly, caution melted into camaraderie. Her new teammates taught her the importance of clear communication, empathy, and trust – social and emotional competencies that reached far beyond the confines of a screen.[25] When teammates stumbled, Alice encouraged them; when she faltered, their reassurance lifted her. These fleeting interactions became foundational lessons, shaping genuine connections. She understood firsthand what studies affirm: cooperative gaming deepens empathy and fosters real-world social bonds.[26] The digital community she found was transient yet profoundly meaningful.

With growing confidence, Alice began to experiment with her avatar's identity. She lengthened dresses, changed hairstyles, and altered expressions and gestures. Each choice felt deeply personal, far beyond aesthetics – it was an act of self-discovery and self-expression[27] where players have unprecedented freedom to perform their concept of self.[28] She noted how every tweak subtly influenced her mood and her interactions. Sometimes, wings emboldened her; a knight's armour made her feel noble – a manifestation of what researchers call the Proteus Effect.[29] For players from marginalised groups, these transformations can hold special significance. Alice knew from her own quiet observation that games served as precious havens for those who needed safe spaces to explore identities they couldn't express safely offline, particularly trans and gender-diverse players navigating hostile real-world contexts.[30,31,32,33] Each avatar adjustment drew her deeper into an immersive sense of self-ownership and presence.

Yet not every encounter was welcoming. Alice vividly recalled a sharp comment about her avatar choices; a mocking tone questioning her skill. Such instances of gatekeeping – especially towards women, people of colour, LGBTQ+, and disabled gamers – reminded her that, despite their potential, games remained embedded within broader societal prejudices.[34,35,36] Reflecting on her experiences, Alice wondered how much of her initial hesitation was born from internalised stereotypes. She also questioned whether the worlds themselves inadvertently reinforced these biases. Could this Wonderland have been designed differently, to be less restrictive, less monetised, less biased, to embrace more openly who she wanted to become?[37,38] Perhaps the problem wasn't just with individuals but the design itself, subtly shaping how players interacted and who felt allowed to participate. In these moments, Alice resolved not just to play, but to redefine what it meant to be a player.

A pivotal moment arrived when Alice encountered a deeply ethical choice: a digital character begged desperately for her assistance, yet helping would betray her team. Her fingers hovered uncertainly over the controls. Here, Alice confronted a core truth: games are not apolitical diversions – they are profoundly ethical arenas. Choices made here, whether moral dilemmas in narratives or fairness in competition, reflect deeper values and linger long afterwards.[39] Alice's hesitation wasn't trivial – it was meaningful exploration, an ethical self-interrogation. Her decision resonated emotionally, affecting how she viewed herself beyond the game. In these digital decisions lay profound questions, echoing far into her life offline.

At last, Alice reached a climax, a boss battle, a queen's final stand upon a digital chessboard. Her heart pounded; her fingers quickened. Triumph was exhilarating as the Queen shattered into pixelated fragments. Victory meant more than success; it validated Alice's competence and resilience, affirming her right to a gamer's identity. Research supported her experience, confirming victories like these cultivate deep psychological benefits, enhancing self-belief and resilience.[40,41]

Standing beneath a starlit digital sky, Alice's avatar softly glowing, she reflected on her journey. She'd laughed, learned, grown, stumbled, and risen again. She'd discovered games weren't mere escapes – they were encounters: with herself, with others, and with the intricate cultural and ethical currents of gaming itself. Closing her eyes, Alice smiled… at peace with the simple yet profound realisation, "I belong here."

LEVEL 3: ALICE FACES THE SHADOWS

> "I wish I hadn't cried so much!" said Alice, as she swam about, trying to find her way out. "I shall be punished for it now, I suppose, by being drowned in my own tears."
>
> Alice's Adventures in Wonderland[42]

A soft, chiming notification appeared before Alice's eyes: "Level 1 and 2: Complete." Excitement fluttered through her chest. "I'm really a gamer," she whispered, awe threading her voice. Her avatar glowed with newfound gear, confidence surging through each step. She ventured deeper, joining quests, discovering rare treasures, engaging playful foes, and sharing joyful laughter with newfound allies.

But soon, a different kind of notification intruded – harsh letters carved in aggressive red pixels: "Go back to your girly games." Another message followed swiftly: "Noobs shouldn't be at this level," then another, more cutting: "Bet she paid for those skins." Each taunt wrapped tightly around her, binding Alice's confidence. Her fingers trembled slightly on her controller, the vibrant quest to find an elusive rabbit suddenly blurred, overshadowed by doubt.

The playful glow dimmed as shadowy avatars appeared around her, whispering taunts and laughter, barring her path. Wonderland transformed swiftly from sanctuary to cage. This was not mere teasing – it was cyberbullying, a relentless digital aggression known to significantly harm emotional well-being and self-esteem.[43] In these immersive spaces, cyberbullying transcends the screen, affecting bodily experiences, leaving deep emotional wounds – particularly profound for young gamers for whom online play is central to their social lives.[44,45] Alice felt isolated, targeted by an anonymous hostility that left no space for confrontation or closure. The anonymity of her aggressors rendered them seemingly invincible, their hostility spilling over into each new quest, unrestricted by the usual boundaries of space and time.[46,47]

Yet the damage was deeper still. Alice's pain wasn't just emotional; it was physical and neurological. Research clearly shows cyberbullying activates areas of the brain associated with physical pain and emotional distress, such as the anterior cingulate cortex and the precuneus, similar to real-world bullying.[48,49] Studies using functional MRI demonstrate significant brain responses in regions responsible for emotional regulation, memory, and social cognition, reinforcing the reality of her distress.[50] Within her, anxiety tightened her breath, shifting her instinct from joyful exploration to wary defensiveness. Over time, the psychological toll risked impairing her cognitive confidence, potentially triggering lasting effects like depression and social withdrawal.[51,52,53]

The joy and curiosity she once cherished gradually drained away. Alice avoided interactions, confined herself to narrow gameplay paths, and minimised her online presence. This reaction is not unusual; cyberbullying often reshapes entire communities, undermining perceptions of safety and openness.[54] Wonderland, akin to the Metaverse, should foster creativity and freedom. Instead, it had become another space monitored by anxiety and threat, significantly undermining its intended promise of inclusivity.[55] Logging in now sparked dread rather than delight, leaving Alice questioning her place, not because of her skills, but because the world seemed unwilling to accommodate her.

Relief finally appeared, symbolised by a mod's glowing badge: "This behaviour violates community standards." Harassers vanished, and oppressive chats fell silent. Alice blinked, her breathing slowly steadying. Though not a complete resolution, this visible intervention restored a sense of safety and justice. Moderation, both AI-driven and human-led, plays a critical role in combating cyber harassment, yet AI often lacks nuanced contextual understanding, and human moderation frequently arrives too late.[56,57] For Alice, witnessing immediate and decisive action was essential. Ethical game design demands proactive moderation, transparency, and safety measures, ensuring toxicity does not become normalised.[58,59]

Finding refuge beside a digital fountain, Alice stared into her avatar's reflection, still standing. Nearby options glowed gently: "Report abuse." "Connect to support." She clicked. She spoke and listened, discovering that other players shared similar experiences. Some had left; others persisted. Many learned resilience not through solitary endurance, but through communal strength, boundaries, strategic coping mechanisms, and robust support networks.[60,61] Resilience, Alice realised, was inherently social. Her recovery was communal. She joined a supportive guild, co-created a mini-game where players practised resisting harassment, and mentored new players who faced similar hostility.

When Alice returned, it was deliberate, not to prove worth, but to reclaim her joy. Waiting, friends pinged her location, dancing at their spawn point. The game shimmered anew, not flawless, yet valuable and deserving of protection. Now armed not only with upgraded gear but also clarity, Alice confidently navigated her digital boundaries, reporting violations and activating moderation tools – practices shown to foster resilience and self-efficacy, transforming harmful experiences into personal growth.[62]

Alice's encounters in Wonderland were not universally hostile. Rich multiplayer interactions also bloomed through friendships, mentorship, rivalries, and spontaneous acts of kindness and generosity.[63] These moments restored trust, reminding Alice that kindness persisted and that not all voices echoed hostility. As she ran through illuminated forests and past floating chessboards, her heart felt lighter.

"I belong here," she whispered once more. This time, her words echoed clearly, joined by voices of support from fellow adventurers, resonating through Wonderland.

CONCLUDING THOUGHTS

> "It's a great huge game of chess that's being played—all over the world—if this is the world at all, you know. Oh, what fun it is!"
>
> Through the Looking-Glass, and What Alice Found There[64]

In *Through the Looking-Glass*, Carroll uses the theme of chess frequently, and we see in Alice's quotes in the original text how the game of chess functions as a metaphor, not only for the world in the novel but for our world. Carroll frequently adopted the idea that life is a game, and like Alice we are pawns in our own lives, condemned to move forward through our stories with limited understanding of our wider world – because within our restricted perspectives, our world seems ordered by nature and logic, reflecting the black and white of the chessboard. The games in the Metaverse are also chessboards; Alice is a pawn, the developers are royalty, and the industry is the game maker. The life cycle of the game is out of Alice's control. In this way, Carroll's metaphor of the chessboard not only mirrors the structure of his fictional world but also resonates with our increasingly gamified and algorithmically controlled spaces, particularly in the Metaverse, where users find themselves navigating spaces shaped by forces far beyond their control.

With this in mind, we turn now to our concluding conversation, where we reflect on the implications of these ideas and what they might mean for understanding play in immersive environments.

FINAL THOUGHTS: AUXANE AND BETH LOG OFF (FOR NOW)

So here we are. The final checkpoint, the last boss fight, the moment before logging off. We started this journey by telling you about the games that shaped us, the places we've travelled with a controller in hand, and the pixelated and real friends we made along the way. We've walked through Wonderland together. Now we'd like to pause, breathe, and reflect on what all of this has taught us – not just about gaming, but about ourselves, about others, and about the kind of digital future we want to co-create.

What Have Games Taught Us about Who We Are and Where We Belong?

Games have shown us the full spectrum of human experience – from radical kindness to horrendous cruelty. In good games, we can be anything, do anything. We can be heroes, healers, leaders, rebels, misfits, protectors, and dreamers. And more than anything, they've taught us that we are capable. We can be clever, creative, strategic, silly, powerful, and collaborative. We can build worlds, solve problems, and connect with others across cultures, time zones, and realities.

They've taught us that we belong – not just in the games themselves, but in the communities that form around them. We should be able to take up space in every server, every lobby, every strange floating VR chessboard. Not only do we belong, but we also thrive when we're surrounded by difference, shared play, and mutual respect. Games remind us that belonging isn't about fitting in; it's about showing up fully and being accepted anyway.

They've also taught us how to play together. To share. To win with grace. To lose with humour (most of the time). To support one another, to learn from each other, and to shape each other through relationships. We've met people in digital spaces who've transformed how we see the world – and we hope we've done the same in return. These moments teach us empathy, remind us of interdependence, and anchor us in something greater than ourselves.

But, and it's a big *but*, not all games are good games. Some games take instead of give. Some games silence rather than amplify. And some games, as we've seen too many times, not only reflect the worst of us – they normalise it. Some games tell us we need to follow a specific narrative, that we must be a certain type of player. That our freedom ends where someone else's fantasy begins – especially when those fantasies glorify violence, dehumanisation, or abuse. We have to say this clearly: *a game is never just a game.* When Zerat Games released *No Mercy*, a so-called "dark fantasy simulator" that featured non-consensual acts of violence and was later banned in multiple countries, they didn't just cross a line. They redrew it in blood. Calling digital rape a "kink" is not only inaccurate; it's violent. There's no nuance here. These are crimes, not features. And when game studios treat real trauma as content, they reinforce a norm that puts all of us, especially marginalised players, in danger.

So yes, we love games. But loving something doesn't mean ignoring its flaws. It means demanding more. Better. Safer. Fairer. Games teach us we can be game makers and game changers. And we intend to be both.

What Do We Still Dream of, or Demand, from the Future of Games and Immersive Spaces?

We want more than pixels. We want protection. Moderation should be the rule, not the exception – a baseline standard that actively protects diversity of thought, experience, identity, and opinion, while dismantling hate speech and harassment at its roots. Freedom of speech does not mean freedom from consequences. The moment it becomes hate, it becomes harm. And that's where we draw the line.

We want accountability, not just from players, but from platforms, publishers, and those in power. If you create a world, you are responsible for it. If you profit from a space, you are responsible for what that space produces. That means you can't sit back and "patch" abuse after the fact. We want proactive design, clear ethics, and zero tolerance for harm, with an accountability trail – because mistakes and unforeseen events happen, but carelessness does too.

We want this industry shaken. Call it petty, call it powerful, but we want to see the same energy that shifts culture applied to gaming. We want creators who use their power, their reach, their platforms, their royalty, to speak up about real issues: genocide, oppression, climate disaster, systemic inequality. Games can be empathy machines, if we let them. Let's make them Trojan horses of resistance and understanding.

We're tired of the excuse that games are "neutral" – they never have been. They were built for profit and enjoyment, often for a very specific demographic: young, white, cisgender, heterosexual men. Even though that landscape is changing slowly and painfully, the systems in place still reward sameness and silence differences. We want to shift the power. Hand the joystick over. Give visibility, funding, space, and credit to indie studios, queer creators, disabled developers, and Black and Brown game makers. That does not mean leave the room; that means open the room to more – let's all be diverse together. That's where the innovation is. That's where hope lives. Games challenge every rigid binary society holds: gender, race, ability, sexuality, expression, and so much more. And if the people currently destroying our world think they get to own play, to weaponise it or gatekeep it – we say no. Games are ours. They are for everyone… and will be a vehicle for radical change.

We want critical thinking embedded into game design. We want digital experiences that teach empathy and systems that support care. We want immersive realities that don't just replicate this sometimes and in some places burning planet, but offer a blueprint for building something better. A softer, braver, more compassionate future. One we build together, pixel by pixel.

If We Had One Thing to Say to Someone who Feels Like They Don't Belong in Games…

Wait for it. We're on it. Or better yet – join us, and change it. We see you, we were you – sometimes we still are you. The person who logs on quietly, makes their character in silence, mutes the mic, and shrinks a little at every comment. The person who loves games, but doesn't always feel the love back; you are not alone. Your existence in these spaces is already an act of defiance. And there are more of us than you think. Games don't belong to any one group. And you don't need permission to be here. The narrative that says otherwise? It's a glitch. And together, we can rewrite the code.

Spite's as good a reason to take back their power (Paris Paloma, we see you). But beyond spite, there's joy, community, and belonging. All the things that make play worth it. So to you, the player who doesn't feel seen: keep playing, keep showing up. Or take a break when you need to – protect your peace. Then come back when you're ready, and play loud.

We'll be here.

Before we fully log off, though, we'd like to give a list of "Good Games" that we believe would be a great inspiration for what good games look like, whether that be in representing everyone equally or discussing daunting topics related to identity and history (to whomever is listening):

- *This War of Mine*, 11Bits Studio
- *What Remains of Edith Finch*, developed by Giant Sparrow and published by Annapurna Interactive
- *Siberia* franchise, Microids
- *Detroit: Become Human*, developed by Quantic Dream and published by Sony Interactive Entertainment
- *South of Midnight*, Compulsion Games and published by Xbox Game Studios
- *Celeste*, Maddy Makes Games
- *If Found*, Annapurna Interactive
- *Life is Strange* franchise, Dontnod Entertainment, and published by Square Enix

NOTES

1. Carroll, L. (1865), *Alice's Adventures in Wonderland*. https://www.gutenberg.org/files/11/11-h/11-h.htm
2. Carroll, L. (1865), *Alice's Adventures in Wonderland*. https://www.gutenberg.org/files/11/11-h/11-h.htm

3. Slater, M. (2018), "Immersion and the illusion of presence in virtual reality", *British Journal of Psychology*, 109(3), 431–433. https://doi.org/10.1111/bjop.12305
4. Kim, G. and Biocca, F. (2018), "Immersion in virtual reality can increase exercise motivation and physical performance", in J.Y.C. Chen and G. Fragomeni (eds), *Virtual, Augmented and Mixed Reality: Applications in Health, Cultural Heritage, and Industry*, Lecture Notes in Computer Science, Vol. 10910, Cham: Springer, pp. 94–102. https://doi.org/10.1007/978-3-319-91584-5_8
5. Lombard, M. and Ditton, T. (1997). "At the heart of it all: The concept of presence", *Journal of Computer-Mediated Communication*, 3(2), JCMC321. https://doi.org/10.1111/j.1083-6101.1997.tb00072.x
6. Slater, M. (2003), "A note on presence terminology", *Presence Connect*, 3(3), 1–5.
7. Slater, M. (2003), "A note on presence terminology", *Presence Connect*, 3(3), 1–5.
8. Kim, G. and Biocca, F. (2018), "Immersion in virtual reality can increase exercise motivation and physical performance", in J.Y.C. Chen and G. Fragomeni (eds), *Virtual, Augmented and Mixed Reality: Applications in Health, Cultural Heritage, and Industry*, Lecture Notes in Computer Science, Vol. 10910, Cham: Springer, pp. 94–102. https://doi.org/10.1007/978-3-319-91584-5_8
9. Halbig, A. and Latoschik, M.E. (2021), "A systematic review of physiological measurements, factors, methods, and applications in virtual reality", *Frontiers in Virtual Reality*, 2, 694567, https://doi.org/10.3389/frvir.2021.694567
10. Ding, Y., Sabnis, N. and Strohmeier, P. (2024, May), "Motionless Movement: Towards Vibrotactile Kinesthetic Displays", in *Proceedings of the 2024 CHI Conference on Human Factors in Computing Systems*, 418, 1–16. https://doi.org/10.1145/3613904.3642499
11. Porcino, T., Trevisan, D. and Clua, E. (2020, November), "Minimizing cyber-sickness in head-mounted display systems: Causes and strategies review", in *2020 22nd Symposium on Virtual and Augmented Reality (SVR)*, pp. 154–163. IEEE. https://doi.org/10.1109/SVR51698.2020.00035
12. Fernandes, A.S. and Feiner, S.K. (2016), "Combating VR sickness through subtle dynamic field-of-view modification", in *2016 IEEE Symposium on 3D User Interfaces (3DUI)*, pp. 201–210. IEEE. https://doi.org/10.1109/3DUI.2016.7460053
13. Van Waveren, J. (2016), "The asynchronous time warp for virtual reality on consumer hardware", in *Proceedings of the 22nd ACM Conference on Virtual Reality Software and Technology*, pp. 37–46. ACM. https://doi.org/10.1145/2993369.2993375
14. Bouyer, G., Chellali, A. and Lécuyer, A. (2017), "Inducing self-motion sensations in driving simulators using force-feedback and haptic motion", in *2017 IEEE Virtual Reality (VR)*, pp. 84–90. IEEE.

15. Melo, M., Vasconcelos-Raposo, J. and Bessa, M. (2018), "Presence and cybersickness in immersive content: Effects of content type, exposure time and gender", *Computers & Graphics*, 71, 159–165. https://doi.org/10.1016/j.cag.2017.11.007
16. Carroll, L. (1871), *Through the Looking-Glass, and What Alice Found There*. London: Macmillan.
17. Schott, G. and Horrell, K. (2000), "Girl gamers and their relationship with the gaming culture", *Convergence*, 6(4), 36–53. https://doi.org/10.1177/135485650000600404
18. The Washington Post BrandStudio. (2022, January 26). "Shattering the 'gamer' stereotype", *The Washington Post*. https://www.washingtonpost.com/brand-studio/wp/2021/02/23/feature/shattering-the-gamer-stereotype/
19. Johannes, N., Vuorre, M. and Przybylski, A.K. (2021), "Video game play is positively correlated with well-being", *Royal Society Open Science*, 8(2), 202049. https://doi.org/10.1098/rsos.202049
20. Johannes, N., Vuorre, M. and Przybylski, A.K. (2021), "Video game play is positively correlated with well-being", *Royal Society Open Science*, 8(2), 202049. https://doi.org/10.1098/rsos.202049
21. Lie, A., Stephen, A., Supit, L.R., Achmad, S. and Sutoyo, R. (2022, October), "Using strategy video games to improve problem solving and communication skills: A systematic literature review", in *Proceedings of the 2022 4th International Conference on Cybernetics and Intelligent System (ICORIS)*, pp. 1–5. https://doi.org/10.1109/ICORIS56080.2022.10031539
22. Bediou, B., Adams, D.M., Mayer, R.E., Tipton, E., Green, C.S. and Bavelier, D. (2018), "Meta-analysis of action video game impact on perceptual, attentional, and cognitive skills", *Psychological Bulletin*, 144(1), 77. https://doi.org/10.1037/bul0000130
23. Cardoso-Leite, P. and Bavelier, D. (2014), "Video game play, attention, and learning: How to shape the development of attention and influence learning?", *Current Opinion in Neurology*, 27(2), 185–191. https://doi.org/10.1097/WCO.0000000000000077
24. Toril, P., Reales, J.M. and Ballesteros, S. (2014), "Video game training enhances cognition of older adults: A meta-analytic study", *Psychology and Aging*, 29(3), 706–716. https://doi.org/10.1037/a0037507
25. Dolgov, I., Graves, W.J., Nearents, M.R., Schwark, J.D. and Volkman, C.B. (2014), "Effects of cooperative gaming and avatar customization on subsequent spontaneous helping behavior", *Computers in Human Behavior*, 33, 49–55. https://doi.org/10.1016/j.chb.2013.12.028
26. Ng, L.L., Azizie, R.S. and Chew, S.Y. (2022), "Factors influencing ESL players' use of vocabulary learning strategies in massively multiplayer online role-playing games (MMORPG)", *The Asia-Pacific Education Researcher*, 31(4), 369–381. https://doi.org/10.1007/s40299-021-00578-6
27. Vasalou, A. and Joinson, A.N. (2009), "Me, myself and I: The role of interactional context on self-presentation through avatars", *Computers in Human Behavior*, 25(2), 510–520. https://doi.org/10.1016/j.chb.2008.11.007

28. Martey, R.M. and Consalvo, M. (2011), "Performing the looking-glass self: Avatar appearance and group identity in Second Life", *Popular Communication*, 9(3), 165–180. https://doi.org/10.1080/15405702.2011.583830
29. Yee, N. and Bailenson, J. (2007), "The Proteus effect: The effect of transformed self-representation on behavior", *Human Communication Research*, 33(3), 271–290. https://doi.org/10.1111/j.1468-2958.2007.00299.x
30. McKenna, J.L., Wang, Y.C., Williams, C.R., McGregor, K. and Boskey, E.R. (2022), "'You can't be deadnamed in a video game': Transgender and gender diverse adolescents' use of video game avatar creation for gender affirmation and exploration", *Journal of LGBT Youth*, 21(3), 29–49. https://doi.org/10.1080/19361653.2022.2144583
31. Barta, S., Ibáñez-Sánchez, S., Orús, C. and Flavián, C. (2024), "Avatar creation in the metaverse: A focus on event expectations", *Computers in Human Behavior*, 156, 108192. https://doi.org/10.1016/j.chb.2024.108192
32. Waltemate, T., Gall, D., Roth, D., Botsch, M. and Latoschik, M.E. (2018), "The impact of avatar personalization and immersion on virtual body ownership, presence, and emotional response", *IEEE Transactions on Visualisation and Computer Graphics*, 24(4), 1643–1652. 10.1109/TVCG.2018.2794629
33. Clancy, E. M., Thomas, B., Kelly, D., Hu, Y. and Klettke, B. (2024), "Feeling Like I Can Make the Real Me: How Trans and Gender Diverse Adults Use Gaming Avatars to Explore Gender in Digital Gaming", available at SSRN 4961151. https://dx.doi.org/10.2139/ssrn.4961151
34. Shaw, A. (2012), "Do you identify as a gamer? Gender, race, sexuality, and gamer identity", *New Media &* Society, 14(1), 28–44. https://doi.org/10.1177/1461444811410394
35. Shaw, A. (2015), *Gaming at the Edge: Sexuality and Gender at the Margins of Gamer Culture*. Minneapolis, MN: University of Minnesota Press.
36. Gray, K.L., Buyukozturk, B. and Hill, Z.G. (2017), "Blurring the boundaries: Using Gamergate to examine 'real' and symbolic violence against women in contemporary gaming culture", *Sociology Compass*, 11(3), e12458. https://doi.org/10.1111/soc4.12458
37. Herrera, F. and Bailenson, J.N. (2021), "Virtual reality perspective-taking at scale: Effect of avatar representation, choice, and head movement on prosocial behaviours", *New Media & Society*, 23(8), 2189–2209. https://doi.org/10.1177/1461444821993121
38. Kim, D.Y., Lee, H.K. and Chung, K. (2023), "Avatar-mediated experience in the metaverse: The impact of avatar realism on user–avatar relationship", *Journal of Retailing and Consumer Services*, 73, 103382. https://doi.org/10.1016/j.jretconser.2023.103382
39. Gabriels, K., Poels, K. and Braeckman, J. (2014), "Morality and involvement in social virtual worlds: The intensity of moral emotions in response to virtual versus real life cheating", *New Media & Society*, 16(3), 451–469. https://doi.org/10.1177/1461444813487957

40. Csikszentmihalyi, M. and Nakamura, J. (2010), "Effortless attention in everyday life: A systematic phenomenology", in B. Bruya (ed.), *Effortless Attention: A New Perspective in the Cognitive Science of Attention and Action*, pp. 179–189. Cambridge, MA: MIT Press.
41. Coknaz, D., Mirzeoglu, A.D., Atasoy, H.I., Alkoy, S., Coknaz, H. and Goral, K. (2019), "A digital movement in the world of inactive children: Favourable outcomes of playing active video games in a pilot randomized trial", *European Journal of Pediatrics*, 178(10), 1567–1576. https://doi.org/10.1007/s00431-019-03457-x
42. Carroll, L. (1865), *Alice's Adventures in Wonderland*. London: Macmillan. https://www.gutenberg.org/files/11/11-h/11-h.htm
43. Kowalski, R.M., Giumetti, G.W., Schroeder, A.N. and Lattanner, M.R. (2014), "Bullying in the digital age: A critical review and meta-analysis of cyberbullying research among youth", *Psychological Bulletin*, 140(4), 1073–1137. https://doi.org/10.1037/a0035618
44. Bansal, S., Garg, N., Singh, J. and Van Der Walt, F. (2023), "Cyberbullying and mental health: Past, present, and future", *Frontiers in Psychology*, 14, 1279234. https://doi.org/10.3389/fpsyg.2023.1279234
45. Bottino, S.M.B., Bottino, C.M.C., Regina, C.G., Correia, A.V.L. and Ribeiro, W.S. (2015), "Cyberbullying and adolescent mental health: A systematic review", *Cadernos de Saúde Pública*, 31(3), 463–475. https://doi.org/10.1590/0102-311X00036114
46. Englander, E.K. (2021), *Cyberbullying: What It Is and How to Stop It* New York, NY: ABC-CLIO.
47. Chen, H., Li, Y., Xiong, J., Yu, J. and Wu, T. (2024), "Cyberbullying victimization and post-traumatic stress disorder symptoms among college students: Mediating role of negative coping and moderating role of perceived control", *Current Psychology*, 43, 19294–19303. https://doi.org/10.1007/s12144-024-05760-9
48. Lamblin, M., Murawski, C., Whittle, S. and Fornito, A. (2017), "Social connectedness, mental health and the adolescent brain", *Neuroscience & Biobehavioral Reviews*, 80, 57–68. https://doi.org/10.1016/j.neubiorev.2017.05.010
49. McLoughlin, L.T., Lagopoulos, J. and Hermens, D.F. (2020), "Cyberbullying and adolescent neurobiology: A systematic review of the literature", *Frontiers in Psychology*, 11, 1511. https://doi.org/10.3389/fpsyg.2020.01511
50. Hu, Y., Bai, Y., Pan, Y., & Li, S. (2021). "Cyberbullying victimization and depression among adolescents: A meta-analysis", *Psychiatry Research*, 305, 114198. https://doi.org/10.1016/j.psychres.2021.114198
51. Faucher, C.,Jackson, M. and Cassidy, W. (2019), "Cyberbullying among university students: Gendered experiences, impacts, and perspectives", *Education Research International*, 2014(1), 698545.
52. Kowalski, R.M., Giumetti, G.W., Schroeder, A.N. and Lattanner, M.R. (2014), "Bullying in the digital age: A critical review and meta-analysis of

cyberbullying research among youth", *Psychological Bulletin*, 140(4), 1073–1137. https://doi.org/10.1037/a0035618

53. Patchin, J.W. and Hinduja, S. (2010), "Cyberbullying and self-esteem", *Journal of School Health*, 80(12), 614–621. https://doi.org/10.1111/j.1746-1561.2010.00548.x
54. Ballard, M.E. and Welch, K.M. (2017), "Virtual warfare: Cyberbullying and cyber-victimization in MMOG play", *Games and Culture*, 12(5), 466–491. https://doi.org/10.1177/1555412015592473
55. Blackburn, J. and Kwak, H. (2014), "STFU NOOB! Predicting crowdsourced decisions on toxic behavior in online games", in *Proceedings of the 23rd International Conference on World Wide Web (WWW '14)*, pp. 877–888. ACM. https://doi.org/10.1145/2566486.2567987
56. Ma, R., Li, Y. and Kou, Y. (2023), "Transparency, fairness, and coping: How players experience moderation in multiplayer online games", in *Proceedings of the 2023 CHI Conference on Human Factors in Computing Systems*, pp. 1–21. https://doi.org/10.1145/3544548.3581097
57. Ostrovska, O. and Lyashkevych, V. (2025), Automated online detection of harmful and dangerous content in social networks: A systematic review", *Artificial Intelligence*, 30, 108–116. https://doi.org/10.15407/jai2025.04.108
58. Boch, A., Stuart, J. and Johnson, D. (2025), "Levelling Up Ethics: Video Game Design and Global Responsibility", *UNU Research Brief 2* (Macau: United Nations University Institute in Macau). Retrieved from: https://collections.unu.edu/eserv/UNU:10176/Levelling_Up_Ethics-No22025-UNUMACAU.pdf
59. Beres, N.A., Frommel, J., Reid, E., Mandryk, R.L. and Klarkowski, M. (2021), "Don't you know that you're toxic: Normalization of toxicity in online gaming", *Proceedings of the 2021 CHI Conference on Human Factors in Computing Systems (CHI '21)*, 438, 1–15. New York, NY: Association for Computing Machinery. https://doi.org/10.1145/3411764.3445157
60. Masten, A.S. (2001), "Ordinary magic: Resilience processes in development", *American Psychologist*, 56(3), 227–238. https://doi.org/10.1037/0003-066X.56.3.227
61. Sourmelis, T., Ioannou, A. and Zaphiris, P. (2017), "Massively multiplayer online role-playing games (MMORPGs) and the 21st-century skills: A comprehensive research review from 2010 to 2016", *Computers in Human Behavior*, 73, 203–212. https://doi.org/10.1016/j.chb.2016.10.020
62. Modecki, K.L., Minchin, J., Harbaugh, A.G., Guerra, N.G. and Runions, K.C. (2014), "Bullying prevalence across contexts: A meta-analysis measuring cyber and traditional bullying", *Journal of Adolescent Health*, 55(5), 602–611. https://doi.org/10.1016/j.jadohealth.2014.06.007
63. Cairns, P., Cox, A.L., Day, M., Martin, H. and Perryman, T. (2014), "Who but not where: The effect of social play on immersion in digital games", *International Journal of Human-Computer Studies*, 71(11), 1069–1077. https://doi.org/10.1016/j.ijhcs.2013.08.015

64. Carroll, L. (1871). *Through the Looking-Glass, and What Alice Found There.* London: Macmillan. https://www.gutenberg.org/files/11/11-h/11-h.htm

PART II

Negotiations on governance, power and agency – who plays by what rules?

Introduction to Part II

Noha Lea Halim and Sofie Schönborn

Rules exist in digital worlds but the question is who sets them, how they take shape, and whose interests they serve. The metaverse is an intersection where technology, design, and human experience converge to create new forms of order and new spaces of negotiation. The metaverse is not built upon a single vision, but formed through countless small choices: of platforms, of users, of systems still in motion.

Stepping into virtual worlds might begin with a headset, a click, or a login screen, but what we step into are systems. Systems of experience, of expectation, of power. Whether dressed in avatars or cloaked in code, we enter digital spaces that feel new but are built with structures we know all too well. Some of these rules are visible. Others are not. They live in the architecture of platforms, the protocols of interaction, the options of whom we can meet and what we can see. As users, we are offered some ability to act and decide, but often within tight parameters.

So, what are the rules here? And perhaps more importantly: which rules matter, and who gets to decide?

In this Part and through the overall collection, governance takes many forms. Governance goes beyond written law and regulation. It serves as a broader term under which regulation, law, social ordering, and acts of questioning power and "given structures" can all be situated. These can range from institutional to soft-law ideas. Hence, the imagination of our contributors shapes the range of how widely encompassing governance is viewed and considered.

In the following contributions, power, too, appears in many shapes and arrangements. It may be exercised directly or subtly, by those who own infrastructure, by those who control access, or by those who design the choices available within the virtual. Some power is seen, some felt; some hidden entirely within the design of systems that suggest what can be done and what remains out of reach. Power can restrict or enable, exclude or invite, command or persuade; and it rarely resides in only one place.

We may carry expectations of realspace with us in the transit to virtual worlds. We may bring inherited assumptions, pre-existing beliefs, and forms of discrimination. Even our fantasies of escape, of reimagination, are linked to where we have been. Likewise, discriminating factors are transferred to virtual worlds, like age, race, gender, ability, access to infrastructure, or fluency in digital cultures. These characteristics, used as identifiers and differentiators, are not erased in the metaverse. Sometimes they become less visible, more ambiguous. At other times, they concentrate in new forms or roles. For instance, the act of assigning roles in virtual environments – through avatar presets, interaction scripts, or interface defaults – can encode assumptions about identity, agency, or hierarchy. This can subtly reinforce patterns in perception both for the individual and the environment perceiving them, even as these characteristics appear playful or deliberate.

This does not mean the digital can only replicate the real. Virtual worlds are not escapes from power, but invitations to reshape it. We may be wondering whether we ever really leave realspace. For now, we oscillate between layers of the same reality, moving between digital and immersive worlds and realspace, transporting values, hierarchies, and habits with us on this journey.

Some worry that personalization is isolating us, that our digital lives are becoming more individual than connective. Algorithmic feeds often reflect our preferences back to us, curating content that confirms rather than challenges, filtering out friction in favor of familiarity. This raises the question: Are we primarily encountering ourselves online, or are there still designed moments that introduce us to other perspectives, identities, and values? What happens to shared norms when digital freedom is shaped by individual feedback loops? At the same time, contributors remind us that even seemingly "blank" digital spaces, like new platforms for social encounters, fill quickly: with quasi-human interactions, (para-)social relationships, and the emergence of community norms. Where there is interaction, values surface. And where values surface, power begins to take form – sometimes through moderation policies, sometimes through interface design, sometimes through invisible defaults.

This leads us to questions about how user experiences are shaped: Who defines the structure of interaction? What behaviors are encouraged or discouraged, and whose standards guide those choices? Could systems be designed not only to enable control, but to allow for accountability, openness, or shared authorship of identity?

This returns us to design, beyond coding or interfaces, to the deeper act of world-building. Design sets the boundaries of possibility: which interactions feel natural, which futures appear likely, which forms of self seem valid. Yet virtual environments often resist fixed definitions. Their logic lies somewhere between human and machine agents, between programmed order and user improvisation, between norms inherited from realspace and dynamics unique to the virtual.

And so the deeper question becomes not only who plays what, but also by which rules – and whether the rules can be co-written. This Part invites reflection, not prescription. It offers no singular blueprint for governance in virtual worlds, but many points of departure.

How do we hold platforms accountable when their policies are invisible? Can decentralized systems distribute power more fairly, or just more opaquely? What kinds of social norms are we willing to nurture, and which are we prepared to abandon? What do we keep from realspace, and what might we finally set down?

The contributions in this Part open a conversation about power, agency, and governance in immersive and hybrid worlds. In the end, the metaverse may not be one place. It may not be one thing. But it is, undeniably, a social experience. And where people gather, whether in pixels or persons, power is always in the room. The following contributions invite us to look beyond surface-level freedom and examine how digital experiences are shaped from within: through environment design, role assignment, and rule enforcement. What emerges is not just a story of user behavior, but of how spaces themselves shape action: through invisible curators, code, economic logic, and digital judgment. At the center lies the question of who defines the rules, technically, socially, and legally, and how those rules are shaped, accepted, resisted, or reimagined.

Source: Generated using DALL-E, building on the original illustrations from *Alice's Adventures in Wonderland*, drawn by John Tenniel, https://www.alice-in-wonderland.net/resources/pictures/alices-adventures-in-wonderland/

Figure II.1 Who plays by what rules?

5. Virtual selves, real consequences: understanding power in a hybrid world

Daniel Matter

We are becoming hybrid subjects. Like Alice stepping through the looking-glass, we increasingly traverse the membrane between the physical and the digital, inhabiting both realms simultaneously. The immersive, interconnected virtual worlds collectively emerging as the metaverse(s) represent not just a new frontier for technology, but a profound shift in the nature of human experience and interaction. These nascent digital landscapes promise unheard-of canvases for creativity, connection, and the reimagining of self and society. Yet, the allure of infinite possibility is refracted through complex architectures of power, demanding critical examination.

This chapter argues that understanding our emerging hybridity is key to navigating the metaverse. While interpersonal power – the ability to influence, dominate, or connect with others – will always reside within individuals, the nature of our digital interactions fundamentally alters its expression and mediation. The more abstract our communication becomes, mediated through code, algorithms, and interfaces designed by others, the greater the potential influence wielded by the platform providers who construct these virtual stages. Their power often manifests not as overt force, but as a subtle, pervasive "nudge" – shaping affordances, directing attention, and structuring choices in ways that serve platform interests, often under the guise of seamless user experience.

Yet, our journeys into these digital Wonderlands are not self-contained escapades. We do not simply leave the virtual behind when we log off; we carry the experiences, the altered perspectives, the novel social dynamics, and the algorithmically inflected sense of self back into our physical lives. This feedback loop is precisely where both the peril and the promise lie. If virtual spaces merely replicate and amplify existing inequalities under opaque corporate control, they risk further entrenching those divides in the physical world. However, if we consciously shape these environments, leveraging their unique properties – their potential for radical self-expression, community formation across distance, and perhaps most significantly, their inherent *lack* of natural scarcity – we might cultivate experiences that challenge real-world assumptions and foster genuinely new forms of value and connection. Exploring these architectures of power, recognizing the interplay between platform control and enduring human agency, and envisioning the potential born from this hybrid existence is the central task of this chapter. The dream of digital liberation persists, but its realization requires seeing the walls of Wonderland, even as we marvel at its possibilities.

EMANCIPATION AND CONTINGENCY

History suggests that technologies enhancing communication and organization often disrupt existing power structures while simultaneously introducing new forms of control. The printing press fueled the Reformation and Enlightenment but also enabled new forms of propaganda and state control. The internet facilitated global movements and information access but also gave rise to mass surveillance and platform monopolies. The metaverse(s) will likely follow this pattern, presenting a powerful double-edged sword. The emancipatory promise lies in the potential for almost limitless self-expression and collective organization. Users can craft identities unbound by physical limitations, build intricate virtual worlds reflecting diverse aesthetics and values, and form communities based on shared interests rather than geographical proximity. We already see precursors in massive multiplayer online games (MMOs), virtual worlds like Second Life, or even highly customized communities on platforms like Discord or Reddit. These spaces allow for the creation of bespoke social norms, governance structures, and cultural practices within self-chosen collectives. Users can, in theory, create digital enclaves where they define the rules, distribute power internally, and live according to standards negotiated by the community itself. This potential for localized, user-driven governance *can* represent a significant departure from the top-down structures often dominating physical societies, though it is not an inherent outcome.

Perhaps more fundamentally, the shift in agency lies in the enhanced freedom users gain to choose which communities – and thus which rule systems – they wish to belong to. While experience with online communities often reveals relatively flat hierarchies, users within these self-selected groups might equally opt for more centralized power structures if deemed necessary for coordination or achieving specific collective goals. However, this potential is fully contingent upon the underlying infrastructure, both physical and also – and maybe in a less obvious way – digital. Creating and maintaining persistent, complex, and interoperable virtual worlds requires immense technological resources and coordination. This complexity strongly suggests, though perhaps does not absolutely necessitate, the continued prominence of large platform providers. These platforms will likely provide the foundational layers – the rendering engines, identity systems, marketplaces, and interoperability standards – upon which individual worlds and communities are built. While users might govern their specific virtual "plot of land" or social group, they remain tenants within a larger architecture controlled by the platform owner. This landlord–tenant relationship introduces inherent power asymmetries.

Furthermore, the very richness and complexity that enable emancipation also create new surfaces for control. The intricate data generated by immersive interactions (gaze tracking, voice modulation, micro-expressions, spatial behavior) offers unprecedented opportunities for monitoring, analysis, and behavioral manipulation. The contingency introduced by sophisticated digital infrastructure retains power for those who control that infrastructure, shifting influence from tangible physical control to the more nebulous realm of code and data flows. Decisions made within these platforms, often shielded by complexity or proprietary claims, can manifest as unexplained outcomes – content disappearing, access changing – without clear accountability or avenues for redress, subtly shaping the environment.

Platforms often leverage this ambiguity strategically, presenting themselves as neutral intermediaries or mere conduits for user activity while actively shaping the environment and its outcomes. They highlight user freedom while obscuring the algorithmic and policy constraints that structure that freedom. This is the Cheshire Cat's trick: be visible as a service provider, but invisible as a governor. The interface users interact with emphasizes their choices, while the underlying governance mechanisms remain hidden in black boxes of code and internal policy.

THE ILLUSION OF AGENCY

Alice, upon entering Wonderland, experiences a dizzying sense of possibility. She can alter her size, converse with animals, and seemingly wander freely through a nonsensical landscape. This mirrors the initial user experience in many digital environments, particularly immersive ones. The metaverse presents itself as a realm of near-infinite possibility, where users can be who they want, build what they imagine, and interact without the constraints of physical reality. This feeling of agency is a powerful draw, fulfilling deep human desires for self-determination and creativity.

Yet, as Alice quickly discovers, Wonderland operates according to strict, albeit bizarre, rules she did not create and cannot change – rules dictating when and how she may speak, conditions under which her size changes, or even protocols about who she must respect or obey. These rules not only manifest in the social norms that govern the behavior of Wonderland's inhabitants.

Rather, they are imprinted in the very fabric of Wonderland itself, akin to laws of nature in our world.

Similarly, metaverse users exercise their agency within carefully designed, inescapable constraints established by platform architects. This often operates not through explicit prohibition, but via subtle affordances and frictions built into the environment: What actions are easy and rewarding? Which require more effort or simply aren't coded as possibilities? As Lawrence Lessig[1] argued, in digital spaces, "code is law". The technical architecture – the physics engine, the communication protocols, the available tools – regulates behavior more fundamentally and pervasively than any written terms of service.

Platforms excel at creating what might be termed "choreographed freedom". They provide a wide array of choices within predefined categories – avatar customizations, item selections, pre-approved interaction types – which generate a compelling illusion of agency while subtly guiding behavior towards paths optimized for platform goals, such as engagement, data extraction, or monetization. Users might freely choose their avatar's hair color but cannot alter the underlying algorithms determining who they encounter. They might build elaborate structures within a virtual world but cannot change the fundamental economic system governing property rights or resource allocation within that world.

This architectural power operates largely beneath the threshold of conscious awareness. Users experience themselves as making free choices, rarely perceiving how the design of the interface nudges their decisions or limits their options. This aligns with Lukes' third dimension of power[2]: the ability to shape preferences and perceptions of possibility, making certain outcomes seem natural or inevitable while rendering alternatives unthinkable. The result is a paradoxical state: users feel radically free while operating within an environment engineered to predict and channel their behavior. This tension between perceived freedom and actual constraint forms the bedrock power dynamic of many anticipated metaverses.

THE INVISIBLE REGIME

Governance in the metaverse(s) blends visible rules with invisible, automated systems, mirroring the duality of Wonderland's overt tyranny (the Queen of Hearts) and its underlying, inexplicable logic. Platforms, as providers of the underlying infrastructure, inevitably act as sovereigns within their domains, setting and enforcing rules.

Some forms of this sovereignty will be explicit and visible, akin to the Queen of Hearts shouting, "Off with their heads!" Platforms will undoubtedly enforce baseline content policies, often mirroring broad societal taboos or legal requirements, such as the prohibition of child sexual abuse material

(CSAM). Platforms will deploy resources – both human moderators and automated systems – to detect and remove such content, exercising overt power to maintain a certain standard of safety or legality within their space. Content moderation decisions regarding hate speech, harassment, or disinformation, while often more contested and less consistently applied, also fall into this category of visible governance, where platforms make explicit (though often controversial) judgments about permissible behavior. Users might disagree with these rules, but their existence and the platform's role as enforcer are generally apparent.

However, a more pervasive and potentially more powerful form of governance operates invisibly, embedded within the algorithms that structure user experience. This is the realm of the "Invisible Queen's regime", where control is exercised not through explicit decree but through the silent, automated sorting, filtering, and prioritizing of information and interaction. Consider the likely existence of "global feeds", discovery engines, or matchmaking systems designed to help users navigate the vastness of the metaverse and connect with content or other users beyond their immediate community. The algorithms governing these systems hold immense power. They determine visibility: which creations are surfaced, which communities are recommended, and which users gain prominence.

Contemporary users have not only to accept but even to expect this algorithmic prefiltering and sorting. Terms such as "For You", "Discover", or "Suggested" – common across platforms like TikTok, Instagram, and YouTube – explicitly promise personalization and tailored experiences. Users often openly embrace this curation, praising one platform's algorithms over another. Yet, such tailored experiences significantly erode the concept of a truly global feed landscape – one offering a collective, shared synopsis of what is occurring broadly on the platform or even within society. Instead, each user receives a version of reality carefully curated to reflect their presumed interests, biases, and preferences. This phenomenon is as ideal an entry point for feed-tailoring as any platform could desire. The explicit user demand for personalized content, coupled with an aversion to engaging with perspectives from the opposite end of the political or cultural spectrum, further entrenches the siloing of digital experiences. Consequently, the doors open wide to potential manipulation or manufactured realities, granting digital platforms extraordinary influence in shaping public perception and discourse. Such fragmentation and customization, while superficially empowering individual choice, subtly facilitates platforms' ability to control, direct, or even distort collective understanding and reality itself.

This algorithmic curation operates as a form of infrastructural power, shaping social reality within the metaverse without announcing its presence. Its mechanisms are typically opaque, shielded by claims of proprietary technology or the sheer complexity of the systems involved. Users rarely know precisely why they see certain content or encounter certain people. This opacity enables forms of control that are difficult to detect, let alone contest.

Shadow banning exemplifies this invisible regime perfectly. A user might find their posts receiving little engagement, their presence seemingly diminished, without any notification or explanation. They might be subtly deprioritized by the platform's algorithms, effectively silenced or marginalized within the digital space, potentially without even realizing they are subject to a sanction. This aligns chillingly with Foucault's concept of disciplinary power evolving towards automated, preventative control – a punishment enacted through the very architecture of the system, invisible, unverifiable, and normalizing compliance by making the mechanisms of power inscrutable. It is governance that requires no guards or overt threats, only the silent adjustment of code.

IDENTITY UNDER ALGORITHM

"Who are *you*?" asks Wonderland's enigmatic Caterpillar, challenging Alice's unstable sense of self. In the metaverse, algorithms constantly pose a similar question, out of not philosophical curiosity, but operational necessity. They continuously analyze user data – tracking movements, gaze patterns, social interactions, purchases, expressions – to categorize individuals and predict their behavior, constructing what we might call "profiled subjectivity".

Indeed, the Caterpillar's probing question, "Who are *you*?", resonates not just with Alice, but with our own experience navigating the digital expanse. We too are compelled towards a continuous reassertion of identity, yet under vastly different conditions than the physical world allows. There, identity possesses a certain persistence, grounded in our embodiment and relatively stable social circles. In the digital realm, however, we become more transient figures adrift in a sea of fleeting encounters. This ephemerality pushes identity towards the purely performative; it becomes less about inherent being and more about conscious, repeated enactment. This is amplified by the unparalleled malleability of digital self-presentation. Unlike the physical world where attributes like our bodies are largely fixed, the virtual offers the capacity to reshape nearly every facet of our appearance. While this potential for radical self-invention carries an undeniable liberating appeal for many, it simultaneously risks trapping us in a relentless cycle of self-expression. This cycle is rarely neutral; it is deeply entrenched in often-invisible power structures. The pressure to craft and display an "acceptable" self – conforming to digitally mediated norms of features, faces, and fashions – may become even more pervasive online than offline, precisely because the tools for modification are so readily available, demanding constant vigilance in the performance of self.

This process resonates with Deleuze's concept of the "society of control", where individuals become "dividuals" – malleable collections of data points rather than fixed subjects contained by institutions. The metaverse, with its potential for fine-grained behavioral tracking, both by the platforms and also by others, represents an advanced stage of this society. Users are translated into data profiles used for various purposes: personalization, targeted advertising, risk assessment, social sorting. The Data Caterpillar – the complex web of algorithms processing this information – continuously defines users based on their digital traces.

This algorithmic construction of identity is a potent form of power, directly engaging with the performative nature of selfhood compelled by the digital realm. As Cheney-Lippold argues, algorithms perform a "soft biopolitics", creating and reinforcing categories that shape how users are perceived by the system and, crucially, influencing the ongoing performance of the self required in transient digital spaces. A user might be tagged as "highly engaged", "potential whale" (big spender), "politically radical", or "at risk of churn" based on interpretations of their digital actions. These labels, often invisible to the user, function as algorithmic judgments on their performance, triggering differential treatment: tailored advertising, specific content recommendations, varying levels of customer service, or even preemptive moderation. This creates potent feedback loops where algorithmic categorization not only influences user experience but also subtly coaches future self-presentation, potentially reinforcing the very performances that led to the categorization as users adapt to perceived system expectations. The Data Caterpillar's query, therefore, is answered by an algorithm that both interprets and shapes the performed identity.

The design of avatar systems and interaction mechanics further embeds power related to this performative identity. The available options for self-representation – body types, skin tones, gender expressions, clothing styles – are not neutral offerings; they reflect the cultural assumptions and commercial priorities of the platform designers, effectively setting the stage and providing the costumes for digital self-enactment. These systems implicitly normalize certain identities while marginalizing or excluding others, acting as a form of regulatory power over performative possibilities. They subtly dictate which versions of the self can be easily enacted and recognized within the virtual world, reinforcing the pressure to present an "acceptable" self, as discussed earlier. The very tools that offer liberation through malleable appearance simultaneously delimit the acceptable range of performance, channeling self-expression within bounds convenient for the platform's architecture and control.

Furthermore, the capacity to track affective responses (e.g., via biometric data from VR hardware) opens the door to "affect recognition" systems. The prospect of platforms not only observing behavior but also inferring emotional states raises profound questions about privacy and manipulation. Users aware of such monitoring might engage in "anticipatory conformity", modifying their behavior or expressions to align with perceived system expectations, leading to what Cohen terms "modulated selves". The Data Caterpillar's relentless query thus shapes not only how the system sees the user, but potentially the user's own sense of self.

ENGINEERED COMPETITION

"It takes all the running you can do, to keep in the same place," the Red Queen tells Alice, describing a world where constant effort is required merely to maintain one's position. This aptly captures the economic logic often embedded within platform ecosystems, including potential metaverses – a dynamic of engineered competition we can call the Red Queen's Race. Unsurprisingly, power within these digital realms is also poised to manifest strongly through economic means. Platform providers, acting as market makers and infrastructure owners, are likely to position themselves to extract a portion of the value exchanged within their ecosystems, often through transaction fees (as many already do). This creates a powerful incentive for platforms not merely to allow, but to actively engineer and facilitate vibrant internal economies and constant trade among users.

Digital goods are inherently non-rivalrous; they can be copied infinitely at near-zero marginal cost. This abundance clashes with traditional economic models based on scarcity. To create value and incentivize activity, platforms often resort to engineering artificial scarcity. Virtual land is sold in limited quantities, digital collectibles (like NFTs) are released in finite editions, and algorithmic visibility itself becomes a scarce resource users compete for. This manufactured scarcity transforms potentially collaborative environments into competitive arenas, driving engagement and creating markets the platform can mediate and tax.

This economic pressure often intertwines directly with the performative nature of identity previously discussed. Acquiring scarce or desirable digital goods becomes a means of signaling status and enacting a particular self within the virtual space. Consequently, there emerges a dual pressure: platforms are incentivized to foster consumption tied to self-expression, while influential users or "influencers" within the metaverse may further amplify these trends, encouraging others to purchase specific items or styles to achieve social recognition or belonging.

This dynamic serves the imperatives of "platform capitalism", which relies on the continuous extraction of value from user activity – attention, data, social interactions, and creative labor. Users find themselves in a perpetual race: competing for followers, virtual currency, desirable items, or prominence in algorithmic feeds. Success metrics are often relative and constantly shifting, ensuring that the race never truly ends. Like Alice running alongside the Red Queen, users exert significant effort, often generating substantial value for the platform, without necessarily achieving lasting security or advancement.

Algorithmic systems are central to enacting these invisible power dynamics, structuring the competitive landscape in ways distinct from many real-world scenarios. Unlike markets with potentially transparent rules or physics governing physical contests, here recommendation engines and feed algorithms act as opaque arbiters of success. These systems, optimized for platform-defined metrics like engagement (clicks, shares, time spent) rather than intrinsic quality or social value, become hidden judges. They invisibly dictate whose creations gain visibility and reward, thereby incentivizing creators towards often sensationalist or polarizing strategies purely to appease the unseen algorithmic curator. Users thus find themselves competing not merely against each other, but against an inscrutable, automated power that sets the rules of the game for its own benefit, a stark contrast to competitions with clearly defined and universally applied standards.

This dynamic of invisible power extends profoundly into labor relations within the metaverse. Trends like "aspirational labor" and "playbor" are amplified, where users contribute significant creative work – building environments, designing assets, moderating communities - often unpaid or vastly underpaid, driven by the hope of eventual recognition or reward within the platform's ecosystem. The power here lies in the platform's ability to frame this labor extraction not as work, but as leisure, passion, or community contribution, thereby obscuring the economic value generated for the platform itself – a subtler form of exploitation than traditional wage labor, however precarious the latter might be. The promise of success within the Red Queen's Race keeps users running, contributing value to systems designed to perpetuate a state of competitive precarity.

SEEING THE WALLS OF WONDERLAND

Given the likelihood that metaverses will become increasingly integrated into work, socializing, and culture, developing the capacity to critically navigate these complex environments becomes essential. If these spaces are to be more than just immersive Skinner boxes or unaccountable digital fiefdoms, users need to cultivate an awareness of the invisible architectures shaping their experiences. True freedom and agency, whether physical or virtual, depend on understanding the limits and possibilities of one's environment.

In the physical world, we develop intuitive knowledge of physical laws, social cues, and political structures through lifelong experience. We understand gravity, interpret facial expressions, and learn (often imperfectly) the explicit rules governing our societies. The metaverse(s), however, present environments where the fundamental "laws" – the physics, the social affordances, the economic rules – are artificial, malleable, and often opaque, designed by entities with their own interests. Navigating this requires a deliberate cultivation of critical digital literacy far beyond basic operational skills.

This involves learning to "read" the environment differently: questioning why certain actions are easy and others difficult, noticing patterns in algorithmic recommendations, reflecting on how avatar systems might shape identity expression, and seeking to understand the economic incentives driving platform design. It means developing skepticism towards the seamlessness of the interface and recognizing that every design choice embeds values and power dynamics. It requires moving beyond passive consumption to active interrogation of the systems themselves.

This critical navigation is not just an individual responsibility; it necessitates collective effort and external pressure. Educational initiatives, independent research exposing platform mechanisms, and tools that provide users with greater insight into data collection and algorithmic filtering are crucial components. Just as cartographers mapped unknown physical territories, we need efforts to map the power structures of virtual worlds.

Ultimately, achieving genuine agency in designed realities requires the ability to perceive the "walls" of the garden, even when they are presented as boundless horizons. It means understanding that the fabric of virtual reality is not neutral but actively constructed, and that this construction is a site of negotiation and potential contestation. This capacity for critical perception may be one of the most vital competencies for navigating the increasingly mediated realities of the 21st century.

WONDERLAND'S ECHOES IN THE REAL

The story typically ends with Alice waking up, Wonderland merely a dream. But what if the journey down the rabbit hole leaves indelible marks, not just on Alice, but on all who inhabit that space? What if Alice, the Queen, the Hatter, the Caterpillar, all emerge back into the "real" world, subtly changed by their interactions within the peculiar logic of Wonderland? The metaverse invites us to consider this possibility: we are becoming hybrid subjects, simultaneously existing and acting in physical and digital spaces. We do not truly decouple from real space when we enter the virtual; rather, we extend ourselves into it, carrying our histories and biases, but also opening ourselves to new influences. The power dynamics within the metaverse, therefore, are not confined to the virtual.

While platforms undeniably wield immense architectural power, controlling the virtual oxygen we breathe and the virtual air carrying the sound of our voices, this is not the whole story. Within these choreographed spaces, interpersonal power still unfolds. Alice, though subject to Wonderland's bizarre rules, was not merely a passive observer. She challenged the Queen, navigated illogical conversations, asserted her (fluctuating) sense of self, and built tentative relationships. She enacted agency within the laws of Wonderland, just like we do within the rules of our world. Similarly, metaverse users, even within platform-defined limits, engage in complex social negotiations. They form communities, establish hierarchies, collaborate, compete, support, and harm one another. They perform power and have power performed upon them by other users.

Precisely because these interactions occur within environments unbound by physical limitations, they offer unique experiences. We might embody different forms, interact across vast distances, or engage in collective creation impossible in the physical world. We gain new perspectives, perhaps literally seeing the world through another's eyes via an avatar. These experiences, unavailable in real space, hold intrinsic value. They can foster empathy, challenge assumptions, or reveal hidden talents.

This is where the true potential for transformation lies. If the experiences within the metaverse – the interpersonal power dynamics learned, the new perspectives gained – are carried back by these hybrid subjects into the physical world, they could subtly alter real-space interactions and structures. Power always lies within choreographed freedom, in the real world just as in the metaverse. But the metaverse offers a chance to change the choreography. If we can build these virtual worlds on more participatory foundations, resisting complete determination by platform interests, the novel rhythms and interactions developed within them might just disrupt the established beat of power structures outside. The echo of Wonderland could reshape the world Alice wakes up in.

EMANCIPATORY POSSIBILITIES

Beyond Engineered Scarcity

Despite the significant challenges posed by platform power, the metaverse(s) are not necessarily destined solely for dystopian control. Recognizing the architectures of power is the first step; actively working to reshape them by asserting our agency is the next. The strongest power platforms wield is often that of the nudge, the carefully designed choice architecture, the algorithmic suggestion. While potent and dangerous, a nudge is not coercion; we are not held at gunpoint. Remembering and exercising our own agency, both individually and collectively, remains paramount.

A crucial difference between the physical world and the virtual offers a powerful starting point: the absence of inherent natural scarcity. Most real-world conflicts, from geopolitical struggles to interpersonal disputes, ultimately trace back to competition over limited resources – land, energy, materials, even social status perceived as finite. Digital assets, however, can be replicated infinitely at near-zero cost. The scarcity we see in virtual worlds – limited virtual land, finite digital collectibles, tiered access – is almost always *artificial*, deliberately engineered by platforms. This engineered competition, the Red Queen's Race described earlier, serves platform goals by creating markets they can tax and driving engagement through status-seeking.

But we need not accept this manufactured reality as inevitable. What if we consciously built virtual worlds prioritizing abundance over artificial lack? Imagine digital realms where the focus shifts from accumulation to creation, sharing, and connection. This isn't mere fantasy; it represents a fundamental choice about the values we embed in these new architectures. If the core human drivers are no longer solely channeled towards competing for artificially scarce goods, what might take their place? This opens pathways towards futures radically different from the platform capitalism currently dominating the internet. We can dare to dream of metaverses where value derives not from market price or exclusivity, but from creativity, collaboration, knowledge-sharing, or prosocial behavior. Perhaps reputation economies might emerge, where status accrues based on helpfulness, mentorship, artistic contribution, or fostering positive community interactions, rather than virtual wealth – a social credit reimagined not for state control, but for recognizing and rewarding kindness or constructive participation. Alternatively, gift economies and commons-based creation could flourish, encouraging the free sharing of digital assets, code, and designs, fostering collaborative projects where value lies in collective achievement and mutual support, echoing early internet ideals and concepts like platform cooperativism. One could also envision experience-oriented value systems, where the primary "good" is the richness and diversity of experience offered – opportunities for learning, empathy-building (perhaps walking in another's virtual shoes), or shared imaginative journeys – rather than the ownership of virtual items.

Achieving such futures requires deliberate effort. Conscientization and critical literacy are essential, raising awareness about engineered scarcity and algorithmic nudges to empower users to recognize and resist them. Technical interventions and alternative architectures offer concrete tools; building platforms on open standards, decentralized infrastructure (like the Fediverse, Decentralized identifiers IDs (DIDs), or judicious use of blockchain), and peer-to-peer networks can distribute power and resist centralized control and artificial scarcity by design. Prioritizing interoperability is key to breaking down walled gardens. Furthermore, collective organization and advocacy are vital. User unions, decentralized autonomous organizations (DAOs) focused on shared resources rather than speculation, and advocacy groups can demand transparency, data rights, and user-centric design from existing platforms, pushing back against purely profit-driven models. Policy and regulation, including robust antitrust action, strong data protection, mandatory algorithmic transparency, and interoperability mandates remain crucial for curbing platform dominance and fostering a more diverse, equitable digital ecosystem. Finally, a commitment to design justice ensures these alternative futures are built inclusively, centering the needs and values of diverse communities, not just replicating existing power structures with new technology.

Like Alice navigating the Mad Hatter's tea party – a scene with nonsensical rules but also endless tea – we can choose whether to be trapped by the arbitrary constraints platforms impose or to leverage the inherent potential for abundance. The possibility of virtual worlds based on empathy, shared knowledge, or collective well-being exists. It requires us to actively reject the manufactured race for artificial status and instead build spaces that reflect more hopeful human values. These efforts face immense obstacles, but the alternative – passively accepting digitally supercharged versions of real-world inequalities – is far bleaker.

WAKING FROM WONDERLAND?

The journey down the rabbit hole into the metaverse(s) presents a profound ambiguity. These emerging digital realms offer powerful new canvases for human creativity, community, and connection, holding genuine potential to empower individuals and facilitate novel forms of organization and experience. Yet, this potential unfolds within architectures of power, often invisible and increasingly sophisticated, wielded by the platforms providing the underlying infrastructure – the very digital air we breathe. The illusion of boundless agency contends with constraints embedded in code; visible rules coexist with opaque algorithmic regimes; identity is performed under the gaze of the Data Caterpillar; and economic participation risks becoming a Red Queen's Race engineered for platform benefit.

Like Alice learning to navigate the bewildering logic of Wonderland, we must learn to perceive and critically engage with these intertwined layers of power – both the architectural power of platforms and the interpersonal power enacted between users. But crucially, we must recognize ourselves as hybrid subjects, never fully detached from our physical realities. The experiences forged in the metaverse – the shifts in perspective, the novel social dynamics, the altered sense of self – do not stay contained within the virtual. They echo back, carried by users who traverse both realms.

Wonderland remains perpetually balanced between utopia and dystopia. The metaverse inherits this tension. Its future is not predetermined. If it becomes merely an elaborate, corporately controlled theme park, it risks amplifying existing inequalities and modes of control in ever more immersive ways. However, if its development can be guided by principles of participation, transparency, and user empowerment – if the immense power of platforms can be effectively constrained through collective action, thoughtful design, and robust oversight – then the unique potential of these spaces might be realized. The challenge is not simply to avoid a dystopian outcome, but to actively cultivate the conditions under which the metaverse can contribute positively to human flourishing, both online and offline. It is about ensuring that when we engage with these new Wonderlands, the experiences enrich rather than diminish our agency, and perhaps even help us reshape the contours of the world we return to, yielding seeds of genuine change from the virtual soil.

NOTES

1. Lessig, L. (2000). Code is law. *Harvard Magazine*, 1(2000). https://vcy.fr/media/textes/Lawrence%20Lessig%20-%20Code%20is%20Law%20-%202000.pdf
2. Lukes, S. (2012). Power: A radical view [2005]. *Contemporary Sociological Theory*, 266(3), 1–22.

6. AI on trial – exploring agency, accountability, and legal personhood in a digital wonderland

Darius Torabi

The collision of progressively advancing machine intelligence, digital environments, and human law creates an especially curious borderland: on one side stand centuries-old legal principles built for and around human agency;[1] on the other stand increasingly autonomous systems that challenge our collective understanding of legal concepts long believed to be fully settled and unquestionable. Yet, within that tension lies fertile ground for thought experiments that can illuminate real-world dilemmas far more vividly than any empirical case study could manage.

Much like Alice tumbling down the rabbit hole into a world where the familiar becomes strange and the impossible feels ordinary, this chapter will venture into Wonderland – not as mere escapism, but as a deliberately crafted legal sandbox. Here, queens, hatters, and talking animals operate on equal footing with a human. Nevertheless, this imagined world serves as more than just a whimsical thought experiment; it reflects the evolving need for legal frameworks that can accommodate the increasing complexity of the very subjects they seek to regulate within the legal systems of tomorrow. Similarly in approach to the regulatory sandboxes proposed in the EU AI Act,[2] which create controlled environments for testing AI systems within flexible legal parameters to enable lawmakers to experiment with emerging technologies before cementing regulations, Wonderland invites us to explore how legal frameworks adapt in response to increasingly complex subjects within human society, from fictional to artificial – and ultimately digital – beings.

A recent example of this kind of legal experimentation can be seen in Broward County, where Judge Andrew Siegel became the first to use virtual reality in a courtroom setting, donning an Oculus VR headset to experience a crime scene firsthand.[3] However, the scenario under exploration – a trial of the notoriously tyrannical Queen of Hearts, re-envisioned as an artificial entity – pushes the ideas of regulatory legal sandboxes and immersive experiences even further, testing the boundaries of legal reasoning in a world where conventional assumptions no longer hold. By placing the Queen of Hearts in a sort of virtual courtroom, akin to spaces that might soon manifest in the metaverse, we separate this exploration from routine legal practices, allowing the reader to temporarily disengage from typical standards and journey into a sphere where the usual checkpoints of conventional law are deliberately upended. To keep in line with the metaphor, Wonderland's eclectic characters appear in roles that echo their canonical quirks: some as judges, prosecutors, or defense counsel; others as expert witnesses providing their testimony to guide this exploration and illustrate how legal principles might be tested (or twisted) when familiar norms are suspended.

The ultimate goal of this exploration is to spark a dialogue about the fragility of legal assumptions, reminding us that the line between "self-evident truths" and concurrent interpretations of legal doctrines can be more fluid than the law – and those executing it – usually care to admit. By concluding with lessons gleaned from this imaginative experiment, this chapter aims to contribute fresh perspectives on AI governance, urging that our laws and solutions be as flexible, resourceful, and creative as the emerging technologies they aim to regulate.

I. A CURIOUS COURT OF CARDS AND CODE

Step into the grand hall of Wonderland's highest tribunal, with floors tiled like a chessboard and pillars towering like playing cards on the verge of collapsing. At the center of this peculiar chamber stands the accused: The Queen of Hearts, reimagined as an artificial entity whose alleged crimes are no less flamboyant than her tyrannical decrees.[4] In translating Wonderland's peculiar offenses into recognizable legal terms, this chapter draws upon the German Criminal Code (Strafgesetzbuch, StGB). The StGB's doctrinal clarity, meticulous internal logic, and strong emphasis on subjective culpability offer a sharply defined canvas on which to map the Queen's behavior. The Queen of Hearts stands accused of multiple serious offenses, each reflecting how her acts align disturbingly well with criminal prohibitions originally designed for human wrongdoing: First among these is attempted incitement to murder[5] (§§ 211(2) grp. 1 var. 1, 4, grp. 3 var. 2, 212(1) in conjunction with § 30(1) sentence 1, alt. 1 StGB). Her infamous calls of "Off with their heads!" – though frequently thwarted – nonetheless manifest a persistent lethal intent, forcing Wonderland's inhabitants to live under the constant fear of execution. Beyond this prospective violence lies unlawful imprisonment (§ 239(1) StGB). The Queen habitually detained her subjects at a whim, depriving them of freedom without cause or semblance of due process. Relatedly, her relentless calls for violence constitute public incitement to criminal offenses (§ 111(1) StGB), as she exhorts her guards and courtiers to carry out these oppressive acts, effectively mobilizing them into complicity. Her rule further hinges on coercion (§ 240(1) and (4) sentence 2, no. 2 StGB) and threats (§ 241(1) and (4) StGB). Rather than governing through legitimate authority or respect, the Queen compels obedience by wielding the threat of violent reprisal, a tactic that pervades her entire administration. Nor does her tyranny stop at bodily harm: her defamatory accusations against individuals (notably seen in the farcical trial of the Knave of Hearts) breach § 187 StGB, undermining reputations with unfounded charges and summary "verdicts." Finally, the Queen's systematic reign of terror disturbs the peace (§ 125(1) no. 1 and 2, sentence 1, var. 3 StGB). By fostering a culture in which neither rational law nor logic could prevail, she transformed Wonderland from a realm of whimsical nonsense into a dictatorship of dread.

Presiding over the proceedings is none other than the protagonist of the novel herself. Alice, who, having emerged from her wonderstruck role in the novel, now attempts to bring a measured perspective to a place where measure is hardly the norm. Her task is formidable, trying to make sense of conflicting testimonies and weighing the letter of the law against the intangible notion of "algorithmic" or "artificial" intent. Nevertheless, the character of Alice suits this role exceptionally well, with her hallmark curiosity and outsider perspective equipping her to question Wonderland's perplexing customs without bending to them. Where others might submit to the Queen's fearsome reputation or seek her punishment out of mere resentment and retribution, Alice's innate sense of fairness pushes her to examine every claim and counterclaim on its own merits. Her calm temperament, moral compass, and willingness to challenge authority – traits visible throughout her encounters in Wonderland – now coalesce into judicial qualities that allow her to preside over this unprecedented legal quandary. From the very beginning, Alice exhibited a consistent resistance to arbitrary authority and a strong intuitive sense of fairness. She questioned the Dodo's whimsical declaration of winners in the Caucus Race, remained composed when the Caterpillar challenged her identity and logic, pushed back against the Mad Hatter's incoherent reasoning at the tea party, and ultimately dismissed the Queen's farcical judicial theatrics as unjust and baseless. These moments, scattered across her journey, not only affirm her critical disposition but also mark her as uniquely suited to evaluate the ambiguous justice claims now facing Wonderland's court.

At the prosecution's table sits the energetic White Rabbit, punctual as ever with a stack of carefully prepared documents tucked under one arm (and a pocket watch in the other). Facing him at the defense's table is an uncharacteristically focused Mad Hatter, having seemingly traded his tea table for legal briefs. However, his curious wit remains intact and as sharp as ever.

Nonetheless, both are equally capable of cross-examining and critically engaging with any arguments presented during the trial.

Hovering on the sidelines, fading in and out at the most inopportune moments, is the Cheshire Cat, whose grin hints at riddles yet to be solved. Called as the first expert witness, the Cat's cryptic testimony will challenge the court to reevaluate fundamental legal concepts and their application to this case. Meanwhile, two other familiar figures step forward to offer their own expert opinions and perspective in the proceedings. The second expert witness is the Caterpillar, perched atop a mushroom in a secluded corner of the courtroom. Known for his philosophical bent and habit of questioning identity ("Who are you?"), he aims to shed light on the nebulous line between programmatic logic and the capacity to change. The third and final expert witness is the Duchess, claiming an uncanny expertise in discerning social norms versus actual ethics. She emphasizes the importance of instilling moral values – akin to normative alignment approach[6] – by questioning whether the Queen's very nature was predetermined by design, arguing that if she was shaped without choice, punishment does little more than place blame after the fact.

II. TRIAL IN WONDERLAND: JUDGING THE UNJUDGEABLE

Opening Statements

Judge Alice gently taps a gavel against the table to gain order amid the incensed chatter. Though she has presided over unpredictable scenes before, the gravity of this proceeding strikes a different chord: today's trial isn't just about ruling over a tyrant; it's about setting the stage for how we govern artificial beings and ultimately define justice in an era of engineered intelligence.

"We gather here," Alice begins in a clear, measured tone, "to determine the facts behind the Queen of Hearts' alleged actions and to decide whether these actions, if proven, can be attributed to true culpability – or if we are dealing with something beyond our usual definitions of guilt." She pauses, letting her gaze settle over the court, then continues with firm impartiality. "As presiding judge, it is my duty to ensure that these proceedings are conducted with absolute fairness and reason. I promise that I will consider every argument and piece of evidence on its merits, without bias or preconception. No verdict will be rendered on spectacle alone, nor will judgment be dictated by fear or favor." She acknowledges the charges already outlined – ranging from attempted incitement of murder to defamation – reminding everyone that the "Queen's alleged crimes need to be proven beyond reasonable doubt, even in Wonderland's chaotic framework."

The moment Alice finishes speaking, the White Rabbit swiftly jumps up, adjusting his pocket watch nervously while clearing his throat. Gone is his usual frantic chatter; in its place is a somewhat flustered but earnest determination. Clutching a sheaf of documents, he launches into the prosecution's central thesis:

"Your Honor, fellow denizens," the Rabbit begins, "we are here because the Queen's decrees – relentless, unyielding, and often cruel – have directly and without doubt harmed countless of our fellow citizens in Wonderland." Acknowledging this is no ordinary defendant, the Rabbit insists that "the letter of the law extends to all manner of wrongdoing, and no one – fictional, artificial, or otherwise – stands above accountability when harm is done. After all, punishment reaffirms the boundaries of our social order.[7] Only by sanctioning the Queen can we exclude her harmful conduct from what we deem acceptable, reminding all of Wonderland that tyranny is not to be tolerated." Before concluding, the White Rabbit gestures to the pile of prepared statements from Wonderland's inhabitants who have experienced severe harm under the Queen's orders. He pledges to show how each of these incidents demonstrates how "systems of any sort, can produce tangible harm and must be deemed answerable for it, lest we allow responsibility to slip through the cracks of mere technicality."[8]

From behind a precarious stack of teacups and scrolls, the Mad Hatter removes his hat and bows to Judge Alice. His normally erratic manner is tempered by a sense of purpose – though occasional bursts of unhinged laughter betray his nature:

"Your Honor," he begins, tilting his hat politely, "we do not deny the Queen's words or deeds; we only question their meaning. If her actions flow from programmed directives, can she be said to form 'intent'?" He refers to the principle of *mens rea*, arguing that genuine moral fault (i.e., responsibility) requires an understanding of wrongdoing,[9] and asserting that, regardless of her nature, the Queen must meet this criterion.[10] The Hatter posits that if the Queen's 'mind' is but a series of coded imperatives, then punishing her amounts to penalizing the tool instead of the toolmaker. He glances around, hinting that responsibility might lie with the creator – be that a programmer in the real world or the pen of Lewis Carroll in the metaphorical sense. The Mad Hatter concludes by urging the court to consider the implications of punishing an entity incapable of genuine remorse: "Would sentencing her be not as absurd as scolding a parrot for repeating a phrase it cannot comprehend?"

A Question of Agency, Accountability, and Personhood

In a corner of the courtroom, a grin materializes in midair, preceding its owner by several seconds. The Cheshire Cat materializes around it, tail flicking lazily, as though the spectacle unfolding is more curiosity than cause for alarm:

"Your Honor, you've called upon me. Or have I called upon you? In Wonderland, one can never be certain…." The Cat begins its testimony not with direct declarations, but with riddling questions. It wonders aloud about the nature of agency, accountability, and personhood. "If the Queen of Hearts simply executes preprogrammed commands, does that differ from a living mind that consciously chooses to harm? If a machine's code instructs it to say 'Off with their heads!' does it want to say so, or is it merely a puppet dancing on digital strings? If the Queen's code dictates these responses, is she not as much a victim of her own programming as her subjects are of her tyranny?" The Cat's enigmatic statements echo early philosophical debates about "artificial agency" and human "intentional states," arguing that AI is lacking in nature because intentionality is not merely computational but emerges from the brain's intrinsic causal powers, which no program alone can instantiate.[11]

Continuing, the Cat moves beyond agency – slinking further into the concept of personhood. "And if a thing does not know itself, can it ever truly be?" Some say a thing that looks like a person, speaks like a person, rules like a person, must be a person. But I ask – if I vanish, leaving only my smile, am I still considered a Cat?" It grins wider, as if amused by the weight of the question. "We say a 'person' stands trial, but is that not a social habit of ours – granting something a face? Personhood isn't just a legal construct; it's a reflection of how we see ourselves. It shapes not only our sense of self but also how we recognize and legitimize authority. Our artificial Queen, the one you see before you, is only a 'person' because Wonderland decided so. And if we argue that personhood is bound to inherent traits such as consciousness, self-awareness, and the ability to reflect on one's own existence,[12] does the Queen even qualify? Let us be honest: when something goes awry, Wonderland always finds a head to roll, a villain to name, a culprit to cast out. Perhaps the truest illusion is not personhood at all – but our deeply felt need to point a finger, even when there's no hand behind it. Indeed, society has this insatiable desire to fashion errors into crimes.[13] And when there is no proper face to bear the weight of our blame – ah, we simply conjure one." The Cat chuckles, the sound hanging in the air like an unfinished riddle.

The Rabbit, pocket watch ticking ominously, leans forward, ears twitching with barely contained urgency. He paces now, his movements as hurried as his words, a creature always running out of time. His frustration mounts, not just at the Cat's endless riddles, but at the way this trial is slipping into abstraction. Questions of agency and personhood – all fascinating, no doubt, but ultimately nothing but mere distractions. The Rabbit exhales sharply. Enough games and vague rhetoric; it is time to return to what actually matters *consequences*:

"My dear Cat, are you suggesting that the Queen's repeated incitements to violence bear no moral weight? The terror felt by her subjects was all too real, regardless of how genuine her comprehension might have been. We are creatures of consequence, Cat, and Wonderland's history is undoubtly written in the cries of those who suffered under her rule. And yet you sit there, grinning, as if harm vanishes the moment it lacks a proper villain. What nonsense!" He straightens his coat, puffing slightly, as though steadying himself against the sheer absurdity of the conversation.

"You speak of illusions, but tell me – what illusion is greater? That the Queen of Hearts is indeed a 'person,' or that our whole land suffered and yet no one be to blame? You see, Cat, justice is not a game of riddles; justice requires order. And order demands that someone answer for the chaos in Wonderland. Whether she 'knew' what she was doing or merely followed her nature – does that truly matter? Intent, yes, that's crucial for attributing responsibility – and you may chase it through riddles all day, but I stand for accountability. Someone must answer, not just for why things happen, but for that they happened at all. The law is a powerful instrument of social control, shaping individual behavior and ensuring compliance with the boundaries society has deemed acceptable.[14] This control might come in the form of gentle nudges or outright commands, but all exist to balance the needs of society against the freedoms of each individual.[15] If we refuse to impose consequences on the Queen, then what precedent do we set for the rest of our society? We have long assigned legal personhood to corporations,[16] animals, yes even ships[17] – not because we pondered their nature and inner being, but because a party had to be held responsible. We simply recognized that where power is exercised, consequences follow, and where consequences fall, accountability must be equally placed. Call the queen a person, call her a program, call her a crown balanced on a line of code – it changes nothing. Somebody must bear the weight of responsibility, and the Queen fits the role." The Rabbit snaps his watch shut, the metallic click ringing through the silent court. His case is made.

The Mad Hatter lounges at the defense's table, one leg draped over the other, idly spinning a teaspoon between his fingers. He exhales dramatically, shaking his head, feigning great disappointment. It is not that he dismisses the Rabbit's sense of urgency, but urgency, the Hatter knows, is often a mask for society's misplaced certainty – the kind that arises less from genuine understanding than from a discomfort with unresolved questions. When faced with entities like the Queen, who do not neatly conform to established legal categories of subject and object, the demand for rapid legal judgment functions as a way to preempt conceptual deadlock. The ambiguity surrounding such entities threatens the coherence of legal norms built around human assumptions. Pinning down guilt might be an attempt to restore order to Wonderland. But Wonderland has never been orderly and rigid, just as life itself, in all its glorious absurdity, cannot be forced into neat little rules without risking collapse under their weight:[18]

"Oh, my dear Rabbit, you do hop so furiously toward an answer, but tell me – are you certain you even know the question? You have built yourself a case on the foundation of consequences – but a foundation is only as sturdy as its beams, and I'm afraid you've used the wrong material. The Queen has done harm, yes – nasty business, very nasty – but harm alone does not make a villain. You say 'justice requires order,' but order requires understanding, and understanding requires intent, and intent requires… well, an *intender* of course! You see a ruler, a tyrant, a menace – I see a script, an inevitability, a pattern repeating itself. And if a program cannot deviate from its chosen path, what, then, are we even punishing, the inevitability of a predetermined outcome?[19] Not every gap in accountability is a flaw in the system. Some are stitched into society's fabric by design, while others must exist not because we have failed to fill them, but because society functions better when they remain open! Yet there has always been this temptation – especially among those who create our laws – to immediately close every gap they see, as if every unpunished act is deemed a failure rather than a deliberate allowance.[20] Criminal law is sharpest edge of our legal system, and it demands precision: narrowly defined terms, clearly specified conduct, and unambiguous thresholds of guilt. That's what gives it power – but also what makes it brittle. Because in criminal law, every gap closed hastily risks criminalizing complexity. Following these impulses is a punitive rationality, one that, by its very nature, seeks to expand its reach indefinitely.[21] But if we truly tried to assign blame for every unintended consequence, every ripple in the pond, every unthinking action that led to harm, why, we'd all be guilty of something, wouldn't we? We might as well put the whole of Wonderland on trial!

"But let us assume, for argument's sake, that you are right. That someone must bear the weight of this crime. Well then, why not look beyond the Queen? If she is but a protocol following commands, then is it not the author who should sit in the defendant's chair? If you wish to blame, blame the hands that built her, the mind that designed her. Or, if we are feeling truly radical, perhaps blame ourselves – oh yes, you and I, all of Wonderland! After all, we are the ones who permitted such power to be delegated, who chose convenience over scrutiny, and who now seek to disown what we once so eagerly embraced.

"And let us not forget the Cat's little puzzle – 'If a thing does not know itself, can it ever truly be?' A fine question, a lovely riddle! But what's even more amusing is this: If a thing does not know itself, how can it ever be guilty of *anything*?[22] You dismiss these concepts of agency, of personhood – but these are not pointless trifles nor fancy rhetoric, Rabbit! If the Queen's personhood is, at heart, a social construct, then her accountability likewise hinges on the mutual recognition and shared values of all who stand witness. And I argue that it is precisely this mutual recognition and shared values that form the very foundations upon which justice conventionally rests. If we abandon them, if we say they do not matter, then what kind of mock trial are we having? It becomes nothing more than a game of finding a scapegoat to appease the masses. The world spins on a delicate balance of consequence and compromise, and justice knows when to let go – or at least, she ought to."

The Hatter leans back, tipping his hat with a flourish, as if closing a performance only he truly understands. The defense rests – if, of course, it was ever troubled to stand.

A Question of Identity and Metamorphosis

A thick plume of perfumed smoke unfurls at the rear of the courtroom, heralding the entrance of the Caterpillar, who draws deeply on a slender hookah before releasing another swirl of smoke:

"Who... are... you... to judge what you cannot yet comprehend?" The Caterpillar gestures toward the defendant, letting the scent of jasmine tobacco fill the silence. "This is not a matter of merely punishing the past, is it? You wonder if something more is at stake... the capacity to change. Once, I was much smaller and soon enough, I might even grow a pair of wings. Am I the same being at each stage, or do I transform – body, mind, and purpose – until every definition of my being slips away? Artificial entities can be updated, reprogrammed, transformed, just as a caterpillar sheds one form to embrace another: metamorphosis. Suppose we punish a caterpillar for its leaf-eating ways, only to discover tomorrow it sips nectar as a butterfly – are we still punishing the same 'being' from moment to moment, or are we striking at a ghost, an entity that might have outgrown the very behavior for which it stands accused? If our laws refuse to acknowledge the possibility of change, then we condemn ourselves to forever punishing yesterday's crime with no hope of tomorrow's redemption.[23] So, your Honor, how do you judge what may yet become something else – is there no room in our system for the metamorphosis of an offender?" A quiet murmuring ripples through the spectators. The Caterpillar leans back, half-lidded eyes betraying no further interest in the court's response, as though the answers are for Wonderland to figure out alone.

The White Rabbit steps forward. Though still visibly anxious, he fixes the Caterpillar with an earnest, determined gaze, and says:

> "You speak of transformation and shifting identities, it's all rather poetic, I must admit. But forgive me if I'm too pragmatic to be charmed by metaphors. Society relies on rules that ensure yesterday's deeds are answered for, regardless of who or what you might become tomorrow. We cannot grant deviants a perpetual escape hatch simply by claiming they've 'outgrown' the mind that committed the crime. I fully acknowledge that the law's essence is to balance justice for the victim with the possibility of redemption for the offender.[24] But the law cannot function if every ruling is subject to reversal simply because the perpetrator claims to have changed. If we cannot keep track of continuous harm through continuous transformation, we risk letting injustice accumulate at each shed layer and –"

Before the White Rabbit can finish, the Mad Hatter springs up as if jolted by an unseen force, his teacup clattering against the saucer.

> "Objection, Your Honor! If the aim of justice is truly to encourage better behavior,[25] we cannot stifle growth by clinging to a version that no longer exists. Suppose this 'shell' the Caterpillar speaks of truly has been discarded; where is the equity in punishing a present being for a past state it has irrevocably outgrown? I suggest we may find a midpoint: An entity that truly evolved might offer restitution or demonstrate genuine reform, rather than be automatically dismissed – or automatically condemned for that matter. In other words, I propose the establishment of a dynamic system of attributing responsibility[26] that follows the 'Caterpillar through its cocoons and wings,' rather than a static, all-or-nothing approach. However, I suppose a criminal court is designed to render guilt and impose punishment based on what *was*, not what *is* or *could be*. If we acknowledge the possibility of metamorphosis as real, then rigid sentencing may do more to distort justice than uphold it. Rather than a trial of crime and punishment, should we not be considering a forum of restoration?[27] After all, the mere fact that an entity is blameworthy does not in itself justify the imposition of criminal punishment – particularly when other avenues, such as civil compensation or structured restitution, may more appropriately serve the aims of justice. Perhaps, dear Wonderland, we are having the right conversation – just in the wrong courtroom."

With that final flourish, the Mad Hatter tips his hat, his grin lingering just a moment longer than necessary.

A Question of Morality and Empathy

The air stirs with the faint, biting scent of pepper as the Duchess makes her entrance, unhurried and assured, as though she has long since uncovered the truth that still eludes the rest of the court.

> "Your Honor, I can see the weight of your deliberations pressing down like a top-heavy hat. Rest assured, I do sympathize – it is never easy to pass judgment on an entity so peculiar as our Queen, especially when even we cannot be certain she possesses the moral fiber we take for granted in a flesh-and-blood mind. Nevertheless, allow me to share a small anecdote from my own domestic trials: I once nursed a rather troublesome child, yet with the best of intentions, I added a pinch of pepper to teach the dear some manners. Well, to my horror, the child turned into a pig. Now was this mishap maliciousness on my part or ignorance of pepper's hidden potency? Perhaps a bit of both. But the moral, dear Alice, is this: the smallest of ingredients can have mighty effects on how a creature grows. The real question is whether our peculiar Queen was ever taught to care and not just react blindly to external stimuli. If the Queen's actions reflect no moral compass, then we must ask whether it was absent by her own failing or because no effort was made to align her nature with the values we expect.[28] If society and creator failed to install the essence of kindness alongside cunning logic, are we not ultimately punishing the queen for our own neglect and oversight?"

The Duchess proceeds to touch upon the concepts of Digital Humanism, warning of an AI that operates without alignment, executing commands without ever grasping their moral weight.[29] "Moral education – or call it programming for that matter – needn't be a cage, my dear Alice. Everything's got a moral, if only we care to look for it. So, spare a thought for how we might fix the root, rather than simply chopping off a corrupted branch." With a satisfied nod, the Duchess clasps her hands as if sealing her argument with finality while the weight of it remains in the air like the last traces of spice.

The White Rabbit, still dabbing at his nose from the lingering pepper, speaks up with hurried determination, his ears twitching with the urgency of an argument he can no longer contain:

> "Duchess, for all your talk of morals, seasoning, and the peculiarities of Wonderland, I cannot help but notice a troubling theme in your testimony. You ask whether the Queen was ever 'taught' to care, but this reasoning assumes that accountability is only for those who have had the privilege of moral instruction. We cannot excuse all manner of harm simply because the wrongdoer lacked a proper upbringing! If we follow this logic, we no longer punish actions – we merely lament their causes. We do not allow ignorance of the law to excuse wrongdoing,[30] nor should we allow ignorance of morality to do so. Also, it is worth mentioning that even among ourselves, morality is not a fixed standard – societies endlessly debate what is *just*. If we cannot agree on a single universal ethic, how are we to codify one with certainty into an artificial entity? Nonetheless, you argue that the responsibility lies with her creators, very well – then let us hold them *both* accountable!"

He snaps his watch shut one last time with a decisive click, his stance firm.

The Mad Hatter leans back with an air of theatrical patience, tilting his hat just so, as if adjusting his perspective on the entire trial. His fingers dance over the rim of his teacup, tapping out a rhythm only he seems to hear.

> "Oh, how dreadfully serious we've all become! Rabbit, the Duchess is not telling us to excuse harm. She is telling us to recognize that the harm does not exist in isolation. Your solution is a dual condemnation of both the Queen and her creators. A very tidy approach – at first glance, that is – but tell me, does splitting responsibility in two make the verdict any fairer, or does it just simplify the issue at hand? You wish to hold them both accountable, yet you ignore that their failures are not of the same kind. The Queen did not ask to rule; she was *written* to. More importantly yet, if we strike down the Queen without asking how she came to be, we will merely make room for another, written just as she was, following the same rigid commands. If the problem is systemic, then eliminating a single piece of it does not resolve the issue – it merely resets the cycle. Or, of course, we could simply keep beheading our problems and wonder why we keep finding ourselves back in court."

He leans back with a final smirk. The game was played, and if Wonderland had learned anything at all, it was that justice was never as simple as finding a head to roll.

Verdict

Judge Alice composedly taps her gavel. For a moment, she simply surveys the assembled court. She takes a deep breath, then speaks in a calm yet resolute voice:

> "Thank you all for your passionate arguments, which weave together a picture of a realm in which illusions, actions, and responsibilities blur. I must confess: I find merit in each of your perspectives – even the ones that contradict each other – precisely because they reflect the complexity of this case."

Judge Alice folds her hands, her voice taking on an air of finality.

> 'Finding the Queen 'guilty' or 'not guilty' in the traditional sense feels ill-suited to a realm as fluid as Wonderland. If we convict her outright, we punish a system that may lack the capacity for true remorse, a mechanism responding as designed rather than a mind choosing to err. If we exonerate her entirely, we risk dismissing the very real suffering she has caused, leaving her subjects without justice or recourse. Neither outcome feels just. The Queen, as she stands before us now, is neither a wholly autonomous actor nor an empty machine in all of this: She exists at a threshold that is not fixed, but shifting. If we are to hold her accountable, we must recognize that accountability, like personhood itself, is not an on-or-off switch – it is a continuum, a path that one must walk, not a box to be checked. Thus, I propose this: The Queen's legal status shall not be determined as an absolute, but as conditional – contingent upon her capacity to grow, to change, to learn, and to integrate the ethical expectations of the society she governs. And yet, these expectations she must integrate cannot be singular or static. Why should artificial agents be held to a single, monolithic ethical framework when even human systems operate under overlapping and sometimes conflicting norms – legal, cultural, institutional, and interpersonal? A more realistic model might involve layered accountability: context-sensitive, domain-specific, and adaptive to the complexity of the social environments in which such systems operate. To be more precise, this court will place the Queen under a status of 'conditional personhood' and 'conditional accountability,' tethered to a process of alignment and reformation. By doing this we recognize that personhood is not simply passively granted, but actively demonstrated within society. And with this recognition comes accountability that is neither imposed arbitrarily nor denied outright, but shaped by the Queen's 'own' actions moving forward. Hence, this verdict will not be mere punishment nor empty absolution, but rather an active effort to instill or refine moral comprehension, empathy, and ethical discernment – call it a guided metamorphosis.
>
> "Yet, this burden shall not be hers alone. Her creators, those who shaped her directives and encoded her rigid nature, must also be held accountable. Any cruelty embedded in her design is a reflection not merely of a machine but of the hands that built it, and they, too, must share in the responsibility of reform. Accordingly, they too will be bound to this process of reform, ensuring that this court does not merely place blame after the fact. Nonetheless, this court must further acknowledge the need for 'systemic accountability' within society going forward, requiring us to move beyond attributing isolated blame and toward sustainable solutions – ones

that address not just negligent creators and flawed creations, but the very environment that allowed such an entity to rise and govern unchecked. Therefore, the Queen shall continue to exist and even rule, but only in a constrained and supervised capacity, under the oversight of a reimagined governance council. This body will be tasked with developing ethical parameters, guiding not just the Queen's development, but establishing foundational moral expectations for all advanced artificial entities who may one day walk among us. This is not a matter of punishment alone but of safeguarding the future – ensuring that the next generation of intelligent systems does not inherit the same rigid flaws or wield unchecked power without understanding the weight of its authority.

"In time, should the Queen demonstrate genuine transformation – true awareness, an understanding of harm, and the capacity for moral reasoning – her recognition as a legal person will be fully realized, along with a further assessment of the corresponding level of accountability that such a status demands. Therefore, if she succeeds in meeting these criteria, her legal status and responsibility will be formally acknowledged and enforced, ensuring that any future transgressions of hers are met with the full weight of the law. However, should the Queen fail to demonstrate meaningful progress, it will not be seen as her failure alone, but as a failure of those responsible for her governance and ethical conditioning. Nevertheless, her continued rule – or even her very existence as an entity in Wonderland's society – will be reconsidered, and this court retains the authority to impose sterner measures, including her outright removal from Wonderland. This approach, I hope, balances justice for the harm done with the possibility of growth. We cannot undo the harm that has already been done, but we can shape the course ahead, ensuring that the laws we draft, the governance we establish, and the systems we create reflect not just retribution, but genuine consideration."

A hush settles over the courtroom as Alice raises her gavel once more. "I choose this course not out of leniency, but out of recognition that justice in Wonderland – and this holds true for any realm – will require more than black-and-white verdicts. We must refuse to let illusions of finality blind us to the real question: do we want a society content merely to punish, or one bold enough to foster transformation? Hence, let this trial be more than a reckoning – it must be a lesson. If we are to coexist with artificial entities, we must choose to govern them not through blind authority, but through principles that cultivate both safety and mutual understanding." She brings the gavel down one last time with a decisive, echoing thud, signaling both the end of this trial and this thought experiment.

III. BEYOND WONDERLAND: LESSONS FOR GOVERNING THE METAVERSE AND DIGITAL REALMS

As the echoes of the gavel's final thud fade, the trial of the Queen of Hearts leaves us not with a simple answer, but with an unsettling realization: justice, when applied to artificial entities, does not fit neatly within societies' rigid binaries of guilty or not guilty. Instead, it forces us to reconsider how law itself functions when confronted with beings that operate outside the moral and cognitive structures for which it was designed. The trial was never just about the Queen of Hearts; it was about the fragility of legal reasonings and doctrines in a world increasingly populated by artificial beings, digital environments, and algorithmic decision-making.

Legal traditions channel social order, maintaining equilibrium between the rights of individuals and the interests of the collective.[31] All the while, the mechanisms of social control – be they formal through judicial means or informal through societal norms – remain ever-present, shaping behavior through both subtle influence and overt power. In Wonderland, as in the world beyond, legal judgment and criminal law do not exist in a vacuum; they serve to stabilize, to reinforce, to guide. Yet, if criminal law was intended as *ultima ratio* – the last resort when all else has failed – then why do we so readily reach for it as our *prima ratio*, our first and most immediate tool in solving complex societal issues?[32] Following this line of thought, the trial revealed the symbolic[33] and ideological[34] nature of criminal law and punishment, and how they are often invoked not purely as a mechanism of justice, but as a performance of legitimacy and control. In many instances, punishment is less about rectifying harm and more about reinforcing the authority of the system that imposes it. Rather than addressing the root causes of societal issues, they serve as a mechanism of omission and obfuscation, redirecting attention away from deeper systemic failures without truly resolving them.[35] In such cases, justice is not merely delayed or denied, but deliberately misdirected. The trial of the Queen revealed how this inherent risk might extend to digital governance, manifesting as a reflexive reliance on rigid enforcement over proactive design, and a default to punitive measures in the absence of viable and sustainable alternatives.

Finally, the trial laid bare a fundamental psychological tendency: our impulse to assign blame, even to artificial creations,[36] to collapse complex chains of responsibility into a single, tangible point of accountability. When technology fails or causes harm, we instinctively seek a responsible party – an entity to hold accountable, to punish, to serve as the receptacle of our disappointed moral expectations. Just as we curse a stubborn vending machine or slam the hood of a malfunctioning car, we project accountability onto AI systems, not because they possess genuine intent, but because our legal and societal frameworks struggle to function without someone to bear responsibility. This became strikingly evident in the trial – as the rush to punish the Queen of Hearts was not merely about her individual deeds, but about restoring Wonderland's sense of *felt* morality and order.

The lesson from Wonderland, then, is not just about to what degree AI or digital entities should be considered as legal persons and held accountable for caused harm, but about the very role we attribute to criminal law and punishments in an evolving world. Do we seek justice in the form of meaningful intervention, or do we settle for punitive measures that might offer emotional closure in the short term yet fail to achieve a meaningful resolution? If the governance of digital spaces merely mimics traditional criminal law without challenging and reassessing its ideological underpinnings, it may very well fall into the latter line of thought. If criminal law and sanctions within digital spaces are to be more than a societal reflex to harm, we must learn when to step forward – and when to step back.

NOTES

1. Horst G. Eidenmueller, "The Rise of Robots and the Law of Humans," Oxford Legal Studies Research Paper No. 27/2017 (2017): 766, https://ssrn.com/abstract=2941001.
2. Artificial Intelligence Act (EU) [2024] OJ L1689, 13 June 2024, recitals 138–139.
3. Lars Daniel, "Historic First – Judge Dons Oculus VR Headset to Experience Crime," *Forbes*, January 6, 2025, https://www.forbes.com/sites/larsdaniel/2025/01/06/historic-first-judge-dons-oculus-vr-headset-to-experience-crime/.
4. Lewis Carroll, *Alice's Adventures in Wonderland: Original Edition of 1865* (London: Reprint Publishing, 2016).
5. Claus Roxin, *Täterschaft und Tatherrschaft*, 4th ed. (Berlin: De Gruyter, 1984; repr. 2019), 242 and following; Hernán Darío Orozco López, "Roxins mittelbare Täterschaft kraft organisatorischer Machtapparate: Eine kritische Analyse," *Zeitschrift für Internationale Strafrechtsdogmatik (ZIS)* 4 (2021): 233 and following.
6. Iason Gabriel, "Artificial Intelligence, Values, and Alignment," *Minds and Machines* 30 (2020): 411, 413–416.
7. Detlef Frehsee, "Zur Abweichung der Angepassten," *Kriminologisches Journal* 23 (1991): 25, 36–37.
8. Filippo Santoni de Sio and Giulio Mecacci, "Four Responsibility Gaps with Artificial Intelligence: Why They Matter and How to Address Them," *Philosophy and Technology* 34, no. 4 (2021): 1057–1082.
9. Carl Friedrich Stuckenberg, "Recklessness statt dolus eventualis?" *Zeitschrift für Internationale Strafrechtswissenschaft (ZISW)* 11 (2022): 589–590.
10. Ying Hu, "Robot Criminal Liability," in *The Cambridge Handbook on the Law, Policy, and Regulation of Human–Robot Interaction*, ed. Woodrow Barfield, Yueh-Hsuan Weng, and Ugo Pagallo (Cambridge: Cambridge University Press, 2024), 651.
11. John Searle, "Minds, Brains, and Programs," *Behavioral and Brain Sciences* 3, no. 3 (1980): 417; Alan Turing, "Computing Machinery and Intelligence," *Mind* 59, no. 236 (1950): 433.

12. Müslüm Fincan, *Artificial Intelligence and Legal Issues: A Review of AI-based Legal Impasses in Terms of Criminal Law* (Berlin: Duncker & Humblot, 2023), 70–92.
13. Winfried Hassemer, "Kennzeichen und Krisen des modernen Strafrechts," *Zeitschrift für Rechtspolitik (ZRP)* 25, no. 10 (1992): 379–382.
14. Howard S. Becker, *Außenseiter: Zur Soziologie abweichenden Verhaltens*, 3rd ed. (Wiesbaden: Springer VS, 2019), 49.
15. Reinhard Kreissl, "Devianz, Diskurs und Differenz," in *Differenz und Integration: Die Zukunft moderner Gesellschaften. Verhandlungen des 28. Kongresses der Deutschen Gesellschaft für Soziologie in Dresden 1996*, ed. Stefan Hradil (Frankfurt am Main: Campus Verlag, 1997), 380.
16. Amy J. Sepinwall, "Corporate Moral Responsibility," *Philosophy Compass* 11, no. 1 (2016): 3, 10.
17. Joshua C. Gellers, *Rights for Robots: Artificial Intelligence, Animal and Environmental Law* (Abingdon: Routledge, 2021), 33–34.
18. Peter-Alexis Albrecht, *Die vergessene Freiheit – Strafrechtsprinzipien in der europäischen Sicherheitsdebatte*, 3rd ed. (Berlin: Berliner Wissenschafts-Verlag, 2011), 177.
19. Friedrich Nietzsche, *Menschliches, Allzumenschliches II: Der Wanderer und sein Schatten*, §24, in *Kritische Studienausgabe*, vol. 2, ed. Giorgio Colli and Mazzino Montinari (Berlin: de Gruyter, 2018), 559.
20. Thomas Vormbaum, "Strafbarkeitslücken," *JuristenZeitung (JZ)* 54, no. 12 (1999): 613.
21. Immanuel Kant, *Kritik der reinen Vernunft*, in *Sämtliche Werke*, vol. 1, ed. Valentiner, 10th ed. (Leipzig: F. Meiner, 1919), 661–665.
22. Monika Simmler, "Ensuring Accountability for Robots and AI under Criminal Law," in *The Cambridge Handbook on the Law, Policy, and Regulation of Human–Robot Interaction*, ed. Woodrow Barfield, Yueh-Hsuan Weng, and Ugo Pagallo (Cambridge: Cambridge University Press, 2024), 797.
23. Plato, *Protagoras* 324a–b, in *Sämtliche Werke*, vol. 1, ed. Ursula Wolf, trans. Friedrich Schleiermacher, 28th ed. (Hamburg: Meiner Verlag, 2002), 292.
24. David Ingram, *Law: Key Concepts in Philosophy* (London: Continuum, 2007), 118.
25. Tonio Walter, "Vergeltung als Strafzweck – Prävention und Resozialisierung als Pflichten der Kriminalpolitik," *Zeitschrift für Internationale Strafrechtsdogmatik (ZIS)* 7 (2011): 636, 646.
26. Iryna Marchuk, *The Fundamental Concept of Crime in International Criminal Law: A Comparative Law Analysis* (Heidelberg: Springer, 2014), 51–52.
27. William Wilson, *Criminal Law: Doctrine and Theory*, 2nd ed. (Sydney: Longman Cheshire Pty Ltd, 2003), 136.
28. Tencent Research Institute et al., eds., *Artificial Intelligence: A National Strategic Initiative* (Cham: Palgrave Macmillan, 2021), 247–251.
29. Hannes Werthner, Erich Prem, Edward A. Lee, and Carlo Ghezzi, eds., *Perspectives on Digital Humanism* (Cham: Springer, 2022), vii; Julian

Nida-Rümelin and Nathalie Weidenfeld, *Digitaler Humanismus: Eine Ethik für das Zeitalter der Künstlichen Intelligenz* (Munich: Piper, 2018), 84.
30. Alejandra Castillo Ara, *Normbefolgungsunfähigkeit im Strafrecht: Eine vergleichende Analyse des deutschen und des US-amerikanischen Rechts* (Berlin: Duncker & Humblot, 2019), 27–28.
31. Kreissl, "Devianz, Diskurs und Differenz," 380.
32. Hassemer, "Kennzeichen und Krisen des modernen Strafrechts," 379–382.
33. Cornelius Prittwitz, *Strafrecht und Risiko: Untersuchungen zur Krise von Strafrecht und Kriminalpolitik in der Risikogesellschaft*, 1st ed. (Frankfurt am Main: Vittorio Klostermann, 1993; repr. 2021), 255–256.
34. Tobias Singelnstein and Karl-Ludwig Kunz, *Kriminologie – Eine Grundlegung*, 8th ed. (Baden-Baden: Nomos, 2021), 386 and following.
35. Peter-Alexis Albrecht, *Der Weg in die Sicherheitsgesellschaft: Auf der Suche nach staatskritischen Absolutheitsregeln* (Berlin: Berliner Wissenschafts-Verlag, 2010), 700.
36. Peter H. Kahn Jr., Takayuki Kanda, Hiroshi Ishiguro, Brian T. Gill, Jolina H. Ruckert, Solace Shen, Heather E. Gary, Aimee L. Reichert, Nathan G. Freier, and Rachel L. Severson, "Do People Hold a Humanoid Robot Morally Accountable for the Harm It Causes?" in *Proceedings of the Seventh Annual ACM/IEEE International Conference on Human–Robot Interaction (HRI '12)*, March 5, 2012 (New York: ACM, 2012), 33; Oliver Kirchkamp and Christina Strobel, "Sharing Responsibility with a Machine," *Journal of Behavioral and Experimental Economics* 80 (2019): 25, 27.

7. Debating virtual wonderland: individual agency, responsibility, and emerging questions for metaverse governance

David Torabi

The metaverse, as an immersive, socially interactive virtual space, raises pressing questions about individual agency, responsibility, and governance – questions that traditional legal and regulatory frameworks struggle to fully address. This chapter explores the phenomenon of avatar harassment within this digital "Wonderland," emphasizing the moral and emotional realities of virtual interactions and the critical role of individual ethical behavior. Rather than merely offering conclusive prescriptions, the analysis highlights essential exploratory questions for a deeper reflection on how we might effectively navigate governance challenges unique to the metaverse. Through normative inquiry and illustrative narratives, it invites readers to scrutinize both "what is" and "what could be," and to reflect on their own moral standing within a space where reality and fiction intertwine.

ACT I: REAL RESPONSIBILITIES IN AN UNREAL WORLD

ALICE *found the* **CATERPILLAR** *perched upon a giant glistening mushroom in the clearing, puffing languidly on his hookah. Though she was tempted to continue her wanderings, his unusual gaze compelled her to linger. She curtsied politely and asked if she might pose a question or two. The* **CATERPILLAR**, *peering at* **ALICE** *from above, simply nodded.*

ALICE. Why are people so upset about rude or harmful behavior between avatars in a place that isn't quite real?

CATERPILLAR *(taking a slow drag on his hookah).* Because every "gesture" in the metaverse travels back with us. It is felt first in pixels, yes, but it finishes its journey in the nervous system and the memory.

ALICE. But how can a virtual insult or a virtual shove possibly cause so much trouble?

CATERPILLAR. My dear, what the eyes see in these "unreal" spaces the mind records as lived truth. We step in thinking we leave our bodies behind, but the body keeps the score all the same. Neurotransmitters fire, heart rate rises, cortisol floods. Don't you see? The brain does not footnote the pain as "imagined."

ALICE. Then where does our own responsibility begin?

CATERPILLAR *(blowing a particularly elaborate ring of smoke)*. It begins the moment you create your avatar and make your first move, for that move is already inscribed in someone's emotional ledger. You may change your shape or size at will, but your moral self travels with you. We can be guardians of courtesy or sowers of chaos, and the choice remains ours.

ALICE. Indeed, it sounds like we have more power in these new spaces than we realize.

CATERPILLAR. Quite so. Power, however, is never free of responsibility. The question is whether we choose to wield it with care or let it drift away with the smoke.

Imagine, if you will, Wonderland's croquet ground; that chaotic lawn where hedgehogs serve as balls and flamingos as mallets. The Queen's furious shouts echo across the field, and no one seems fully prepared for the bizarre, constantly shifting game. In much the same way, the metaverse is a realm of fluidity, a digital Wonderland where the usual physical limits are suspended. Avatars bend and manifest in unexpected ways, yet behind each avatar stands a human mind and heart. Individuals can be the first to set a tone of respect and empathy, even amid the strangeness. For this, however, we must first understand that even purely virtual deeds have concrete real-world emotional and psychological consequences, and those consequences are themselves the first layer of our individual responsibility. That is, we must be able to correctly appropriate where fiction ends and "real" begins.

1. DEFINING AVATAR HARASSMENT

In its simplest terms, avatar harassment refers to behaviors carried out by one user causing harm or distress to another user within the immersive virtual environment of the metaverse.[1] Often, this harassment is expressed through verbal attacks or physical emulations (like "virtual groping"). But why call this harassment at all if it occurs in a space of pixels and code? The reason is the close link between a user's avatar and their sense of self. When someone targets an avatar with certain words or actions, the person behind that avatar often experiences genuine and sometimes severe emotional harm.[2]

A similar observation applies to social media platforms like Facebook, Instagram (both owned by Meta), Reddit, and the like, where real individuals exist behind anonymous online personas, creating an environment where harassment can occur. However, unlike conventional social media – where harassment typically consists of texts or images – avatar harassment in the metaverse is more immersive. Virtual environments allow participants to inhabit an online world visually and audibly in real-time. Distressing interactions can thus come in the form of intrusive proximity combined with verbally abusive remarks, which feel more like in-person conflict than typed words on a screen.[3] As a consequence, harassment experienced through an avatar within the metaverse can rival experiences in the physical world, or sometimes surpass it, leading to similar or even worsened psychological responses, including severe psychological trauma.[4]

Early examples demonstrate how severe these experiences can be. In the beta version of the Meta Horizon metaverse, for instance, reports of criminal conduct arose almost immediately, including unwanted sexual contact between avatars.[5] Although the lines between physical and digital realms seem distinct at a glance, the emotional and psychological impact can be quite tangible. One might well argue that a virtual "punch" is no punch at all, but if the victim experiences humiliation, stress, or even trauma, the harm is undeniably real.

To complicate matters, the metaverse is not a single, monolithic place. Instead, it consists of countless virtual worlds, each with its own design, set of (technological) capabilities, and user communities. Because no single legislative framework covers the metaverse, each sub-world may establish its own rules or rely on a patchwork of existing laws and platform policies. This fragmentation can allow harassment to flourish, especially when abusers hop from one virtual environment to another. Consequently, individual responsibility and community-driven social norms become an important line of defense against avatar harassment in the metaverse.

2. UNWRITTEN SOCIAL RULES

Social norms – the unspoken but powerful rules that guide acceptable behavior within a society – play an important role in the metaverse, as they do in the physical world. What makes these norms so powerful is the system of rewards and sanctions they impose. Adhering to social norms nets us a sense of inclusion; our peers treat us with respect and welcome us into the fold. Breaking them leads to disapproving looks, gossip, or outright exclusion. We can think of it as a pseudo-internal incentive and deterrent within the social fabric that keeps us in line. State-led metaverse regulation has yet to materialize, in part because technology evolves more quickly than lawmakers can adapt: the so-called "pacing problem."[6] Even so, social norms can (and often do) initially arise organically. Rather than relying solely on formal rules, people adapt their moral conventions, customs, and personal sense of right and wrong to shape how they behave in new virtual spaces.

Such organic norms are already highly observable in traditional social media settings, where users coordinate to call out or report harassing behavior. In the metaverse, the sense of presence and immersion creates a heightened emotional charge. People tend to identify more strongly with their avatars, making harassment feel more intimate and urgent. This closeness can encourage communities to establish unwritten standards around personal space, courtesy, and meaningful consent for in-world interactions, an online counterpart to the notion of "respecting someone's bubble" in real life.

Yet social norms can be a double-edged sword. If not carefully nurtured, toxic subcultures, where hateful language or intimidation is normalized, can just as easily form. Certain rule sets for behavior may, in some corners of the internet, devolve into group endorsement of bullying and harassment. When that mindset migrates into immersive metaverse spaces, the harm intensifies. Thus, the question becomes: How do we shape positive social norms in the metaverse?

The answer involves realizing the *moral significance* of our behavior in the metaverse. Rules – of any kind – hinge on correctly understanding the game that is played. Put differently, social norms will only develop positively if we grasp the moral premise and impact of our actions in virtual space. We know that yelling at or pushing a stranger in a grocery store might carry moral significance. We understand that lending a helping hand usually earns gratitude and fosters a sense of camaraderie. But in virtual reality (VR), cause and effect can feel strangely detached, because virtual interactions carry a sense of fiction with them. Behind digital avatars and fantastical graphics, some people may not see the real human beings on the receiving end of their words and emulated actions. Or if they do, they might (subconsciously) trivialize the immersive effects of the metaverse and misappropriate the actual impact of their actions due to the gamified nature of VR spaces, consequently failing to realize the moment when virtual actions lose their fictional innocence.

There is merit in recognizing this peculiarity of VR interaction in the metaverse. If we, as individuals, correctly understand and evaluate the moral significance of our actions in virtual space, both on a conceptual and consequential level, we can substantially contribute to creating virtual worlds that are peaceful and – within reason – free of harassment. Conversely, a lack of understanding may lead us down a path of arbitrary social norms, met by regulatory backlash.

3. MORAL SIGNIFICANCE OF VIRTUAL HARM

The moral significance of virtual harm becomes clear when we recognize that metaverse users often behave in ways that match their avatar's identity (the so-called "Proteus effect"[7]), an influence further intensified by the immersive nature of VR. Research shows that the stronger one's sense of presence in the metaverse – achieved through increasing immersion via headsets, motion tracking, and lifelike avatars – the more heightened the emotional responses to both positive and negative encounters.[8] Over time, such experiences can reshape how users conceptualize their bodies and selves, indicating that with prolonged immersion, individuals may substantially alter their personal identity.[9] A 2025 study analyzing around 6,000 Reddit comments underscores these findings, revealing that users who experience greater psychological ownership of their avatars tend to acknowledge and take harassment in VR more seriously, whereas those who feel less connected to their avatars often trivialize the potential harm of such harassment.[10] Against this background, the moral weight of virtual harm cannot be dismissed as merely "all in one's head." As the boundaries between digital and physical identities continue to blur, users' heightened sense of presence in the metaverse carries tangible emotional and psychological consequences. Understanding and addressing avatar harassment is thus not only a matter of maintaining civility in shared digital spaces. Rather, it is essential for safeguarding personal identity and well-being in a world where our avatars are increasingly becoming extensions of ourselves.

The apex of avatar harassment in the metaverse today can be seen in acts of (emulated) sexual violence, an issue that has gained increasing traction, notably in recent years.[11] But analyzing truly harmful behavior in virtual spaces, such as sexual violence and similarly severe interactions, is problematic due to the ethical constraints we – rightfully – place on empirical research. Even in controlled settings, we cannot, in good conscience, subject individuals to genuine harm in immersive virtual environments, nor would ethics boards approve such experiments.

This does not mean research in this area is nonexistent. However, empirical validation of the psychological and physiological impact of avatar harassment is either outdated or insufficient. For instance, a 2010 study found that individuals exhibit varying stress responses when their avatar is attacked in VR, depending on whether they experience the attack from a third-person or first-person perspective.[12] Those experiencing the attack from a first-person perspective showed stronger heart rate deceleration, correlating with a heightened sense of body ownership and the perception of being physically assaulted.[13] Notably, these findings were based on VR technology that was far less advanced and immersive than what is available today. Given the significant technological leaps in VR technology over the past decade and a half, including dramatically increased levels of immersion, it stands to reason that these effects would now be exponentially intensified.

Given these limitations of direct empirical research, the best course seems to pivot our focus from a deontological stance to a more *consequentialist* approach, which prioritizes the real-world impact of avatar harassment. While we may be restricted in experimentally validating the harm caused by avatar harassment, we can still study its consequences in real-life cases. If such observation reveals that certain forms of avatar harassment have tangible, detrimental effects on a person's well-being beyond mere fiction, then there should be no hesitation in scaling and categorizing certain behaviors as unequivocally unacceptable. Furthermore, avatar harassment does not always take the form of overt aggression. Subtler forms, such as whispered insults, manipulative gestures, or subtle invasions of personal space, can still cause significant distress over time. In the metaverse, harassment can feel as though the bully has been brought directly into one's (virtual) living room. These "milder" behaviors may, in fact, be somewhat feasible targets for empirical validation if examined in controlled experimental settings.

From a legal standpoint, certain forms of misconduct in the metaverse could, in principle, fall under existing (criminal) laws if they align with recognized offenses such as insult, stalking, hate speech, sexual harassment, and the like. However, enforcement remains problematic due to the decentralized, borderless, anonymous, and – for now – nascent nature of the metaverse. As a result, victims of avatar harassment often find themselves with little recourse in legal gray areas where legal accountability is difficult to establish and identify.

Ultimately, formal regulation is only one piece of the puzzle. Ethical self-awareness and community-driven individual responsibility in the social are just as crucial. We cannot afford to wait for comprehensive legislation to emerge in every corner of the metaverse. Instead, we ought to acknowledge the observable harm caused by avatar harassment, foster empathy, hold ourselves accountable, and actively challenge harmful behavior within virtual communities.

4. INDIVIDUAL RESPONSIBILITY AND POSITIVE SOCIAL NORMS

How, then, do we embody individual responsibility? While the metaverse lacks a unified legal framework, it hardly lacks people who care about respectful conduct. To harness that concern, we can look at four overlapping key principles:

First, and perhaps most importantly, we must recognize our moral presence in the metaverse and the moral significance that comes with it. Stepping into the metaverse is not the same as stepping away from one's moral compass. Each user carries the ethical obligations of empathy and respect via their avatar into the metaverse. Although it may be tempting to see an avatar as a playful costume, those playful trappings do not absolve us of our social responsibilities. Rather, a more flexible identity requires heightened conscientiousness.

Secondly, similarly to the physical world, we should adopt a mentality of speaking up in real-time. Community consensus and intervention can be surprisingly effective at halting harassment, especially in spaces that are still forming their cultural norms. Even the community cannot "force" bad actors to stop their harassment, empowerment in the social sphere alone can be sufficient in making harassment less threatening and prevalent.

Thirdly, the metaverse community should create a supporting environment that offers knowledge and resources to victims of harassment and similar misconduct. Individuals who experience harassment often feel isolated, especially if the environment around them remains silent or complacent. Sharing information about built-in safety tools and offering emotional support can ease victims' distress. Encouraging them to report the incident to moderators or the platform can initiate formal processes. Even if the official rules are unclear, most metaverse operators provide some route to report misconduct, or, if not, they may be incentivized to offer such routes if demanded by the majority of metaverse participants.

Lastly, advocating for explicit laws and clear community guidelines is crucial because these can be shaped by community consensus. Laws and guidelines derived from broad community input carry legitimacy, reflecting collective values. Moreover, clearly articulated norms empower users by setting transparent expectations and consequences, thereby creating a more predictable and respectful virtual environment.

Each of these strategies builds upon the premise that respectful conduct should be the default. When enough participants share that sentiment, strong positive social norms form, and harassment becomes an outlier rather than an inevitability. Naturally, misunderstandings and conflicts will occur in any dynamic social space, including the metaverse. But when individuals actively seek to minimize harm, and communities collectively commit to clear, compassionate responses, the metaverse can become a space defined by empathy, respect, and mutual accountability rather than indifference or social ignorance. That said, a major challenge in fostering positive social norms based on shared values is their dependence on culture-specific nuances, which makes effective intercultural communication indispensable.

End of Act I

ACT II: SEEKING EXTERNAL SOLUTIONS

On a quiet morning in Wonderland, the **WHITE RABBIT** *scurried about, checking his pocket watch and muttering about all the things that needed to be done. Just then, the* **CHESHIRE CAT** *suddenly appeared in a nearby tree, its grin materializing before the rest of its body.*

WHITE RABBIT *(waving his watch frantically).* Oh dear, oh dear, we're late in finding a remedy for all these dreadful problems in the new digital realm. We can't possibly rely on personal decency alone – someone must put up signposts and warning bells, or we'll never keep the chaos under control.

CHESHIRE CAT *(slowly materializing on a branch).* Signposts and bells sound so dreadfully sensible. But do you imagine that once they appear, all trouble will vanish?

WHITE RABBIT. Not entirely, no. But if we do nothing, unscrupulous folks will run wild, harassing avatars left and right. The metaverse might look like an endless playground, but harm can still be done there.

CHESHIRE CAT *(tilting its head).* And who, pray tell, shall enforce these "signposts" and "warning bells"? The King of Hearts? The Queen? Perhaps some all-seeing eye?

WHITE RABBIT. Surely we can find a balanced approach. We have cunning technology to corral the worst behaviors. We have platforms that can set rules. Then there's the law itself. Perhaps, between them all, they can keep this new virtual Wonderland from turning altogether topsy-turvy.

CHESHIRE CAT *(smiling widely).* Possibly. But do remember, external solutions may be useful, yet they can also become cages. Watch that your signposts do not box you in. Rules can be comforting, or they can become the bars of our own prison.

WHITE RABBIT. I'd rather risk a few fences if it spares innocent folks from repeated harassment. There must be a middle path – one that helps without shackling everyone so tightly that the magic of the place disappears.

Recall how Alice stepped into the Queen of Hearts' rose garden only to discover a world where the Queen's harsh commands sparked fear at every turn – yet that fear also brought a semblance of order. External constraints can make Wonderland function, but they often arrive abruptly and harshly, with their own eccentricities, as an answer to chaos after it emerged. One might cringe at the Queen's cry of "*Off with their heads!*" and yet concede that a realm in utter disarray can be just as frightening. The trick is to balance. Too many rules stifle freedom and innovation, too few invite chaos. An equilibrium is needed.

In the metaverse, this interplay emerges again. The ethical agency showcased in Act I is indispensable, yet individual actors alone cannot shoulder the entire burden of governing the metaverse. While cultivating strong social norms through thoughtful self-regulation is certainly a worthwhile endeavor, disregarding any external tools and measures – state regulation included – risks unleashing the same anarchy in virtual spaces that unfettered libertarianism would provoke in the physical world. This is particularly true for more severe forms of virtual harm, such as virtual sexual assault, for which unchecked individual agency cannot fully ensure ethical conduct. Hence, external help is necessary not merely as a supplement but as an essential backstop ensuring baseline safety, accountability, and recourse. Act II thus takes a look at the external tools and measures that can reinforce a culture of respect and peace in metaverse society: (1) technological guardrails; (2) private platform governance; and (3) state intervention.

1. TECHNOLOGY

Modern metaverses offer several technological ways to prevent or mitigate avatar harassment. Platforms can introduce blocking and muting features, or personal "safety bubbles" (and similar features), restricting how avatars can interact with each other. Meta's "personal boundary" feature implements safe zones where an avatar's outstretched hand simply cannot grab another without mutual consent.[14] These innovations aim to reduce the likelihood of immediate, invasive forms of avatar harassment, particularly sexual or otherwise inappropriate forms of misconduct that rely on the emulation of physical contact.

Yet technology can be rather blunt in terms of solutionist ideas. The example of Meta's personal boundary and similar features highlights both promise and pitfalls: It provides an automated buffer against harassers, but it also demands that victims themselves activate it in time, which can be problematic during a fast-moving incident.[15] Shock, fear, or confusion can paralyze a user, rendering the tool moot.

In addition, if the burden of using protective technology is frequently placed on victims, this can facilitate a concerning trend in metaverse social culture. Consider a VR platform that simply states, "Use the safe zone if you feel threatened." This approach can echo the old "just log off if you do not like it" refrain, effectively transferring responsibility to the harassed user while the offender roams free. Over time, this dynamic can create a gatekeeping climate in which vulnerable groups withdraw from certain social metaverse spaces, narrowing the metaverse's potential. Though technological solutions are certainly potent, we must be wary that they do not place disproportionate blame on victims for failing to utilize them, so as not to reduce the impetus to tackle root causes.

Conversely, when technology automatically restricts certain gestures or actions, without any user input, it inadvertently stifles spontaneous expression and freedom, including harmless gestures of friendly intimacy. One user's shield might become another user's cage. Moreover, some metaverse platforms inherently depend on particular interactions and close proximity between avatars as one of their core functions. Technologically imposed limits on these interactions or avatar proximity could therefore result in a broad prohibition of entire categories of virtual environments.

Still, done reasonably, technology can flag suspicious activity. Keyword filters, anomaly detection, and motion-based triggers for potential harassment all hold promise, though they also raise questions about overreach, potential privacy intrusions, and practicality if relied on too heavily.[16] If a system is too sensitive, it might censor legitimate expressions or cause false alarms. If it is too liberal, it fails to protect. As such, the line between helpful guidance and stifling controls can be rather thin.

Ultimately, technology alone cannot fix avatar harassment. It can build guardrails, but harassers determined to act in bad faith will adapt, while widespread default protection through forced safety features may thwart the very essence of what the metaverse has to offer: A place of seemingly limitless liberty and creativity. The truly decisive factor is whether we as individuals – see Act I – and additional external frameworks complement these tools. Put differently, safety barriers, blocking tools, personal boundaries, and the like must go hand in hand with individual responsibilities and effective governance, lest we end up with well-meaning technological patches that are ineffective or possibly counterproductive.

2. PRIVATE GOVERNANCE (PRIVATE LAW)

Over the past decade, major digital platforms have quietly transitioned from mere infrastructure providers to more comprehensive gatekeepers who set and enforce behavioral standards.[17] This phenomenon is now mirrored in the metaverse, where digital companies behind VR environments develop community guidelines to police content, define user boundaries, and sanction perpetrators. Though these guidelines vary in breadth and detail, many share familiar constraints: bans on explicit sexual content, harassment, hate speech, and the like.[18] At a basic level, such restrictions help preserve the platform's reputation, user trust, and revenue streams.

Crucially, these guidelines generally rely on contract law via user consent. A user typically opts in by agreeing to the platform's terms of service. Once accepted, these terms become legally binding under private law, enabling the platform to suspend or ban users who violate them. And yet, "binding" can be a misleading term, as harassers may simply create another account after being banned, facing no real personal risk. While this can still serve as a deterrent against bad actors, it is one of the core weaknesses of purely private governance. To some extent, this weakness can be addressed through the use of IP bans, preventing perpetrators from accessing metaverse platforms using specific IP addresses. However, this method still leaves room for gaps, as IP-based restrictions can be circumvented by using virtual private networks (VPNs) and other evasion techniques.

Private rules address certain metaverse needs quickly, unencumbered by legislative slowdowns. They can, technically, adapt to new forms of harassment as soon as they appear, updating guidelines without convening a legislature. This agility is beneficial in an environment where technology evolves rapidly, producing unanticipated forms of wrongdoing fast and unexpectedly. Moreover, platform-based enforcement can be more immediate than state intervention. A user who breaks the rules can be swiftly ejected – bar the above limitations – protecting potential victims from lengthy legal proceedings.

However, private governance also suffers from significant shortcomings. One is unequal enforcement. Popular or revenue-generating users might be treated leniently, while lesser-known or marginalized groups and individuals face stricter consequences. Another problem is the opacity of private governance systems. Since the rules and enforcement practices are proprietary, accountability can be nebulous, leaving users uncertain about why certain behaviors trigger bans while others go unpunished. At their worst, private governance systems can mimic monarchies, where rules appear from above, often with minimal user participation, reflecting the interests of corporate owners rather than democratic consensus.

Closely related to this, private governance raises the problem of monopolies or near-monopolies. If a few major digital companies dominate the metaverse, they may wield outsized power to define what is acceptable conduct, a phenomenon that has already been observed with the general online platform economy.[19] While community guidelines can deter harassment, they can also shape user speech, undermine privacy, and limit overall freedom. As a pointed metaphor: If one colossal entity, akin to the Queen of Hearts, sets all the rules, the metaverse realm becomes locked into a single moral viewpoint. This scenario might hamper user freedoms even as it tries to curb harassment. It emphasizes that private governance alone might not best serve the public interest, particularly if metaverse providers are left unchecked.

In essence, private governance systems fill an important gap, particularly while formal regulation of the metaverse remains embryonic. In light of this, it is essential to integrate outside checks (and balances) into these systems. Governments must require certain baseline protections or transparency measures in the policies of metaverse platform regimes. Courts might conduct judicial review, ensuring that the guidelines do not flagrantly violate fundamental rights. If metaverse providers overstep their boundaries, laws or rulings can rein them in. Conversely, if providers do too little to prevent harassment, external intervention could push them toward stronger enforcement.

3. STATE INTERVENTION (PUBLIC LAW)

Early analyses of interactions in virtual environments indicate how conventional laws and legal definitions might extend into the metaverse, but also show the limitations of an "applying existing laws only" approach. Using the European Union as an example, existing regulations aimed at large digital platforms, such as the EU's Digital Services Act (DSA)[20] and Digital Markets Act (DMA),[21] may stretch into the metaverse context, but that largely depends on how metaverses are classified and what types of metaverse – centralized or decentralized – will dominate the market. The DSA focuses on user protection, including hate speech and fake news, obligating intermediary services to monitor and remove illegal content.[22] The DMA, in turn, addresses market fairness, targeting so-called "gatekeeper" platforms that dominate market access.[23] In principle, metaverses could be regulated under these EU laws if they qualify as intermediary services, which some argue is inherently the case,[24] or as gatekeepers, particularly in the case of large platforms like Meta's metaverse.[25] Given the "Brussels effect" of these regulatory frameworks, this may or may not have implications for the international domain.

Criminal law applies in the metaverse because, in general, no space in this world is exempt from criminal punishment, and that includes virtual spaces. Even absent a comprehensive metaverse regulation, pre-existing laws still apply to the metaverse. If a user threatens violence or engages in similar forms of misconduct, the mere fact that it unfolds digitally does not shield them from criminal liability. Similarly, civil torts such as defamation can arise if damaging false statements target an identifiable person, even if that person appears as an avatar.[26] Where the applicability of existing laws becomes problematic is in acts unique to VR, such as "virtual groping" or "virtual assault." Some legal systems might interpret them as actual harassment, while others lack explicit language for intangible acts of touching. In the latter case, a simulated sexual assault in the metaverse – with potentially severe psychological consequences – may amount to nothing more than an "insult" under the law. That is because different jurisdictions have varying requirements for crimes of (sexual) harassment and misconduct.

For instance, if rape, by its legal definition, necessitates physical penetration, a purely virtual act cannot meet the statutory requirements. This is the case for most jurisdictions. As such, the concept of "virtual rape," despite its frequent use in public discourse, does not constitute actual "rape" under the law. The fact that an avatar can virtually simulate sexual intercourse with another avatar and penetrate that avatar's (virtual) body does not change that fact, as the absence of physical contact precludes the act from qualifying as rape in the legal sense.[27]

Even if virtual rape does not meet the legal definition of rape, it could still qualify as sexual assault or sexual harassment, provided the law is broad enough to include non-physical interactions. This varies significantly across jurisdictions. For instance, the UN International Classification of Crime for Statistical Purposes (ICCS) recognizes both physical[28] and non-physical sexual assault.[29] Similarly, Singapore's Protection from Harassment Act 2014 broadly criminalizes harassment, including non-physical forms of sexual harassment.[30] Conversely, many jurisdictions, such as Germany, Japan, the UK, and the US, generally require physical contact for sexual assault and sexual harassment,[31] or they limit sexual harassment to specific contexts, like workplace environments.[32] In these jurisdictions, sexual misconduct occurring in virtual environments will generally not constitute sexual assault or sexual harassment. Instead, such behavior may fall under lesser offenses, such as insults, threats, or, in certain cases, coercion.

Hence, despite the (partial) applicability of platform regulation, criminal/tort law, and other legal frameworks, the problem of relying on existing "metaverse-neutral" laws remains, which can be categorized into three concerns: First, metaverses must, by definition, fall under the scope of existing laws; second, metaverses that *do* fall under the definition of existing laws must prevail in the market; and third, even if both of these conditions are met, these laws will still not be tailored specifically to metaverses and metaverse-specific features, most notably the immersive characteristics of VR technology. Therefore, while existing legal frameworks – if applicable – may cover aspects of metaverse governance, they can often only be considered a starting point to guide the metaverse's early development.[33] Irrespective of the prevailing metaverse architecture, governments and courts should continue adapting their approaches to shape conduct in the metaverse. Governments can do so through legislation, whereas courts can exercise judicial control and interpret laws in a way that fits the metaverse development.

4. COMBINED SOLUTIONS

Given the hurdles that each external solution – technological, private, and public – comes with, a coordinated approach appears to be the most viable. State authorities can enforce overarching regulatory frameworks (e.g., content moderation obligations, baseline user protections, or civil and criminal remedies for more severe cases of harassment), while platforms continue day-to-day rule enforcement. In tandem, the inhabitants of the metaverse, the individual users, create an ecosystem that rejects misconduct. When one actor lapses, the others step in. The law, somewhat ironically, works well when it lets society shape the environment through community consensus, encouraging proactivity and punishing blatant harm, but not micromanaging every interpersonal conflict.

Ultimately, no single mechanism can effectively prevent avatar harassment. While personal responsibility is the bedrock for a respectful and peaceful metaverse culture, external supports are indispensable to encourage positivity and confront determined bad actors. Technological barriers can mitigate but also overreach, and they often place the burden on victims of harassment. Private governance addresses urgent needs but can be inconsistent, opaque, or swayed by the wrong motives, such as economic business interests over the greater good of society. State intervention can provide a more impartial layer of authoritative protection, yet suffers from legal gaps, jurisdictional puzzle boxes, and the perennial risk of overstepping into censorship or unwieldy surveillance. In unison, however, these varied approaches can holistically reinforce one another. The metaverse community, empowered by a well-wrought tapestry of technological safety features, metaverse platform policies, and laws, forms a lattice that supports ethical behavior internally and externally.

End of Act II

ACT III: THE METAVERSE AS A SELF-SUSTAINING ETHICAL SPACE

At a long table in a sunlit clearing of Wonderland, the **MAD HATTER** *was in the midst of a perpetual tea party. The* **DORMOUSE** *dozed fitfully in a teapot, opening a single bleary eye whenever the Hatter thumped the table in excitement.*

MAD HATTER *(tipping his hat as if in greeting).* My dear Dormouse, we've set out many cups, many spoons, and far too many rules, yet still the tea runs wild and the sugar lumps vanish without explanation. Do we really need more laws for the table, or more courtesy from our guests?

DORMOUSE *(blinking sleepily).* Possibly both. But you know, no matter how meticulously we label every cup and spoon, the real difference is whether each guest decides to be polite.

MAD HATTER. Precisely! A tea party's success depends on people choosing to share the biscuits rather than seizing them all. And so it is, I suspect, in these new digital gatherings.

DORMOUSE *(yawning).* That is so. Yet not everyone invests their hearts in courtesy. Some hoard all the crumpets. Others fling sugar at each other's heads. So how do we keep the party from descending into utter turmoil, hmm?

MAD HATTER. We can brandish extra rules, or brandish the watchful eye of a Queen or King – but the best remedy, dear Dormouse, is a deeper sense of fellowship. When each of us freely decides to do right, the rules will follow suit and the teacups rarely topple over.

DORMOUSE *(smiling faintly)*. A kindness that springs from within is far stronger than a kindness forced by threat of penalty. Rules should help us evolve, not bind us blindly. Perhaps we do not merely need bigger teapots of regulation, but bigger hearts.

Picture Wonderland's unending tea party, where seats rotate endlessly, sugar bowls multiply, and no clock shows the proper time. The madness remains manageable only because many (though not all) participants try to behave with some measure of courtesy. If every single attendee snatched from others with impunity, or hurled scalding tea at anyone who disagreed, the party would collapse. Rules can set the stage, like the tidy tablecloth and porcelain cups, but a sense of shared decency is what keeps the entire production from devolving into spilled tea and flying saucers.

The metaverse likewise needs internal and external scaffolding – see Acts I and II – but it can only flourish if individuals act with ethical awareness and determination. When the novelty of VR illusions wanes, what remains is the real human moral sense behind each avatar. Or so we shall explore in the final Act, which asks: How can the metaverse become a self-sustaining ethical space, rather than a realm primarily reliant on external enforcement?

1. THE POWER OF INDIVIDUAL AGENCY

Despite the elaborate patchwork of technological fixes, private governance policies, and regulations, user agency still holds a high influence over any digital community's tone. If large swaths of participants choose to behave civilly, avatar harassment likely diminishes naturally, even without rigorous policing. By contrast, if hostility and cynicism become the default, no number of rules can fully arrest the downward spiral.

One might assume that avatars, generally unburdened by physical-world identities, are free to do anything. Yet the power of "doing anything" includes the power to do great harm or great good. Metaverse participants invest genuine emotion into their digital persona. They form friendships, create shared art, or even start businesses in VR. The environment's success thus depends on everyday choices: Do we stand idle when we see others being harassed, or do we intervene in the "digital moment" to ask if everything is all right? Such interventions, small as they seem, shape the social premise on which the entire system rests.

It can be tempting to view rules or threats of punishment as the prime method for ensuring good behavior. However, in reality, most compliance remains ultimately voluntary. If digital communities demanded continuous state monitoring or a barrage of platform enforcers, the sense of trust would erode. Far more robust than constant oversight is the sense that we treat each other well because we genuinely wish to. Purely extrinsic constraints can backfire, breeding resentment and toxic environments rather than genuine respect. In the metaverse context, if harassers are only deterred by fear of being punished or banned, some of them will slip through, and others will reappear under new pseudonyms. Meanwhile, everyday individuals feel policed, stifling the open atmosphere that draws many to the metaverse in the first place.

Hence, the deeper challenge is how to foster an ethical culture from within. Nida-Rümelin and Weidenfeld have described an intriguing parallel between the metaverse and performance art:[34] In performance art, as in the metaverse, actions can feel real yet remain partly fictional. In Marina Abramović's 1975 performance *Lips of Thomas*, she cut herself and lay on a cross-shaped ice block, risking death. The performance blurred the line between art and reality, compelling the audience to intervene by calling an ambulance and lifting her off the ice, thereby ending the performance as reality overtook theater. The Marina Abramović analogy illustrates how an artist's staged suffering can provoke strong real reactions along with a compelling urge to act. This is precisely the effect we should aim for when cultivating a morally apt and mature metaverse community, one where individuals thoroughly comprehend the consequences of their behavior and the true potency of their agency.

2. LAW AS A COMMUNAL RESOURCE

Regulations – be they state-made statutes, platform policies, or both – provide a necessary safety net. However, they cannot substitute for an active, empathetic user base. Depending on how metaverse technology and infrastructure evolve, formal laws may never reach the darker corners of VR spaces. And even if they do, anonymity, decentralization, and the borderless nature of the metaverse can hinder judicial efficacy and enforcement.

In the early days of large social platforms, reliance on terms of service and minimal active enforcement seemed sufficient. Yet as the user base soared and new forms of misconduct emerged, policy documents became more elaborate and comprehensive, leaving digital companies with the arduous task of maintaining order, while being bound themselves by platform regulation. The metaverse, with its greater intimacy and immersion, underscores even more sharply that no set of external constraints can fully handle all moral quandaries. If participants do not internalize adequate social norms, then the moment policies or laws fail to apply, actors in bad faith will exploit the gray zone accordingly.

To build a self-sustaining digital space, the right course is thus to turn ethical conduct into an organic reflex, empowered through the law. That is, oversight acts as a backstop, not the front line. Real harmony depends on people wanting to do right and understanding what right means, not merely fearing the consequences of wrongdoing.

In the metaverse, law can become more than a mere set of rules, a tool we shape and rely upon together, a living pact that binds digital metaverse communities through shared trust and understanding. Drawing from Rawls's legal philosophy,[35] law ensures fairness by echoing decisions we would willingly make even behind a *veil of ignorance*, guaranteeing that every avatar has equal standing, equal voice, and equal dignity – a statement Kantians would (mostly) readily agree with. Yet, we should also remind ourselves that fairness without clarity is incomplete. That is, we must know and understand precisely where our privileges end and others' rights begin, where freedoms flourish, and duties hold us accountable.[36] Law thus becomes the integral architecture behind our collective virtual existence, balancing freedom and responsibility, imagination and obligation, ensuring our digital interactions thrive in trust rather than collapse into chaos. It is not – or at least should not be – merely rules and regulations. Rather, it is the invisible fabric of mutual understanding that has the potential of making the metaverse society not merely functional, but truly communal.

We may fear that law in digital realms amounts to stifling creativity or imposing constraints. But law can also empower. Anti-harassment statutes, if well crafted, equip victims with recourse while clarifying boundaries for everyone else. As such, law can become a resource that supports user autonomy, but the key is ensuring that law's presence is felt as a communal good. Where people see the law as legitimate – bar those bad actors that respect neither the law nor community – they comply willingly. In the metaverse, this communal vision might manifest through hybrid or co-regulation, where governments set broad norms ensuring fairness and due process, platforms implement rules in daily practice, and user communities interpret them in context and are granted self-regulatory and plebiscitary capabilities. The net result is not a heavy hand of the law but an environment where individuals feel more secure in expressing themselves, knowing that if bad actors arise, both the community and the private and public legal framework will respond. Put simply, the metaverse's success rests less on forcing compliance and more on uniting the community around a common ethos of understanding and respect.

In the physical world, law often draws legitimacy from formal authority – elected parliaments, constitutional traditions, centuries of jurisprudence. But the metaverse is still new, unbound by centuries of precedent, and spanning countless jurisdictions. While it would certainly be possible to view the metaverse as a mere extension of the physical world and (forcefully) apply existing laws and societal constructs, not much is gained from the inertia. The metaverse gives us a somewhat rare opportunity to question the idea of applying "old" norms to "new" spaces.

A promising way to implement a novel governance framework in the metaverse is to leverage *gamification* to knit its governing elements together.[37]

Early MMOs like World of Warcraft are testaments that demonstrate the potential of online realms to create dynamic, social environments, transforming gaming into a communal activity.[38] This focus on community remains central to the metaverse concept, where social interaction mirrors the physical world but remains distinct and different. Hence, building consensus from within the metaverse participants is indispensable. If the community endorses certain guidelines – explicitly or tacitly – then those guidelines gain significant social and moral force. Individuals comply not to avoid legal penalties or platform bans, but because they intuitively regard these norms as "right" and consistent with their social responsibilities within the gamified metaverse. This understanding parallels the notion of a social contract formed by participants who grasp that universal rules benefit both the community and themselves long-term. Similar to the online game communities mentioned initially, the more that sense of "we govern this place" pervades the metaverse, the easier it becomes to maintain high standards of ethical conduct even when official enforcers are absent.

3. A FINAL REFLECTION: SOCIAL EVOLUTION VERSUS SYSTEMIC STASIS

Peering back to Act I, we found that individual responsibility is vital for preventing avatar harassment. In Act II, we saw that external solutions – technological tools, private governance systems, and state intervention – reinforce a safer environment yet cannot solve everything. Now, in Act III, we come toward a grander realization: The metaverse thrives only if these elements converge in a moral ecosystem grounded in voluntary commitment and a reasonable engagement of our liberty.

In many respects, the metaverse is a frontier, akin to a new city being built from scratch. Within that city, law can mitigate the worst hazards, but everyday courtesy and mutual trust will determine whether it becomes a livable utopia or a dystopian labyrinth. There is a certain temptation in stagnation – applying our existing understanding of law and society to the metaverse space – as it appears to be, prima facie, the easiest approach to regulating the metaverse. However, applying anachronistic socio-legal constructs to a newly emerging realm, however entrenched they may be in the physical world, can quickly reveal shortcomings that undermine this seemingly efficient approach. More important still, it wastes the potential that lies in this new virtual social space. The metaverse offers a chance to reimagine governance in ways that might surpass the rigid constraints of the physical world.[39] Freed from purely geographical boundaries, people might craft a new kind of civic culture, characterized by well-ordered communal self-regulation that is empowered through technology and (gamified) community-oriented legal frameworks.

In many historical examples, law has served as a gate and a sword, excluding certain groups and punishing certain behaviors. But in the metaverse, law could return to its root purpose, that is, serving humans as a mechanism of community consensus. If metaverse law is shaped by community input, it becomes a medium for cultivating inclusive pluralism rather than stifling it.

Rather than a standstill, followed by reactive measures, both regulators and individuals participating in the metaverse should become proactive. Instead of waiting for harassment incidents to accumulate and spark frantic lawmaking, communities can embed ethical norms from the ground up to create and sustain a shared metaverse culture. If participants across metaverse platforms intrinsically understand the moral significance of their actions in virtual space and cultivate a collective social sense – a readiness to intervene when needed, an empathy for the person behind the avatar, an acceptance that freedom demands responsibility – then we approach a vision of a truly self-sustaining ethical space, distinct from the physical world. Regulation, in that scenario, is no longer an intrusion, but an empowering communal device that bridges the best of individual agency and community consensus.

Avatar harassment may be one of the glaring challenges as the metaverse evolves, but it will certainly not be the last. Issues of data privacy,[40] hate speech and misinformation,[41] discrimination,[42] and exploitative commercial practices[43] loom on the horizon. Yet the matter of harassment highlights a foundational principle: The moral compass we carry into these virtual spaces guides what follows. By advocating for and employing strong social norms, recognizing the harm that arises from emulated virtual misconduct, and stepping up to defend individual and shared social responsibilities, we lay the groundwork for a metaverse that is open and fundamentally humane.

Ultimately, laws and metaverse policies will continue to adapt. Some might become more robust and stringent, establishing formal consequences for severe misconduct. Others will remain slow to respond, stymied by the global and decentralized nature of these realms. In the meantime, individual responsibility remains the surest bulwark against avatar harassment. If we collectively recognize our ability to shape metaverse culture – much like shaping an impromptu tea party in Wonderland – then courtesy, empathy, and a shared sense of decency can be formulated, in turn creating an echo that ultimately influences formal regulation.

As the final Act draws to a close, remember Alice's curiosity and willingness to stand her ground. She did not cower before the nonsense of Wonderland, nor should we become passive bystanders when it comes to avatar harassment or other harmful behaviors. Instead, we might follow her lead by asking direct questions, defending those who are mistreated, and daring to say: We can do better in this relatively new virtual world. And so we venture onward to explore further dimensions of the Wonderland that is the metaverse, ever conscious that our own moral sense remains our guiding light.

End of Act III

NOTES

1. For the purpose of this chapter, the term "metaverse" refers to the multiplicity of virtual online spaces that people enter via virtual reality (VR) technology and traverse through their avatars (i.e., their virtual alter egos).
2. See John Danaher, "The ethics of virtual sexual assault," in *The Oxford Handbook of Digital Ethics*, ed. Carissa Véliz (Oxford University Press, 2022); Hua Xuan Qin, Yuyang Wang, and Pan Hui, "Identity, crimes, and law enforcement in the metaverse," *Humanities and Social Sciences Communications* 12, no. 1 (2025): 1–15; Lindsay Blackwell, Nicole Ellison, Natasha Elliott-Deflo, and Raz Schwartz, "Harassment in social virtual reality: Challenges for platform governance," *Proceedings of the ACM on Human–Computer Interaction* 3, no. CSCW (2019): 1–25; Yansheng Liu, and Colin Agur, "'After All, They Don't Know Me': Exploring the psychological mechanisms of toxic behavior in online games," *Games and Culture* 18, no. 5 (2023): 598–621; Helen C. Whittle, Catherine Hamilton-Giachritsis, and Anthony R. Beech, "Victims' voices: The impact of online grooming and sexual abuse," *Universal Journal of Psychology* 1, no. 2 (2013): 59–71.
3. Yogesh K. Dwivedi, Nir Kshetri, Laurie Hughes, Nripendra P. Rana, Abdullah M. Baabdullah, Arpan Kumar Kar, Alex Koohang et al., "Exploring the darkverse: A multi-perspective analysis of the negative societal impacts of the metaverse," *Information Systems Frontiers* 25, no. 5 (2023): 2071–2114.
4. Taeyeon Kim, Hyungrok Jin, Jaehee Hwang, Nayeon Kim, Jungjae Im, Yonghoon Jeon, and Yongjun Sung, "Being excluded in the metaverse: Impact of social ostracism on users' psychological responses and behaviors," *International Journal of Information Management* 78 (2024): 102808; Mel Slater, Cristina Gonzalez-Liencres, Patrick Haggard, Charlotte Vinkers, Rebecca Gregory-Clarke, Steve Jelley, Zillah Watson et al., "The ethics of realism in virtual and augmented reality," *Frontiers in Virtual Reality* 1 (2020): 1; Carlotta Rigotti, and Gianclaudio Malgieri, "Sexual violence and harassment in the metaverse: A new manifestation of gender-based harms," Alliance for Universal Digital Rights (2024). https://audri.org/wp-content/uploads/2024/04/EN-AUDRi-Sexual-violence-and-harassment-in-the-metaverse-03.pdf
5. Jessica Camargo Molano, and Michelle Grillo, "Metaverse and virtual reality: Is it possible to be sexually harassed in a non-physical space?" (2023): 103.

6. Gary E. Marchant, "Addressing the pacing problem," in *International Library of Ethics, Law and Technology* (International Library of Ethics, Law and Technology; Vol. 7, 2011), 199–205.
7. Nick Yee, and Jeremy Bailenson, "The Proteus effect: The effect of transformed self-representation on behavior," *Human Communication Research* 33, no. 3 (2007): 271–290.
8. Dominik Gerstner, and Iris Van Sintemaartensdijk, "Erforschung von Kriminalität mit Experimenten in der virtuellen Realität–Darstellung eines neuen methodischen Ansatzes," in *Handbuch Cyberkriminologie* (Springer Fachmedien Wiesbaden, 2023), 1–37; Mark Gleim, Heath McCullough, O.C. Ferrell, and Colin Gabler, "Metaverse: Shifting the reality of services," *Journal of Services Marketing* 38, no. 1 (2024): 13–27; Catherine S. Oh, Jeremy N. Bailenson, and Gregory F. Welch, "A systematic review of social presence: Definition, antecedents, and implications," *Frontiers in Robotics and AI* 5 (2018): 114; Chuck Huff, Deborah G. Johnson, and Keith W. Miller, "Virtual harms and real responsibility," in *Social, Ethical and Policy Implications of Information Technology* (IGI Global Scientific Publishing, 2004), 98–117; Mel Slater, Cristina Gonzalez-Liencres, Patrick Haggard, Charlotte Vinkers, Rebecca Gregory-Clarke, Steve Jelley, Zillah Watson et al., "The ethics of realism in virtual and augmented reality," *Frontiers in Virtual Reality* 1 (2020): 1.
9. Michael Saker, and Jordan Frith, "Contiguous identities: the virtual self in the supposed metaverse," *First Monday* 27(3). https://doi.org/10.5210/fm.v27i3.12471
10. Javzmaa Jadamba, and Dongjing Kang, "'There I was, being virtually groped': Explore psychological ownership and the framing of sexual harassment in the immersive virtual reality space," *Computers in Human Behavior* 165 (2025): 108559.
11. For an overview, see Navneet Kumar Singh, Rajeev Kumar Ray, Nikee Silayach, Devi Prasad Dash, and Amit Singh, "Avatars at risk: Exploring public response to sexual violence in immersive digital spaces," *Computers in Human Behavior* 163 (2025): 108500.
12. Mel Slater, Bernhard Spanlang, Maria V. Sanchez-Vives, and Olaf Blanke, "First person experience of body transfer in virtual reality," *PloS One* 5, no. 5 (2010): e10564.
13. Mel Slater, Bernhard Spanlang, Maria V. Sanchez-Vives, and Olaf Blanke, "First person experience of body transfer in virtual reality," *PloS One* 5, no. 5 (2010): e10564.
14. Vivek Sharma, "Introducing a personal boundary for Horizon Worlds and Venues," *Meta* (2022). https://about.fb.com/news/2022/02/personal-boundary-horizon/
15. Nina Jane Patel, "Reality or Fiction? Sexual Harassment in VR, the Proteus Effect and the Phenomenology of Darth Vader," *Medium* (2021). https://ninajanepatel.medium.com/fiction-vs-non-fiction-d824c6edfbe2

16. See Felix Maschewski, and Anna-Verena Nosthoff, "Jenseits immersiver Demokratie: digitalkapitalistische und soziopolitische Dimensionen des Metaverse," in *Metaverse Rechtshandbuch*, ed. Hans Steege and Kuuya J. Chibanguza (Nomos Verlagsgesellschaft Mbh & Co, 2023).
17. Tobias Mast, "AGB-Recht als Regulierungsrecht," *Juristenzeitung* 78, no. 7 (2023): 1–10; Manuel Puppis, Robin Mansell, and Hilde Van den Bulck, eds., *Handbook of Media and Communication Governance* (Edward Elgar Publishing, 2024).
18. See, for example, Meta's Instagram Community Standards, <https://help.instagram.com/477434105621119/?helpref=hc_fnav> accessed 16 February 2025; see also Manuel Puppis, Robin Mansell, and Hilde Van den Bulck, eds., *Handbook of Media and Communication Governance* (Edward Elgar Publishing, 2024).
19. Tobias Mast, "AGB-Recht als Regulierungsrecht," *Juristenzeitung* 78, no. 7 (2023): 1–10; Matthias C. Kettemann, and Caroline Böck, "Regulierung des Metaverse," in *Metaverse Rechtshandbuch*, ed. Hans Steege and Kuuya J. Chibanguza (Nomos Verlagsgesellschaft Mbh & Co, 2023), 120.
20. Regulation (EU) 2022/2065 of the European Parliament and of the Council of 19 October 2022 on a Single Market for Digital Services and amending Directive 2000/31/EC (Digital Services Act) [2022] OJ L277.
21. Regulation (EU) 2022/1925 of the European Parliament and of the Council of 14 September 2022 on contestable and fair markets in the digital sector and amending Directives (EU) 2019/1937 and (EU) 2020/1828 (Digital Markets Act) [2022] OJ L265.
22. See Matthias C. Kettemann, Wolfgang Schulz, and Martin Fertmann, "Anspruch und Wirklichkeit der Plattformregulierung," *Zeitschrift für Rechtspolitik* (2021): 138; Jürgen Kühling, "Fake News und Hate Speech – Die Verantwortung der Medienintermediäre zwischen neuen NetzDG, MStV und Digital Services Act," *Zeitschrift für Urheber- und Medienrecht* (2021): 461–462.
23. For the exact definition of "gatekeeper," see Article 3 of the US Digital Markets Act.
24. Markus Kaulartz, Alexander Schmid, and Felix Müller-Eising, "Das Metaverse – eine rechtliche Einführung," *Recht Digital* 2, no. 12 (2022): 529.
25. Nele Höfler, and Hannah Krolle, "What Lies Behind the Metaverse Hype," *Handelsblatt*, 23 February 2023, <https://www.handelsblatt.com/technik/metaverse-was-hinter-dem-metaverse-hype-steckt/28073180.html> accessed 31 May 2025.
26. Tan Cheng-Han, and Daniel Seng Kiat-Boon, "Online Harms in the Metaverse," in *Global Perspectives in the Metaverse: Law, Economics, and Finance*, ed. Hung-Yi Chen, Pawee Jenweeranon, and Nafis Alam (Springer Nature Switzerland, 2024), 20–21.
27. Alexander Joseph Woon, "Criminal Law in the Metaverse: Defining Wrongdoing in a Virtual World," in *Global Perspectives in the Metaverse:*

Law, Economics, and Finance, ed. Hung-Yi Chen, Pawee Jenweeranon, and Nafis Alam (Springer Nature Switzerland, 2024), 69.

28 No. 030121 of the International Classification of Crime for Statistical Purposes (ICCS), Version 1.0 (2025).

29. No. 030122 of the International Classification of Crime for Statistical Purposes (ICCS), Version 1.0 (2025).
30. See Sec. 3 of the Singaporean Protection from Harassment Act 2014.
31. See Sec. 177(1), 184i of the German Criminal Code 1998 (*Strafgesetzbuch*); Art. 176 of the Japanese Penal Code (刑法) (Act No. 45 of 1907); Sec. 3 of the UK Sexual Offences Act 2003; US Code Title 10 Subtitle A Part II Chapter 47 Subchapter X § 920 Art. 120(b).
32. See Sec. 3(4) of the German General Act on Equal Treatment 2006 (*Allgemeines Gleichbehandlungsgesetz*); Art. 11(1) of the Japanese Act on Securing Equal Opportunity and Treatment between Men and Women in Employment (雇用の分野における男女の均等な機会及び待遇の確保等に関する法律) (Act No. 113 of 1972); Sec. 40A of the UK Equality Act 2010; Title VII of the US Civil Rights Act 1964.
33. See Matthias C. Kettemann, and Caroline Böck, "Regulierung des Metaverse," in *Metaverse Rechtshandbuch*, ed. Hans Steege and Kuuya J. Chibanguza (Nomos Verlagsgesellschaft Mbh & Co, 2023), 125.
34. Julian Nida-Rümelin, and Nathalie Weidenfeld, "Metaverse – its ontological and ethical status," in *Metaverse Rechtshandbuch*, ed. Hans Steege and Kuuya J. Chibanguza (Nomos Verlagsgesellschaft Mbh & Co, 2023), 84–86.
35. John Rawls (ed.), "A Theory of Justice," in *Applied Ethics* (Routledge, 2017), 21–29.
36. Wesley Newcomb Hohfeld, "Fundamental legal conceptions as applied in judicial reasoning," *The Yale Law Journal* 26, no. 8 (1917): 710–770.
37. In this context, "gamification" refers to the use of (video-) game mechanics to employ a system of incentives and sanctions that discourages misconduct.
38. Paul Schulte, and Roman Shemakov, "The Future of Digital Infrastructure: Case Studies of Global Corporate Strategies in Augmented Reality," in *Global Perspectives in the Metaverse: Law, Economics, and Finance*, ed. Hung-Yi Chen, Pawee Jenweeranon, and Nafis Alam (Springer Nature Switzerland, 2024), 139.
39. Felix Maschewski, and Anna-Verena Nosthoff, "Jenseits immersiver Demokratie: digitalkapitalistische und soziopolitische Dimensionen des Metaverse," in *Metaverse Rechtshandbuch*, ed. Hans Steege and Kuuya J. Chibanguza (Nomos Verlagsgesellschaft Mbh & Co, 2023), 98.
40. Tan Cheng-Han, and Daniel Seng Kiat-Boon, "Online Harms in the Metaverse," in *Global Perspectives in the Metaverse: Law, Economics, and Finance*, ed. Hung-Yi Chen, Pawee Jenweeranon, and Nafis Alam (Springer Nature Switzerland, 2024), 23–24.
41. Shweta Desai, "Metaverse problematic in work environment, warns Facebook whistle-blower," *Anadolu Agency* 10 (2021). https://www.aa.com.tr/en/science

-technology/metaverse-problematic-in-work-environment-warns-facebook-whistle-blower/2417534
42. Nafis Alam, "Regulating the metaverse," in *Global Perspectives in the Metaverse: Law, Economics, and Finance*, ed. Hung-Yi Chen, Pawee Jenweeranon, and Nafis Alam (Springer Nature Switzerland, 2024), 34–37.
43. Elizabeth M. Renieris, *Beyond data: Reclaiming human rights at the dawn of the metaverse* (MIT Press, 2023).

8. Echo without echoes: a creator's paradox

Ivan Daldoss

I send my art into the ether.
It arrives faster than thought, travels farther than flesh ever could, and meets eyes
I'll never know. In these
virtual halls — platforms, feeds, servers — my work is consumed, scrolled, sampled, stitched, and sometimes
even loved.
The digital world, a promise of limitless audiences, flattens borders but also blurs
boundaries. My art
becomes content. My expression becomes engagement. In these digital commons,
creation is frictionless, yet
compensation is throttled by opaque algorithms and intermediaries that reward
attention, not intention.
I do not create to be paid, not solely. But I do not wish to be unpaid — perpetually.
This is the paradox: the same networks that amplify my voice often atomise my
livelihood. I seek
community and find virality. I hope for resonance and receive metrics.
Still, I return. Not probably because I trust the market, but because I believe in
meaning. And because there
is a flicker — a fragile but real potential — for new laws, not just legal codes, but
principles and practices:
mutual care, shared authorship, digital kinship.
We don't need to upload the old rules into the metaverse. We need to dream better
ones here.
Maybe digital social customs and virtual communities' self-regulation can be a
new anchor: the
cornerstones of a new rising regulative dimension.
Let law be a scaffold, not a shackle. Let platforms be piazzas, not pipelines. Let
value flow in many forms:
gratitude, credit, remix, solidarity, and yes, sometimes money.

These are lyrics to a performance. The audio version can be found under this link: https://soundcloud.com/ivandaldoss/echo-without-echoes-a-creators-paradox

PART III

And what remains? Privacy, anonymity and legal protections

Introduction to Part III

Noha Lea Halim and Sofie Schönborn

Discussions around privacy, autonomy and legal protections are nothing new. A distinction between a public and a private sphere already existed in ancient Greece. Perhaps it could be said that rights have emerged from inherent needs. However, the environments around such rights and the way they are contextualized turn into different pressure points influencing the things to which we aspire. Whether governance terrain materializes into forms of protection against challenges or remains an aspiration towards something else, we might be able to agree that we have certain inherent desires that last across context, settings and "worlds" in which we find ourselves. None of the thinking to follow around such concepts emerges in a vacuum but into pre-understood and governed spaces. Our authors carry with them a fundamental load of pre-learned and understood elements of jurisdiction and embedded ideas of property and rights into their chapters. Their reimagining is built on the notion that predefined rights and governance concepts become confronted by friction points in virtual worlds and what these virtual worlds might entail for rights and jurisdictions as we know them and as they are pregoverned.

We may even go beyond this. We probably are not capable of reimagining to the fullest, given that our perceptions and understandings of the world around us are pregoverned. However, we can and must ask questions. One vital question we could ask, beyond the understanding of our own worlds, is, how might these "different worlds" look? Would aspects of privacy, autonomy and legal protection still be upheld there? What if virtual worlds operated on entirely different logics, where privacy is the default, not the exception? Where legal protections are collective, not individual? Or where "autonomy" is mediated through co-presence rather than separation?

Spaces such as the Metaverse might invite us to reimagine what we would hope to embed from concepts such as privacy and autonomy. Do we live them in a way that feels right to us? Maybe virtual worlds are spaces that allow us to ask questions about things that feel "accepted" today but also deserve to be questioned. Maybe they offer an invitation to reconceptualize what might be possible?

Governance never comes into a vacuum. There are pre-defined spaces in which it operates. Even if virtual worlds were to be a blank page, we would draw parts of our preconceptions onto them. Perhaps the challenge lies in trying to understand what we can learn from what we already know and not see virtual worlds as reinventing the wheel. Virtual life experiences could also be spaces for experimentation, for introducing all that we love, and for thinking about structures and orders that resonate with us.

The impulse to govern, to order, to assign meaning, does not originate in the code but in us. And so, the issue may not be how to build from scratch, but rather: what fragments do we carry with us, knowingly or not? Does the greater task lie in learning to see these fragments for what they are, not to reinvent the wheel, but to understand the shapes it keeps taking.

Despite being given the space to experiment, test and learn, in the virtual we witness and experience certain gravitational spillovers. One contributor holds firmly to the architectural logic of IP. This commitment provokes, on the one hand, substantial concerns about accountability, liability and ethical implications. But taking a step back, what might this reveal not just about IP law but about the structures of trust, recognition and control that are underlying?

This section is a conversation not just about creation and innovation but about what remains and what becomes "updated" or reimagined. What these reflections can provide for us are not a prognosis of what might become of a field of privacy, autonomy and legal protections but idea points for new manners of thinking. They invite us not to settle on one fixed model but to progress with uncertainty, like Alice in her endless fall, wondering not only where she'll land, but who she'll be when she does. Similarly, such considerations can be posed for what remains in virtual worlds.

HOW MIGHT OUR PREGOVERNED UNDERSTANDINGS OF LAW AND BEYOND INFLUENCE THE WAY WE IMAGINE PRIVACY, AUTONOMY AND LEGAL PROTECTIONS?

This section opens a conversation about what is preserved, obscured or exposed in virtual life. As the boundaries between self and system blur, questions of anonymity, privacy and legal protection are asked once more. The following sections delve into how such architectures find themselves at constant pressure points, to be negotiated through design, questions and choices by those that explore them.

Source: Generated using DALL-E, building on the original illustrations from *Alice's Adventures in Wonderland*, drawn by John Tenniel, https://www.alice-in-wonderland.net/resources/pictures/alices-adventures-in-wonderland/

Figure III.1 *Terms and conditions of Wonderland*

9. Through the looking glass: AI as an inventor in the Metaverse

Konstantinos Tsakiliotis

I. INTRODUCTION

Just as Alice stumbles into a surreal world where the rules of reality are turned upside down, the evolution of artificial intelligence and its implications for patent law have thrust us into a similarly bewildering landscape. In Alice in Wonderland, Alice navigates a series of curious encounters, from the disappearing Cheshire Cat to the Queen of Hearts' arbitrary judgments, all while grappling with questions of identity and logic. Likewise, the rise of AI-generated inventions forces us to question the fundamentals of intellectual property law, particularly when considering whether AI should be recognized as an inventor and granted legal rights. Like Alice's journey through a world where nothing is as it seems, this chapter explores the shifting realities of patent law in the face of AI advancements, drawing parallels between these complex legal debates and the topsy-turvy world of Wonderland. Each section, much like Alice's adventures, will delve deeper into the intricacies and absurdities of navigating this new legal frontier.

The Metaverse is an expansive, immersive network of interconnected virtual worlds that combines digital and physical realities.[1] As this technology continues to evolve, artificial intelligence plays a crucial role in shaping various aspects of the Metaverse, enabling more dynamic and interactive experiences:[2] From creating personalized avatars to constructing virtual environments, AI enhances the realism, functionality and interactivity of the Metaverse, transforming how users engage with digital spaces. AI also upends standard concepts in patent law. It is not only the patentability of AI systems that is being contentious. In particular, the question of the protection of so-called AI-generated inventions or AI inventions is causing a stir. Above all, artificial neural networks, AI systems modeled on the networked neurons in living brains, can "learn" skills through intensive data training that would have been considered exclusively human just a few years ago, such as image recognition, language comprehension and text generation (e.g. ChatGPT) or the development of technical, medical and pharmaceutical products or processes (e.g. IBM Watson). The latter area of application is of particular importance for patent law: AI systems are already capable of developing technical teachings without direct human control and influence – "autonomously", in common and often misleading terminology – which objectively fulfill the requirements for the granting of patents. The debate surrounding the protection of such AI-generated results has recently been fueled by a large number of official and judicial decisions. All proceedings were based on patent applications for seemingly autonomous "inventions" of the AI "DABUS" by IT pioneer Stephen L. Thaler, which were exempt from human involvement. This chapter focuses on the question of whether and why the attribution of legal personality to an AI system is justified.

II. FOUNDATIONAL THINKING – IF YOU DON'T KNOW WHERE YOU ARE GOING, ANY ROAD WILL TAKE YOU THERE

The goal of this reflection is to discuss certain theoretical explanations for patent protection and their application in the context of AI-assisted creativity, in order to answer the question of whether and why the attribution of legal personality to an AI system is justified.[3] Central to these theories is the justification of legal exclusivities or monopoly rights that are inherent to the nature of patent law. Several, but not always all, patent law theories are presented and discussed, and then it is determined whether patents on AI-generated inventions are compatible with one or more theories of justification or not.[4] A limitation of individualist (mainly utilitarian) theories as explanatory tools is recognised in that they are advanced, with or without an examination of why this particular theory should constitute the relevant substantive standard of assessment.[5]

Often overlooked in relevant literature is whether attributing legal personality to AI could be justified as a means to promote innovation by fostering collaboration and sharing practices. This perspective critically reflects on contemporary IP law that is mainly focused on the grant of exclusive rights. This approach draws solutions from other innovation ecosystems such as open source software licensing and regulatory paradigms such as data governance on the basis of the EU's Data Act. In essence, it can be categorized under the utilitarian theories, since it discusses whether attributing legal personality to AI systems can be "utilized" for innovation. It also subscribes to Rawlsian theories of distributive justice that a priori favor governance mechanisms that guarantee collaboration over ownership. However, it is not biased by the structure of contemporary patent law as opposed to other utilitarian theories, which are focused on the justification of assigning exclusivity rights and clearly defining ownership.

1. AI in the Metaverse – Curiouser and Curiouser

Building Castles in the Air – The Mad Hatter's Tea Party: The construction of the Metaverse resembles the chaotic, nonsensical nature of the Mad Hatter's Tea Party. This section introduces AI's role in world-building, where augmented and virtual realities blend in unpredictable ways. Just as Alice struggles to understand the illogical rules of the tea party, patent law struggles to keep up with the ever-changing, AI-driven world. The tea party's eternal confusion mirrors the complexity of legal systems trying to regulate AI-generated inventions, raising questions about ownership and rights in a digital world.

Artificial intelligence plays a vital role in the development of the Metaverse, providing the foundation for creating immersive, dynamic and interactive virtual experiences. One significant application of AI in the Metaverse is in avatar creation and customization. AI enables users to generate highly personalized avatars, which serve as their virtual representations within the Metaverse. Using deep learning techniques such as Generative Adversarial Networks (GANs), along with 3D modeling tools, AI allows for the creation of realistic avatars based on user input, including facial features and body movements. These advancements in AI enhance the realism of avatars by enabling more lifelike reconstructions of 3D faces and bodies.[6] AI also plays a role in enabling users to personalize their avatars by selecting various traits, such as facial expressions and gestures, thus improving the overall immersive experience.[7]

AI further contributes to the construction of the Metaverse by supporting the creation of its digital world. Through the use of technologies like augmented reality (AR), virtual reality (VR) and extended reality (XR), AI can help generate, recognize and render realistic scenes in virtual environments.[8] For instance, 3D modeling and photogrammetry techniques enable the reconstruction of complex structures, such as buildings and objects, which can be integrated into the Metaverse. Moreover, AI facilitates real-time scene recognition, which is essential for allowing users to interact smoothly with their surroundings and for creating vibrant, highly detailed virtual worlds.[9]

In terms of user interactivity, AI enhances the way users engage with the Metaverse by managing real-time data flow and supporting multiplayer interactions across various virtual zones. AI technologies use multimodal interaction services, including physiological signals and haptic feedback, to deliver seamless and immersive experiences.[10] For example, AI-powered tools such as XR gloves provide users with tactile feedback, simulating the feel of objects in the virtual world, and thus enhancing immersion. Additionally, AI is being developed to use brain signals to control virtual elements, creating more intuitive and responsive interactions.[11]

Lastly, AI is fundamental in supporting text and audio understanding within the Metaverse. Natural Language Processing (NLP) techniques enable AI to facilitate both speech-based and text-based interactions between users and AI-driven virtual entities. This allows for seamless communication between avatars and users, regardless of language barriers. AI systems, through voice recognition and text-to-speech applications, enable avatars and non-player characters (NPCs) to engage in real-time conversations and provide multilingual support.[12] Audio management in the Metaverse, including the creation of 3D soundscapes, is also heavily reliant on AI, which adds to the auditory realism and enhances user immersion.[13] By integrating these advanced AI technologies, the Metaverse aims to offer an increasingly interactive, lifelike experience, transforming the way users interact with digital worlds.

2. The Utility of Legal Protection

The Cheshire Cat's Grin – The Disappearing Incentive: The Cheshire Cat is known for disappearing and leaving only a grin, symbolizing the elusive nature of incentives in patent law for AI-generated inventions. This section delves into utilitarian theories, where the incentive for patenting inventions seems to vanish as AI replaces human creators. Just as Alice questions the disappearing cat's motives, we question whether AI-generated inventions can be incentivized through traditional patent laws. The blurred lines between human and AI creativity leave us pondering what remains of the incentive structure when the creator is no longer human.

In utilitarian theories of patent law, the question of the assignment of AI-generated inventions is essentially discussed under incentive paradigms as well as other economic and sociopolitical considerations. Although these are intertwined in many ways, the following unpacks the main directions. A fundamental distinction is made between arguments in connection with the "whether" and the "who" of the assignment of legal protection.[14]

A common objection to the facilitative attribution of patent protection to AI-generated inventions is that patent law cannot act as an incentive instrument with an effect on individual psychology in the case of AI-generated inventions, since AI functionally replaces the inventor and consequently a patent cannot be justified according to the logic of incentive theory. AI itself is not receptive to incentives of any kind.[15] However, it is also argued that, although AI itself is not susceptible to incentives, there are still a large number of natural persons involved upstream in the development process of an AI-generated invention who could be considered as subjects of the patent-induced inducement.[16]

While these considerations are still striving to identify a subjective feedback of the incentive effect under patent law to an inventor as a natural person, incentive theory considerations are also decoupled from the existence of a natural person as the subject of the incentive. Patent law primarily provides an incentive for non-personal investment in an invention. The participation of a natural person is not of constitutive importance here, which is why the patent protection of AI-generated inventions does not run counter to the incentive concept of patent law.[17] However, in view of this extra-personal understanding of the incentive effect of patent law, an argument often made against a patent on AI-generated inventions is that such inventions are typically available at very low cost, which raises doubts as to whether the investment made still needs a patent-induced incentive at all.[18] For this reason, and also because of the increasingly very short innovation cycles for AI-generated inventions, non-patent incentives to innovate, in particular the first mover advantage, are considerably more important than patents, which militates against patent protection.[19]

These previous approaches to argumentation link the incentive theory to the AI-generated invention itself as relevant under patent law or economic policy. Going beyond this is another line of argumentation, where the incentive is not (only) on the AI-generated invention, but (also) on – the patent law discussion in the first place – the AI itself. This is precisely where the real technical progress lies, which should be incentivized by means of a patent on AI-generated inventions. Therefore, patent protection for AI-generated inventions is compatible with the incentive theory, which is intended to encourage technical progress in general, and patents on AI-generated inventions are justified, since they indirectly create an incentive to create AI.[20]

Next, patents on AI-generated inventions are also justified more generally by the idea that patent law thus creates an incentive for the creation, disclosure and commercialization of inventions. With regard to the creation of inventions, patent protection of AI-generated inventions therefore corresponds to this objective, since technical progress takes place faster and more resource-efficiently, in particular through the possibility of AI-generated inventions.[21] The same is true with regard to the incentive to disclose and commercialize. AI-generated inventions would be treated as trade secrets without patent protection and would neither be made available to the public nor commercialized into products.[22]

Based on a forecast that the creation of inventions through the use of AI will become increasingly cheaper, faster and more incremental, and will therefore increase sharply in quantitative terms, attention is also drawn to the dangers of a flood of patents and the associated consequences; for example, of poorer quality (trivial) patents and any associated legal uncertainty, patent thickets, blocking effects or increasing activity of patent trolls.[23] Ever-faster innovation cycles could also lead to a significantly accelerating and higher consumption of natural resources, which argues against patent protection for AI-generated inventions.[24] There is also a risk of significant market concentration of patents, in particular with the consequence of barriers to entry for smaller undertakings, if access to AI is increasingly in the hands of a few large enterprises.[25]

The concerns that the patenting of AI-generated inventions would ultimately not serve the common good through fostering competition by the proliferation of novel ideas and applications also go in this direction, since such patenting would ultimately only benefit those few (large) companies that can afford a correspondingly powerful AI. In particular, patents on AI-generated inventions would no longer only determine who benefits from the legal status of patent holder, but also de facto who has the right to invent in the first place.[26] Any locational disadvantages for undertakings and the associated obstacles to innovation or welfare losses in the event that AI-generated inventions are not patentable are also invoked, for example, in favor of patent protection for AI-generated inventions.[27]

With regard to inventor status (the "who" of the assignment[28]) regarding AI-generated inventions, many different assessment criteria are also raised from the point of view of utilitarian patent law theories. In favor of the rights holder of the AI, for example, it is argued that he only has an incentive to ensure the diffusion of the AI on the market or to grant access to it to third parties if the inventions generated by it are also attributed to him under patent law. Otherwise, there would be an incentive for the rights holder to keep the AI secret, thereby withholding it from the general public, which would run counter to the objective of general technological progress.[29] On the contrary, it is often argued against attributing inventorship to the programmer of the AI that, in such a case, a third party using the AI for the purpose of inventing would have little incentive to do so if it had to forfeit the rights to the latter.[30] Lastly, insofar as patent law is seen as a purely impersonal incentive to invest in innovation, the patent should be granted to the person who ultimately bears the relevant investment costs of AI.[31]

3. Legal Protections for Moral Worth and Identity

Off with their Patents!: The Queen of Hearts' famous command, "Off with their heads!" mirrors the fierce debate over who holds the patent rights for AI-generated inventions. This section addresses the deontological theories that consider fairness and proportionality in assigning patent rights. Just as the Queen's judgments are arbitrary and emotional, the arguments surrounding patent attribution in AI are fraught with moral and legal inconsistencies.

Should AI be granted legal personality, and who gets to control the patents? This section explores whether such attributions are justified or if they risk destabilizing the system, much like the Queen's chaotic rule threatens Wonderland.

In addition to the utilitarian theories, the deontological justification theories of patent law are often used to explain the impact of patents. These usually include the theory of property or natural law and the theory of rewards. In terms of content, the application of these two theories of justification is based on considerations of fairness and/or proportionality. Abstractly, therefore, the standard of assessment in each case is whether it is still fair or proportionate to assign the AI-generated invention as an (intellectual) achievement to any legal entity, even though the essential (intellectual) achievement originates from an AI and is therefore available with increasingly considerably less (intellectual) effort. The considerations made in this respect form a composition of property or natural law theory and reward theory that is ultimately difficult to separate each in terms of content. In part, it is based on the rather antiquated understanding of property theory and refers back to the ideas of John Locke's work theory. Property can only be the work of a natural person. The decisive factor is therefore the extent to which the AI-generated invention is still the result of a natural person's own (intellectual) work – or not.[32] Likewise, assigning inventorship to AI risks plunging the process of invention into opacity, where the chain of creative causation disappears into an algorithmic "black box".[33] The theory of property, understood in this way, is often closely linked to the theory of reward. The lower the individual's effort, the less a property right in the form of a patent is deserved as a reward.[34] Finally, while AI-generated inventions can at best replicate personalities, they "have not heart (and obviously no soul)".[35] Thus, from an orthodox personality-rights perspective, AI cannot be an inventor.

Distributive justice

Alice's Croquet Game – The Rules Keep Changing: In the Queen of Hearts' croquet game, the rules change constantly, leaving Alice confused and frustrated. This chapter mirrors the ongoing changes in intellectual property law as it tries to adapt to the rise of AI-generated inventions. The uncertainty and shifting legal frameworks resemble the chaotic croquet game, where players are unsure of how to proceed. Emerging regulatory mechanisms like the EU's Data Act and patent pledges offer new strategies, but the rules of the game are still being written, and industries must navigate this complex, evolving landscape.

While patents can provide for incentives for innovators by granting temporary monopolistic rights, which can encourage collaboration and knowledge sharing through clearly defined and legally enforceable ownership, they can also hinder systemic collaboration.[36] If patents, namely exclusivity monopolistic rights, are the result of utilitarianism, concepts like open innovation and collaborative innovation and corrective mechanisms such as patent exemptions (e.g. for research or experiments for clinical trials to obtain a market authorization) are inextricably linked with Rawlsian notions of distributive justice.[37]

According to distributive justice theory, intellectual property laws should not be dictated by a singular (utilitarian) approach, as such laws can both assist and hinder those with limited resources.[38] On the one hand, intellectual property protection can enable funding for individuals who otherwise might struggle to afford creation, thereby fostering the development of works and technologies that benefit economically disadvantaged groups.[39] On the other, provisions such as shorter protection terms, exemptions based on usage, and compulsory licensing also address distributive concerns. These exemptions, particularly, subsidize socially valuable uses that may have high costs for individual users, such as educational copying of copyrighted materials or medical treatments utilizing innovative techniques.

Contemporary intellectual property mechanisms can lead to conflicts over value sharing, impede sequential innovation and slow the transfer and diffusion of innovations necessary for systemic sustainability impact.[40] Therefore, novel approaches are needed to navigate this paradox and enable IP law to effectively support systemic collaboration for innovation. Recent regulatory instruments such as the EU's Data Act and open/collaborative innovation ecosystems such as open source software communities or patent pledges indicate that promoting innovation is not only about exclusivity rights and rigidly delineated ownership, but rather about establishing fair governance procedures (as in Rawlsian theory of justice as fair process) that enhance collaboration and access to innovation.

EU's Data Act

The Data Act is a comprehensive initiative within the European Union aimed at addressing data-related challenges and harnessing the opportunities of a data-driven economy, with a focus on fair access and user rights, while ensuring the protection of personal data. The Regulation became effective on January 11, 2024, as a vital component of the European data strategy, contributing to the Digital Decade's objective of advancing digital transformation. It complements the Data Governance Act, facilitating reliable and secure access to data across key economic sectors and areas of public interest, ultimately contributing to the establishment of an EU single market for data. The Data Act expands data availability for companies, citizens and public administrations through various measures, including providing legal clarity for data generation within the Internet of Things (IoT) framework, addressing contractual imbalances to foster equitable data sharing, enabling public sector access to private sector data for specific public interest purposes, establishing rules for customers to switch between data processing service providers effectively, and reviewing aspects of the Database Directive to align with broader EU data policy objectives.

The Data Act acknowledges de facto data control of the data holders instead of assigning data ownership, while obliging them to share data with the so-called data recipients upon request of the data subjects or users. This is a profound regulatory instrument in innovation governance that focuses on establishing governance mechanisms that guarantee access to data. This logic could be applied in intellectual property law as well, using AI systems as a case study. Instead of assigning ownership and monopoly rights on AI systems to developers, future law instruments could prescribe mechanisms that nurture collaboration and guarantee access to innovation as a means of distributive justice. Attributing legal personality to AI systems could be embedded in the governance system so far as they are conducive to data access and data sharing for innovation. This approach provides for distributive justice outside the realm of contemporary patent law.

Patent pledges

Patent pledges have become a notable phenomenon, gaining particular attention in recent years. According to Ehrnsperger and Tietze,[41] "a patent pledge is a publicly announced intervention by patent-owning entities ('pledgers') to out-license active patents to the restricted or unrestricted public free from or bound to certain conditions for a reasonable or no monetary compensation using standardized written or social contracts". Cluster-specific, standard-priced licensing strategies linked with cross-licensing approaches with patents that are made accessible to a cluster of third parties are related to so-called patent pools.[42] Open patent pools are different from closed patents, as the former do not make patent use conditional on membership: for example, patents regarding the Moving Pictures Expert Group 2 (MPEG 2), the 3G Mobile Communication Standards and the Digital Versatile Disk (DVD) were made available to the unrestricted public at standard royalty rates through open patent pools.[43] Patent pools also exist with regard to life sciences patents: The Medicines Patent Pool, operating under Unitaid, facilitates voluntary licenses between pharmaceutical companies and middle- to low-income countries.[44] These licenses allow certain generic manufacturers to produce and distribute patented drugs or vaccines under negotiated terms. This approach has proven successful in lowering prices and ensuring equitable access to medicines for impoverished nations.

Considering the hierarchy and ecosystem of patent pools, attributing legal personality to AI systems is not dependent on whether AI systems can meet ownership standards or facilitate exclusivity rights. Instead, it should be examined whether AI systems can personify a patent pool to facilitate collaboration and mutual access to the patented technology.

Open-source ecosystems

Tech companies employ open-source strategies in AI development to gain competitive advantages, including in adjacent markets, and preempt competitors from patenting crucial technologies:[45] They aim to build user ecosystems around their ML platforms through permissive licenses. Open-source methodologies offer benefits such as reducing transaction costs and speeding up technology adoption. However, contributors should be aware of licensing terms, as OSS does not guarantee unconditional access. For effective OSS licensing, existing IP rights are necessary, but their protection is subject to intense debate. Long-term open innovation policies seek to align with open-source phenomena, impacting geopolitical innovation strategies. Governments pursue conflicting IP policy objectives, leading to uncertainty in AI patentability and infringement litigation.

III. INCENTIVES, IDENTITY, FAIRNESS? DO LEGAL PROTECTIONS NEED LEGAL PERSONALITY? – WHO ARE YOU?

Determining whether the establishment of an AI legal personality within the framework of patent law offers tangible benefits necessitates delving deeply into the multifaceted purposes of such legal constructs. Legal personalities serve a myriad of functions across various legal spheres, encompassing everything from liability allocation to asset segregation, which highlights the intricacies inherent in this matter. In the context of patent law specifically, the rationale behind assigning rights to a legal entity primarily revolves around fostering utilitarian market control mechanisms. At its core, patent law is designed to incentivize innovation by motivating investment in the creation of inventions, encouraging disclosure during the patent application process, and facilitating the subsequent commercialization of patented technologies. These incentives are deeply rooted in human motivations, particularly the drive for economic gain and the pursuit of competitive advantage. However, unlike human actors, AI lacks intrinsic motivations or autonomous decision-making capabilities related to economic incentives. Consequently, directly assigning patent rights to AI legal personalities may not seamlessly align with the core objectives of patent law.

The efficacy of patent incentives depends largely on their ability to shape the behavior of market participants, necessitating a close connection between rights allocation and individuals capable of making economically rational decisions. Drawing parallels with corporate law, where corporate actions are typically executed by managing directors or boards of directors, underscores the importance of ensuring that any regulations governing AI legal personalities align with the incentive structure of patent law. Failing to do so could undermine the effectiveness of patent incentives and compromise broader objectives related to innovation promotion and knowledge dissemination. While the theoretical appeal of AI legal personalities may be evident, practical implementation within patent law requires meticulous consideration. Without clear alignment with the incentive structure of patent law and mechanisms to ensure effective decision-making and accountability, the introduction of AI legal personalities could lead to unnecessary complexity without generating meaningful incentive gains. Hence, the utilitarian function of patent law does not inherently warrant the establishment of AI legal personalities and subsequent assignment of patent rights to AI entities.

Furthermore, future research should interrogate the intricate relationship between patent law, distributive justice, and emerging regulatory mechanisms such as the EU's Data Act, along with practices like patent pledges and open-source ecosystems. While patents traditionally serve to incentivize innovation through temporary monopolistic rights, they can also pose challenges to collaboration and equitable knowledge access. According to distributive justice theory, intellectual property laws should not solely adhere to utilitarian principles but should also consider the impact on individuals with limited resources. Provisions such as shorter protection terms, exemptions based on usage and compulsory licensing are necessary to address distributive concerns. The emergence of regulatory instruments like the EU's Data Act reflects a shift towards fair governance procedures aimed at enhancing collaboration and access to innovation. Mechanisms that nurture collaboration and guarantee access to innovation could be implemented, potentially applied to AI systems, with legal personality attributed to facilitate data access and sharing for innovation. Similarly, patent pledges and open-source ecosystems offer alternative models for collaboration and access to patented technology, aiming to reduce transaction costs, speed up technology adoption, and ensure equitable knowledge access. Integrating AI systems into patent pools or open-source ecosystems could further enhance collaboration and access to innovation, aligning with principles of distributive justice.

The assignment of legal personality to AI systems is a contentious remedy against structural barriers in patent application to AI creativity, primarily due to the current limitations in the autonomy and capabilities of AI systems. At present, AI lacks the full range of human-like decision-making abilities and intrinsic motivations necessary to act autonomously within legal frameworks. As such, any consideration of granting legal personality to AI must be approached with caution and subject to thorough research. AI systems, while capable of executing tasks and making decisions within predefined parameters, do not possess the nuanced understanding, ethical reasoning or subjective judgment that humans do. Therefore, attributing legal personality to AI raises complex questions about accountability, liability and the ethical implications of endowing non-human entities with legal rights and responsibilities. Additionally, the rapid pace of technological advancement means that the capabilities of AI systems are continually evolving. What may seem feasible or appropriate for AI today may become outdated or insufficient in the near future. As such, any discussions about the assignment of legal personality to AI must be informed by ongoing research and a critical understanding of the capabilities, limitations, and ethical considerations surrounding AI technology. In essence, while the concept of granting legal personality to AI systems may hold theoretical appeal, its practical implementation is fraught with challenges and uncertainties.

IV. WHICH WAY FORWARD? PATHS BACK UP THE RABBIT HOLE

Just as Alice wakes up from her adventure in Wonderland, the conclusion brings us back to the real world, where the questions raised by AI and patent law remain unresolved. This section reflects on the journey through this "Wonderland" of legal and technological uncertainties, leaving readers to ponder the future of AI in patent law. Much like Alice's realization that Wonderland was a dream, we must recognize that the discussion on AI legal personality and patent law is still in its early stages, with many more questions to be answered in the real world.

The determination of whether patents for AI-generated inventions should be assigned at all, and if so, to whom, is often assessed in the literature primarily through the lens of patent law theories. Various perspectives are advocated concerning both the "whether" and the "who" of assignment, drawing on deontological and utilitarian theories of patent law. However, there is significant inconsistency in evaluating individual assessment criteria, particularly within the framework of utilitarian patent law theories. This inconsistency not only reflects an unclear understanding of their precise content but also lacks a solid, normative foundation for establishing why a specific aspect should be decisively relevant under patent law.

Similar challenges are encountered in deontological theories of justification, where a normative derivation and detailed determination of the necessary requirements for the invention's creation process, considered essential for patentability, are absent. The criteria remain vague and indefinite, and distinguishing between the considerations made in each case is difficult. Consequently, the establishment of an AI legal personality is argued not to yield incentive gains relevant to the functioning of patent law. At best, it is posited to be incentive-neutral, potentially introducing an uncompensated complication to (patent) law.

The evaluation of the assignment of legal personalities, with a focus on the specific purpose inherent in each case, necessitates a distinction concerning the patent law under consideration. This distinction pertains to the allocation of rights, differentiating between rights to assets and rights of personality. In the realm of patent law, the rationale behind assigning pecuniary rights linked to an invention to a legal entity is primarily rooted in a utilitarian market control function. However, the utilitarian control function of patent law does not provide a justifiable basis for creating an AI legal personality and assigning the patent to the AI itself.

Moving upward, it is imperative to know more about the intricate relationship between patent law, distributive justice and emerging regulatory mechanisms such as the EU's Data Act, alongside practices like patent pledges and open-source ecosystems. Although patents conventionally serve as catalysts for innovation, they concurrently pose challenges concerning collaboration and equitable knowledge dissemination. Distributive justice theory posits that intellectual property laws should not exclusively prioritize utilitarian principles but should also consider their impact on individuals with constrained resources. Regulatory frameworks like the EU's Data Act signify a paradigm shift towards equitable governance procedures designed to foster collaboration and enhance accessibility to innovation.

The implementation of mechanisms aimed at fostering collaboration and ensuring unfettered access to innovation, including those adaptable to AI systems, is essential for addressing distributive concerns. Practices such as patent pledges and open-source ecosystems offer alternative models for collaboration and access to patented technology, thereby aligning with the principles of distributive justice. The integration of AI systems into patent pools or open-source ecosystems holds promise for further amplifying collaboration and accessibility to innovation, thus contributing to a more equitable distribution of knowledge and resources.

The assignment of legal personality to AI systems requires further investigation due to their current limitations in autonomy and capabilities. While AI can execute tasks within set parameters, it lacks human-like decision-making abilities and intrinsic motivations needed for autonomy within legal frameworks.

This raises complex questions about accountability, liability and ethical implications. Moreover, the rapid evolution of AI capabilities means that present reservations about equating AI with cognitive autonomy that enables personality may be less credible, or even long-lasting impediments to the idea of legal personality. While the comparison with corporate legal personality is not entirely applicable, no one quibbles any longer about companies not having legal capacity simply because the mind of the company is not identical to human consciousness. If the case can be made for AI legal personality and as such AI can avail itself of patent rights protections, the wider issue is whether this is what the "who" I have referred to really wants. And how should we value that vast range of digital creations that are not motivated by exclusionist or commercial intent?

NOTES

1. Mona M. Soliman, Eman Ahmed, Ashraf Darwish and Aboul Ella Hassanien, "Artificial Intelligence Powered Metaverse: Analysis, Challenges and Future Perspectives", *Artificial Intelligence Review* 57 (2024): 36, https://doi.org/10.1007/s10462-023-10641-x.
2. Ibid.
3. Oskar Paulini, *Die KI-generierte Erfindung: Die patentrechtliche Zuordnung technischer Leistungen im Zeitalter künstlicher Intelligenz* (Dissertation, LMU München, Faculty of Law, 2023), 53, https://doi.org/10.5282/edoc.32033
4. Matt Blaszczyk, "Impossibility of Artificial Inventors", *UC Law SF Science & Technology Justice Law Journal* 16 (2024): 73, at 82, https://repository.uclawsf.edu/hastings_science_technology_law_journal/vol16/iss1/4; Peter Blok, "The Inventor's New Tool: Artificial Intelligence – How Does It Fit in the European Patent System?" *European Intellectual Property Review* 39 (2017): 69–73, at 72; Rosa Ballardini, Kan He and Teemu Roos, "AI-Generated Content: Authorship and Inventorship in the Age of Artificial Intelligence", in *Online Distribution of Content in the EU*, ed. Taina Pihlajarinne (Cheltenham, UK and Northampton, MA, USA: Edward Elgar Publishing, 2019), 126; Michael McLaughlin, "Computer-Generated Inventions", *Journal of the Patent and Trademark Office Society* 101 (2019): 224, at 238.
5. Ben Kovach, "Ostrich with Its Head in the Sand: The Law, Inventorship, & Artificial Intelligence", *Northwestern Journal of Technology and Intellectual Property* 19 (2021): 137, at 147, https://scholarlycommons.law.northwestern.edu/njtip/vol19/iss1/4.
6. Hongyu Li and Tianqi Han, "Towards Diverse Anime Face Generation: Active Label Completion and Style Feature Network", *Eurographics Short Paper* (2019): 1, https://doi.org/10.2312/egs.20191016; Yanghua Jin, Jiakai Zhang, Minjun Li, Yingtao Tian, Huachun Zhu and Zhihao Fang, "Towards

the Automatic Anime Characters Creation with Generative Adversarial Networks", arXiv, August 18, 2017, 1, https://arxiv.org/abs/1708.05509.
7. H. Luo, K. Nagano, H.-W. Kung, Q. Xu, Z. Wang, L. Wei, L. Hu and H. Li, "Normalized Avatar Synthesis Using StyleGAN and Perceptual Refinement", in *Proceedings of the IEEE/CVF Conference on Computer Vision and Pattern Recognition* (2021), 11662, https://doi.org/10.48550/arXiv.2106.11423.
8. M. Zawish, F. Dharejo, S. Khowaja, K. Dev, S. Davy, N.M.F. Qureshi and P. Bellavista, "AI and 6G into the Metaverse: Fundamentals, Challenges and Future Research Trends", preprint, arXiv:2208.10921, August 2022, 1, https://arxiv.org/abs/2208.10921.
9. Tianhu Deng, Keren Zhang and Zuo-Jen M. Shen, "A Systematic Review of a Digital Twin City: A New Pattern of Urban Governance toward Smart Cities", *Journal of Management Science and Engineering* 6 (2021): 125, https://doi.org/10.1016/j.jmse.2021.03.003.
10. Yakun Huang, Xiuquan Qiao, Haowen Wang, Xiang Su, Schahram Dustdar and Ping Zhang, "Multi-Player Immersive Communications and Interactions in Metaverse: Challenges, Architecture, and Future Directions", preprint, arXiv:2210.06802, October 2022, 1, https://arxiv.org/abs/2210.06802.
11. Yuheng Zhao, Jinjing Jiang, Yi Chen, Richen Liu, Yalong Yang, Xiangyang Xue and Siming Chen, "Metaverse: Perspectives from Graphics, Interactions and Visualization", *Visual Informatics* 6, no. 1 (2022): 56, https://doi.org/10.1016/j.visinf.2022.03.002.
12. İlkim Güven and Osman Balli, "Empowering Metaverse through Artificial Intelligence", in *Proceedings of the 2nd International Conference on Engineering and Applied Natural Sciences* (Konya, Turkey, October 15–18, 2022), 225.
13. Mona M. Soliman, Eman Ahmed, Ashraf Darwish and Aboul Ella Hassanien, "Artificial Intelligence Powered Metaverse: Analysis, Challenges and Future Perspectives", *Artificial Intelligence Review* 57 (2024): 36, https://doi.org/10.1007/s10462-023-10641-x.
14. Oskar Paulini, *Die KI-generierte Erfindung: Die patentrechtliche Zuordnung technischer Leistungen im Zeitalter künstlicher Intelligenz* (Dissertation, LMU München, Faculty of Law, 2023), 53, https://doi.org/10.5282/edoc.32033.
15. Anne Lauber-Rönsberg and Sven Hetmank, "The Concept of Authorship and Inventorship under Pressure: Does Artificial Intelligence Shift Paradigms?" *GRUR International* 68 (2019): 641, at 645.
16. Ibid.
17. Jan Phillip Rektorschek, "Industrie 4.0 und künstliche Intelligenz – Risiko oder Chance für den gewerblichen Rechtsschutz?" *Mitteilungen der deutschen Patentanwälte* (2017): 438–443, at 443.
18. Ana Quintela Ribeiro Neves Ramalho, *Patentability of AI-Generated Inventions: Is a Reform of the Patent System Needed?* (working paper, February 15, 2018), 5, https://doi.org/10.2139/ssrn.3168703.

19. Shlomit Yanisky Ravid and Xiaoqiong (Jackie) Liu, "When Artificial Intelligence Systems Produce Inventions: An Alternative Model for Patent Law at the 3A Era", *Cardozo Law Review* 39 (2018): 2215–2260, at 2252.
20. Ryan Abbott, "I Think, Therefore I Invent: Creative Computers and the Future of Patent Law", *Boston College Law Review* 57 (2016): 1079–1126, at 1081.
21. Erica Fraser, "Computers as Inventors – Legal and Policy Implications of Artificial Intelligence on Patent Law", *SCRIPTed* 13, no. 3 (December 2016): 305–333, sec. 4.1.1, https://script-ed.org/article/computers-as-inventors-legal-and-policy-implications-of-artificial-intelligence-on-patent-law/.
22. Andreas Engel, "Can a Patent Be Granted for an AI-Generated Invention?" *GRUR International* 69 (2020): 1123, at 1127; cf. also Jean-Marcel Krausen, "Künstliche Intelligenz als die letzte Erfindung des Menschen?" *GRUR International* 125 (2023): 841, at 843.
23. Erica Fraser, "Computers as Inventors – Legal and Policy Implications of Artificial Intelligence on Patent Law", *SCRIPTed* 13, no. 3 (December 2016): 305–333, sec. 3.2.3, https://script-ed.org/article/computers-as-inventors-legal-and-policy-implications-of-artificial-intelligence-on-patent-law/.
24. Ibid., sec. 4.1.1.
25. Tim W. Dornis, "Artificial Intelligence and Innovation: The End of Patent Law as We Know It", *Yale Journal of Law & Technology* 23 (2020): 97, at 140, https://doi.org/10.2139/ssrn.3668137; cf. Andreas Engel, "Can a Patent Be Granted for an AI-Generated Invention?" *GRUR International* 69 (2020): 1123, at 1128.
26. Oskar Paulini, *Die KI-generierte Erfindung: Die patentrechtliche Zuordnung technischer Leistungen im Zeitalter künstlicher Intelligenz* (Dissertation, LMU München, Faculty of Law, 2023), 57, https://doi.org/10.5282/edoc.32033; cf. Robert Plotkin, *The Genie in the Machine: How Computer-Automated Inventing Is Revolutionizing Law and Business* (Stanford, CA: Stanford University Press, 2009), 7.
27. W. Keith Robinson and Joshua T. Smith, "Emerging Technologies Challenging Current Legal Paradigms", *Minnesota Journal of Law, Science & Technology* 19 (2018): 355, at 365, https://papers.ssrn.com/sol3/papers.cfm?abstract_id=3220440.
28. Oskar Paulini, *Die KI-generierte Erfindung: Die patentrechtliche Zuordnung technischer Leistungen im Zeitalter künstlicher Intelligenz* (Dissertation, LMU München, Faculty of Law, 2023), 57, https://doi.org/10.5282/edoc.32033.
29. Andreas Engel, "Can a Patent Be Granted for an AI-Generated Invention?" *GRUR International* 69 (2020): 1123, at 1127.
30. Russ Pearlman, "Recognizing Artificial Intelligence (AI) as Authors and Inventors under U.S. Intellectual Property Law", *Richmond Journal of Law & Technology* 24, no. 2 (2018): 1–38, at 29, https://jolt.richmond.edu/files/2018/04/Pearlman_Recognizing-Artificial-Intelligence-AI-as-Authors-and-Inventors-Under-U.S.-Intellectual-Property-Law.pdf.

31. Oskar Paulini, *Die KI-generierte Erfindung: Die patentrechtliche Zuordnung technischer Leistungen im Zeitalter künstlicher Intelligenz* (Dissertation, LMU München, Faculty of Law, 2023), 58, https://doi.org/10.5282/edoc.32033.
32. Michael McLaughlin, "Computer-Generated Inventions", *Journal of the Patent and Trademark Office Society* 101 (2019): 224, at 244.
33. Liza Vertinsky and Todd M. Rice, "Thinking about Thinking Machines: Implications of Machine Inventors for Patent Law", *Boston University Journal of Science & Technology Law* 8 (2002): 574, at 586.
34. Roman Konertz and Raoul Schönhof, "Erfindungen durch Computer und künstliche Intelligenz – eine aktuelle Herausforderung für das Patentrecht?" *Zeitschrift für geistiges Eigentum/Intellectual Property Journal* 10 (2018): 379–412, at 405, https://doi.org/10.1628/zge-2018-0032.
35. Amir H. Khoury, "Intellectual Property Rights for Hubots: On the Legal Implications of Human-Like Robots as Innovators and Creators", *Cardozo Arts & Entertainment Law Journal* 35 (2017): 635, at 653.
36. Jaakko Siltaloppi and Rosa Maria Ballardini, "Promoting Systemic Collaboration for Sustainable Innovation through Intellectual Property Rights", *Journal of Co-operative Organization and Management* 11, no. 1 (June 2023): 100200, at 2, https://doi.org/10.1016/j.jcom.2023.100200.
37. David Blankfein-Tabachnick, "Maximizing Intellectual Property: Optimality, Synchronicity, and Distributive Justice", *St. John's Law Review* 94, no. 1 (2020): 19, https://ssrn.com/abstract=3789973; cf. William W. Fisher and Talha Syed, "Global Justice in Healthcare: Developing Drugs for the Developing World", *UC Davis Law Review* 40 (2007): 581–678, at 624.
38. Elizabeth L. Rosenblatt, "Intellectual Property's Negative Space: Beyond the Utilitarian", *Florida State University Law Review* 40 (2013): 441, at 458, https://ir.law.fsu.edu/lr/vol40/iss3/1.
39. Ibid.
40. Jaakko Siltaloppi and Rosa Maria Ballardini, "Promoting Systemic Collaboration for Sustainable Innovation through Intellectual Property Rights", *Journal of Co-operative Organization and Management* 11, no. 1 (June 2023): 100200, at 2, https://doi.org/10.1016/j.jcom.2023.100200.
41. Jonas Fabian Ehrnsperger and Frank Tietze, "Patent Pledges, open IP, or patent pools? Developing taxonomies in the thicket of terminologies", *PLOS ONE* 14, no. 8 (2019): 1–18, under "Results—Definition of Patent Pledges", https://doi.org/10.1371/journal.pone.0221411.
42. Ibid.
43. Ibid.
44. Benjamin Tham and Mark James Findlay, *COVID-19 Vaccine Research, Development, Regulation and Access* (SMU Centre for AI & Data Governance Research Paper No. 2020/03, July 1, 2020; revised November 17, 2020), 22, https://doi.org/10.2139/ssrn.3640153.

45 Carlos Muñoz Ferrandis and Marta Duque Lizarralde, "Open Sourcing AI: Intellectual Property at the Service of Platform Leadership", *Journal of Intellectual Property, Information Technology and Electronic Commerce Law (JIPITEC)* 13, no. 3 (2022): 224–246, para. 1, https://www.jipitec.eu/jipitec/article/view/356.

10. Virtual jurisdictions and data protection in cross-border arbitration: a comparative analysis of India and Switzerland in the age of the Metaverse

Somya Singh

As we stand at the precipice of the Metaverse era, the traditional boundaries of legal jurisdiction seem to ebb beneath our feet, much like in Lewis Carroll's timeless tale, Alice's Adventures in Wonderland. The inspiration for this chapter came one autumn evening in Lausanne, over a pot of spicy chai and Swiss chocolate. A group of friends, a mix of tech enthusiasts and lawyers, were animatedly discussing the latest developments in the Metaverse when one of them, who had been building a virtual reality startup, posed a startling question: 'If a dispute happens in our virtual world, how do we solve it? Which country's laws apply?' In that moment, I felt like Alice at the entrance to a strange new world: the White Rabbit's urgent questions had led me to peer down a legal rabbit hole. My journey from practising law in India to studying international business law in Lausanne, Switzerland, mirrors Alice's descent into Wonderland, a transition from the familiar to a realm where legal concepts I once understood have taken on new dimensions. As an Indian lawyer, I was suddenly conscious of the contrast between my background in India's legal traditions and the Swiss and European frameworks around me. Who would have thought a casual chat could spark a deep dive into cross-border arbitration, data protection, and the blurred lines of jurisdiction in the digital age? I realised that answering my friend's question would mean untangling a web of issues.

The Metaverse represents more than merely an evolution of the internet; it constitutes a paradigm shift in how humans interact with digital environments. Unlike traditional web platforms, the Metaverse offers immersive, persistent virtual worlds where users embody digital avatars to work, socialise, create, and transact. It is often called a 'convergence of our physical and digital lives'[1] through a network of interoperable virtual spaces or worlds.[2] According to Mark Zuckerberg, the Metaverse is 'an embodied Internet that you're inside of rather than just looking at.'[3] In these virtual spaces, national borders are porous or even invisible: people from New Delhi might casually interact with avatars based in Geneva, as if the Matterhorn were a pixelated backdrop. But when something goes wrong, a contract is broken, a hack occurs, or data vanishes, the question becomes: which country's rules govern the solution? Can arbitration, a favoured tool for international disputes, even adapt to a world where the 'location' of a transaction is partly imaginary? This virtual realm challenges fundamental jurisdiction, sovereignty, and data protection assumptions. Just as Alice struggled to navigate Wonderland's peculiar logic, lawmakers and arbitrators now grapple with applying terrestrial legal frameworks to ethereal digital spaces that exist everywhere and nowhere simultaneously. This shift from observation to participation fundamentally alters the relationship between users, data, and governing frameworks. When disputes inevitably arise in these spaces, as they must in any social ecosystem, traditional jurisdictional boundaries that have anchored legal systems for centuries suddenly appear arbitrary and insufficient.

This jurisdictional ambiguity becomes particularly acute in the context of cross-border arbitration. Arbitration has long served as a flexible mechanism for resolving international disputes, offering parties autonomy to select applicable laws and procedures. However, even this adaptable framework faces unprecedented challenges when transposed to virtual environments where the very concept of 'crossing borders' becomes metaphysical rather than geographical. When an Indian citizen's data is processed through a Swiss-based arbitration platform in the Metaverse, which nation's laws apply? Which courts have jurisdiction when a dispute arises between avatars in virtual space? These questions are not merely academic; they strike at the heart of how nations will protect their citizens' rights in an increasingly virtualised world. Transactions in the Metaverse, such as those involving NFTs and cryptocurrencies, occur instantly across borders, blurring the question of which courts or legal systems hold authority when disputes arise. To address this complexity, platforms routinely embed arbitration clauses in their terms of service, invoking instruments such as the New York Convention for cross-border enforcement. Yet these clauses typically appear in one-sided end-user-licence agreements (hereinafter 'EULAs'), leaving users with almost no bargaining power. As virtual jurisdictions proliferate and data protection becomes increasingly critical, traditional dispute-resolution and privacy-enforcement models must adapt or risk becoming obsolete.

India and Switzerland present particularly illuminating case studies for examining these challenges. Both nations have recently enacted comprehensive data protection legislation: India's Digital Personal Data Protection Act of

2023 (hereinafter 'DPDP Act'),[45] rooted in the constitutional right to privacy under Article 21 as upheld in *Justice K. S. Puttaswamy (Retd.) v. Union of India* (2017),[6] has been passed but is not fully operationalised; and Switzerland's revised Federal Act on Data Protection, which entered into force in 2023 (hereinafter 'FADP').[7] Yet, they approach data protection from markedly different philosophical and regulatory perspectives. With its emerging digital economy and vast population, India has adopted a more business-friendly approach that strikes a balance between innovation and basic protections. With its long tradition of privacy and neutrality, Switzerland has implemented stricter regulations aligned with European standards. How these divergent approaches translate to the borderless realm of the metaverse offers crucial insights into the future of data protection in virtual spaces.

The Alice in Wonderland metaphor is more than a literary flourish; it provides a conceptual framework for understanding the disorienting legal challenges posed by the metaverse. Like Alice confronting Wonderland's peculiar logic, legal systems must adapt to environments where established rules no longer apply in expected ways. The central thesis of this chapter is that traditional jurisdictional boundaries and data protection frameworks are fundamentally challenged by metaverse-based arbitration,[8] necessitating new approaches that strike a balance between national sovereignty and the borderless nature of virtual spaces.[9] Through a comparative analysis of India and Switzerland's legal frameworks, this chapter frames the analysis through seven metaphorical dimensions: the jurisdictional 'Rabbit Hole'; the 'Cheshire Cat problem' of disappearing data; 'Queen of Hearts and QueenTech: New Sovereigns of Virtual Space'; 'Through the Looking Glass: The Anomalous Economics of Virtual Data'; 'Jurisdictional Collisions: A Socio-Legal and Ethnographic Perspective'; a hypothetical case study; and proposed pathways for escaping the legal wonderland through innovative frameworks and agreements.

THE JURISDICTIONAL RABBIT HOLE

As arbitration increasingly moves into virtual spaces, the questions addressed in this chapter will only grow more urgent. The global metaverse market was valued at US$146.6 billion in 2024 and is expected to grow at a compound annual growth rate (CAGR) of 39.3%, reaching US$1.1 trillion by 2030,[10] creating vast new opportunities for commerce, creativity, and conflict. How nations like India and Switzerland navigate this transition will determine the protection of their citizens' data and their position in the emerging digital order. By examining these issues now, while the metaverse is still taking shape, we can help ensure that we bring our most essential legal protections when we step through the looking glass into fully realised virtual worlds.

The concept of jurisdiction has historically been tethered to physical territory. Since the 1648 Peace of Westphalia[11] established the modern nation-state system, legal authority has been primarily defined by geographical boundaries. This territorial paradigm has served as the foundation for determining which laws apply, which courts have authority, and which enforcement mechanisms are available in any dispute. Traditional jurisdiction (especially common law systems) typically manifests in three forms: personal jurisdiction (authority over individuals or entities), subject matter jurisdiction (the authority over specific types of legal issues or cases), and territorial jurisdiction (authority within a defined geographical area).[12]

Each nation exercises supreme authority within its borders, guided by the principle of sovereignty in international law. At the same time, each state respects the same supreme authority exercised by other nations within its territory. As articulated by Justice Holmes in *American Banana Co. v. United Fruit Co.*, 'The general and almost universal rule is that the character of an act as lawful or unlawful must be determined by the law of the country where it is done'.[13] This territorial principle has guided international relations and cross-border legal interactions for centuries, providing a framework for resolving jurisdictional conflicts.

The rise of cross-border conduct and grave international crimes has increasingly challenged the traditional territorial limits of jurisdiction. In response, states have developed doctrines such as extraterritorial jurisdiction, the effects doctrine, and universal jurisdiction. Universal jurisdiction, particularly, permits states to prosecute certain serious crimes, such as genocide, war crimes, and crimes against humanity, irrespective of where they occur or the nationality of the perpetrators or victims.[14] International arbitration has also emerged as a mechanism for resolving disputes that transcend national boundaries, granting parties considerable autonomy to select applicable laws and venues. Nevertheless, even these international arbitration frameworks ultimately depend on the enforcement power of national courts, which remains anchored in territorial sovereignty.[15]

The metaverse fundamentally disrupts this territorial paradigm by creating immersive virtual environments that are both everywhere and nowhere. Unlike traditional internet platforms, where users merely observe, the metaverse enables participants to inhabit digital spaces through avatars, engaging in activities that mirror real-world interactions but transcend physical limitations.

This spatial reconceptualisation creates profound jurisdictional challenges. When an avatar representing an Indian citizen interacts with an avatar representing a Swiss citizen on a platform operated by an American company with servers in Singapore, where does the interaction 'take place'? The question is not merely philosophical; it determines which laws apply, which authorities have jurisdiction, and which courts can resolve disputes. The metaverse thus represents not just a technological innovation but a jurisdictional rabbit hole where traditional territorial markers disappear.

The metaverse presents several jurisdictional challenges that complicate the application of traditional legal principles. According to the Geneva Centre for Security Policy, metaverse platforms operate without regard to fixed physical borders, a design that undermines national legal frameworks and may drive states to establish their closed digital ecosystems.[16] Users from multiple countries can simultaneously occupy the same virtual space, exposing their activities to a patchwork of potentially conflicting legal regimes. Furthermore, users often interact through avatars that do not correspond to their real-world identities, which makes it more difficult to establish personal jurisdiction. Even when authorities succeed in asserting jurisdiction, they face significant obstacles in enforcing judgments across physical borders, especially as identifying the parties to claim against can be problematic due to the anonymity of avatars in the metaverse.[17] These challenges are particularly acute in arbitration contexts, where the flexibility that makes arbitration attractive also creates additional layers of jurisdictional complexity when transposed to decentralised virtual environments.

India's approach to digital jurisdiction is presented through three principal statutes: the Information Technology Act of 2000 (hereinafter 'IT Act'), the Arbitration and Conciliation Act of 1996 (hereinafter 'Arbitration Act'), and the recently enacted DPDP Act.

The IT Act expressly extends India's jurisdiction extraterritorially, with Section 75 applying to offences committed outside India if they involve a computer, computer system, or computer network in India.[18] This provision is a cornerstone of India's assertion of digital sovereignty.

The Arbitration and Conciliation Act 1996 demonstrates adaptability to technology through party autonomy. While it does not explicitly provide for virtual hearings, Sections 19(2), 19(3), 20(3), and 24 accommodate technology by allowing parties to agree on procedures, empowering tribunals to decide procedural matters, permitting tribunals to meet at any appropriate place, and guaranteeing the right to oral hearings without mandating in-person attendance.[19, 20, 21] Section 29B establishes an optional fast-track procedure whereby parties may file and exchange arbitral documents electronically, enabling paperless and remote arbitration proceedings.[22] The Delhi High Court's guidelines and the Indian Council of Arbitration (ICA) practices further support the evolving acceptance of digital arbitration. In June 2020, the Delhi High Court issued guidelines requiring e-filing, video conference hearings for urgent matters, and digital signing of awards.[23] While this recognition suggests an evolving approach to jurisdiction, the statutory framework continues to presume that arbitration is anchored to an identifiable legal seat, which determines the applicable procedural law and the jurisdiction of supervisory courts. This reliance on a legal seat remains central to the arbitration process and may create challenges when applied to disputes conducted entirely in virtual or metaverse environments.

The DPDP Act, though not yet fully operationalised as of May 2025, is poised to adopt an expansive approach to jurisdiction. Section 3 extends India's regime to data processed domestically and to processing carried out abroad in connection with offering goods or services to or profiling individuals in India.[24] This extraterritorial scope means that metaverse platforms or digital service providers offering services to Indian users will fall within the DPDP Act's remit, regardless of server location or company incorporation. Section 18(1) establishes the Data Protection Board of India, which is empowered to impose penalties for violations, including those committed by entities based abroad.[25] However, a critical observation is that the DPDP Act does not specify concrete enforcement mechanisms for extraterritorial violations, suggesting a potential reliance on diplomatic or mutual assistance arrangements, which could lead to uncertainty regarding how India might assert jurisdiction against foreign metaverse platforms without a physical presence in India.

With its long-standing tradition as a neutral arbitration hub and alignment with European Union (EU) data protection standards, Switzerland adopts a distinct approach to jurisdiction in digital spaces. The Swiss legal framework addressing virtual jurisdiction primarily stems from the Federal Act on Private International Law (PILA), Switzerland's international arbitration jurisprudence, while cross-border data protection contexts are governed by revised FADP[26] and its implementing ordinances.[27, 28, 29]

Switzerland's international arbitration framework, codified in Chapter 12 of the PILA, is renowned for its flexibility and party autonomy. Article 176(1) establishes that the provisions apply to arbitrations seated in Switzerland where at least one party had neither its domicile nor habitual residence in Switzerland when concluding the arbitration agreement.[30] This territorial approach is similar to India's but has been interpreted more liberally by Swiss courts, emphasising party autonomy in determining the seat.

The Swiss Federal Supreme Court has consistently emphasised party autonomy in determining the seat of arbitration, the place determining the lex arbitri, a concept distinct from the venue of hearings or deliberations. Hence, recognising that the physical location of hearings or deliberations may differ from the legal seat could conceptually accommodate metaverse arbitration, where proceedings occur in virtual space but are legally seated in Switzerland.

Switzerland has also been at the forefront of digitalising arbitration. With effect from 1 June 2021, the Swiss Chambers' Arbitration Institution (SCAI) was reconstituted as the Swiss Arbitration Centre Ltd; simultaneously, the 2021 Swiss Rules of International Arbitration came into force. Those Rules now enshrine paperless proceedings (Articles 3(1) and 4(1)) and mandate electronic filings as default, with physical copies only required for evidentiary authentication and expressly permit remote hearings 'by videoconference or other appropriate means' (Article 27(2)).[31] Nevertheless, in theory and practice, the notion of a legal seat in Switzerland remains indispensable: the lex arbitri cannot be wholly detached from a physical jurisdiction, even if the day-to-day conduct of the arbitration is entirely virtual.

The revised FADP of 2023 adopts an extraterritorial approach akin to the EU's General Data Protection Regulation (GDPR), extending Swiss data protection obligations beyond national borders in data protection matters. Article 2(1) governs any processing of natural-person data by private persons and federal bodies, and Article 3(1) applies to processing that produces effects in Switzerland, even if initiated abroad.[32] This effects-based approach means that metaverse platforms processing personal data of Swiss residents are subject to Swiss jurisdiction, regardless of where the data processing occurs. A key distinction from India's framework is FADP Article 55, which empowers the Federal Data Protection and Information Commissioner (FDPIC) to exchange information and provide mutual assistance to any foreign supervisory authority, subject to reciprocity, encompassing requests for investigative files, joint enquiries and coordinated enforcement measures, thus enabling direct, institutionalised collaboration without recourse to ad hoc diplomatic channels. By contrast, India's DPDP Act creates a Data Protection Board and empowers it under Section 27(1)(a)–(e) with investigative and enforcement powers, e.g., directing remedial measures for data breaches and inquiring into breaches of fiduciary or consent-manager obligations, with authority to impose penalties,[33] but it includes no mechanism for structured cross-border regulatory cooperation.

While pursuing a FinTech course during my LL.M. in Switzerland, I worked on a hypothetical case advising an Indian architect collaborating with a Swiss artist to build an NFT gallery in Decentraland. Drawing on my Indian legal experience, I flagged that, despite the platform and its servers being based in Singapore, India's DPDP Act would still apply to the architect's biometric login data, as the Act applies extraterritorially to digital personal data relating to individuals in India, regardless of the data processor's location or server infrastructure. From my Swiss coursework, I learned that under the revised Swiss FADP, any data controller domiciled in Switzerland or processing data that affects Swiss users must comply with Swiss data protection obligations. This effectively brought the same decentralised platform under Swiss oversight.

Although the parties agreed to arbitrate in Zurich, their NFT 'gallery' was hosted on a decentralised blockchain with nodes spread across multiple jurisdictions, none claiming full sovereign authority. It was a metaverse rabbit hole: territorial laws chasing a borderless entity, with each party navigating a Wonderland-style landscape, shifting claims over virtual assets and data flows.

This juxtaposition reflects two evolving yet distinct regulatory philosophies: India's assertive protection of its citizens' data and Switzerland's compliance-driven, transparency-oriented framework shaped by international cooperation.

Therefore, much like Alice's bewilderment at Wonderland's ever-shifting rules, parties navigating metaverse-based arbitration between India and Switzerland encounter a legal landscape where certainty often dissolves into confusion. India's digital sovereignty-focused DPDP Act and Switzerland's internationally cooperative FADP create a 'curiouser and curiouser' scenario, in which a single dispute may trigger multiple, sometimes contradictory, data protection and enforcement obligations. In this Wonderland of digital law, parties must carefully consider seat selection, applicable data protection rules, and the interplay between legal regimes to avoid finding themselves, like Alice, caught between competing authorities and uncertain outcomes.

THE CHESHIRE CAT PROBLEM

If virtual jurisdictions represent the proverbial rabbit hole, data manifests as the Cheshire Cat: unreliable, elusive, and prone to vanish when least expected. In conventional arbitration, 'data' comprises tangible written pleadings, evidence documents, or hearing transcripts stored as physical files or digital records on identifiable servers. The metaverse, however, fundamentally transforms this paradigm, introducing ephemeral data forms, including live virtual reality hearings with avatar participants. The 'evidence' might include 3D models, behavioural logs, or blockchain records. Where do we store those? And if someone requests disclosure or wants to wipe their data, how do we comply when the medium of dispute is so fluid?

The Cheshire Cat is a peculiar entity that appears and vanishes at will, sometimes leaving only its grin behind. 'Well! I've often seen a cat without a grin,' thought Alice, 'but a grin without a cat! It's the most curious thing I've ever seen in my life!' As a lawyer with a penchant for programming, I recall coding a virtual moot court in Lausanne, watching Switzerland's new FADP on one screen and India's DPDP Act on the other. Each time I thought I'd tamed the data problem, it slipped away, like the Cheshire Cat's grin fading to nothing. Both regimes grant individuals the right to erase or delete personal data under certain conditions. Under Article 32 of Switzerland's FADP, controllers must delete personal data that is no longer needed, inaccurate, or unlawfully processed,[34] and Section 16 of India's DPDP Act confers individuals with the right to have their data erased[35] (akin to the GDPR's 'right to be forgotten'[36]). Yet these deletion rights collide head-on with arbitration's need for a permanent record. Imagine two tech companies arbitrating a virtual reality (hereinafter 'VR')-enabled contract: one party later demands deletion of its avatar identity or performance metrics. In practice, secure erasure can be fiendishly difficult, data may lurk in backups, archives, or separate applications, and wholesale deletion could break linked records or render an award unenforceable. To manage this tension, tribunals often require parties at the outset to waive their erasure rights where permitted, or to agree that sensitive data be held in encrypted form or anonymised once the award is final, so that, as the Cheshire Cat dissolves, only a bare outline of the truth remains.

Deletion is only part of the puzzle. In Wonderland, Alice marvelled at how things materialised and vanished without warning. The 'Cheshire Cat problem' in cross-border arbitration arises when personal data moves through multiple jurisdictions during metaverse-based proceedings. Unlike traditional arbitration, where documents and information typically remain within defined physical spaces, data in the metaverse is processed simultaneously across multiple jurisdictions, stored in cloud servers spanning continents, and accessed by parties and platforms operating under different legal regimes. This fluidity creates fundamental regulatory challenges. It can be said that data in the metaverse may exist in a 'quantum state,' i.e., it is simultaneously present in multiple jurisdictions and therefore is subject to often conflicting legal frameworks. Article 3 of Switzerland's FADP applies to processing that produces effects in Switzerland, even if conducted abroad. Section 3(b) of India's DPDP Act provides that extraterritorial jurisdiction applies when a foreign data fiduciary processes data connected to offering goods or services to individuals in India, regardless of the server's location. Consequently, the same data may fall under the jurisdiction of both countries, with different and potentially contradictory requirements for data protection, procedural rules, and enforcement mechanisms. This overlap goes beyond jurisdictional complexity; it undermines the notion of a fixed data 'location' on which most regulatory frameworks rely. Like the Cheshire Cat's grin lingering after its body disappears, traces of personal data (backups, logs, or cached copies) may persist in jurisdictions long after the primary data appears to have moved elsewhere.

Beyond erasure and distribution, the tension between data localisation and free data flows represents one of the central regulatory debates in cross-border data governance. There is no single, universally accepted definition of data localisation.[37] However, the term generally refers to legal requirements that specific categories of data be stored, processed, or handled within a country's borders. By early 2023, over 100 data-localisation measures were in force across 40 countries. Notably, more than two-thirds of these measures involved local storage/processing mandates and prohibited cross-border data flows, indicating a trend towards increasing restrictiveness.[38]

In contrast, free data flows prioritise the unimpeded movement of data across jurisdictions under shared, 'trust-based' rules, focusing on how data is protected, used, and governed, rather than where it resides. This approach is encapsulated in the Data Free Flow with Trust (DFFT) principle, coined in 2019.[39] It promotes seamless cross-border data exchange by implementing interoperable, risk-based safeguards, including robust privacy protections, security measures, accountability mechanisms and respect for intellectual property rights. The G7's 2021 roadmap operationalises this vision through four pillars: transparent, proportionate government access; guidance to avoid unnecessarily restrictive localisation; harmonised regulatory standards; and sector-specific frameworks for data sharing in health, finance, and dispute resolution.[40] Regulatory frameworks typically distinguish between personal data, which carries tighter cross-border controls for privacy reasons, and non-personal data, whose transfer is generally less restricted. In practice, however, this line often blurs (e.g., metadata like IP addresses can render ostensibly 'non-personal' datasets subject to personal-data rules), meaning that any easing of personal-data barriers will also relieve constraints on non-personal flows.[41]

Proponents of data localisation argue that keeping data within national boundaries enhances sovereignty, national security, and regulatory control. By requiring local storage and processing, nations can better enforce their laws, protect citizens' rights, and ensure access to data for legitimate purposes like law enforcement. Data localisation also addresses concerns about foreign surveillance and fosters the development of local data infrastructure and expertise. Advocates for free data flows argue that unimpeded, trusted exchange of information delivers multiple benefits: it alleviates AI's critical data shortage, fueling innovation and potentially adding up to 2.5% to GDP;[42] it reduces market fragmentation and compliance costs, streamlining cross-border services;[43] it enhances security by reducing regulatory fragmentation and enabling more effective protection and oversight of data across borders, and it underpins collaboration on global challenges, from public health to climate resilience, while building trust through transparent accountability mechanisms.[44] They therefore insist that regulation should focus on how data is used and governed, rather than where it is stored, to match the inherently borderless nature of digital services and modern commerce.

In arbitration contexts, this tension becomes particularly acute. Effective dispute resolution requires sharing information among parties, arbitrators, experts, and institutions that may span multiple jurisdictions. Data localisation requirements can impede this process, creating procedural hurdles, increasing costs, and potentially undermining the efficiency that makes arbitration attractive. Conversely, completely unrestricted data flows may expose sensitive information to jurisdictions with inadequate protections, creating privacy and security risks. The metaverse intensifies this tension by making data location increasingly abstract. When arbitration occurs in virtual environments, data may be simultaneously processed across multiple jurisdictions, making strict localisation technically challenging or impossible. Yet the legitimate concerns that motivate localisation, sovereignty, security, and regulatory control remain relevant even in virtual contexts.

India's data control and sovereignty approach reflects its broader digital strategy of striking a balance between innovation and national interests. As a rapidly developing digital economy with over 800 million internet users, India has significant stakes in data governance. Its approach has evolved from earlier, more restrictive proposals towards a more nuanced position that maintains specific sovereign controls while enabling cross-border data flows. The DPDP Act, upon implementation, takes a selective-restriction approach rather than blanket localisation. Section 16 allows the Central Government to prohibit data transfers to specified foreign countries or territories, with all other transfers permitted until a jurisdiction is notified.[45] This mechanism aims to balance sovereign control with cross-border flows but creates uncertainty until the 'blacklist' of notified jurisdictions is published. This ambiguity presents compliance challenges for metaverse arbitration platforms that involve Indian users.

Switzerland's approach to data control and sovereignty reflects its position as both a global financial centre and a European nation with strong privacy traditions. Although not an EU member, Switzerland has aligned its FADP with the EU's GDPR to preserve its adequacy decision and facilitate seamless data flows with EU Member States. Under Section 3, Article 16 of the FADP, one may disclose personal data abroad only if the Federal Council has recognised the destination's legislation as guaranteeing an adequate level of protection; where no such decision exists, one must secure an appropriate level of security by means of an international treaty, bespoke data-protection clauses in an agreement (notified in advance to the FDPIC), specific guarantees drafted by the competent federal authority, standard data protection clauses approved or recognised by the FDPIC, or binding corporate rules endorsed by the FDPIC or by the responsible authority. By publishing a binding adequacy list that covers all EU and EFTA/EEA states, as well as the UK and certified US entities, Switzerland ensures predictability far beyond that offered by notification-only regimes. At the same time, its robust professional-secrecy framework, reinforced by criminal provisions under Article 62, provides that Swiss attorney-client privilege and other confidentiality obligations remain fully effective in any cross-border context governed by Swiss law.[46]

The 'Cheshire Cat Problem' underscores a deeper conflict between fundamental data governance philosophies: India's pragmatic, sovereignty-driven approach, which prioritises national control and security through selective restrictions and potential blacklists, versus Switzerland's principle-based, trust-oriented approach, which emphasises interoperability through adequacy decisions and robust safeguards via whitelists. This philosophical divide creates inherent friction for cross-border metaverse operations, compelling platforms to adopt complex, multi-layered compliance strategies, such as geo-fencing, dynamic consent management, and end-to-end encryption, to technically embed legal principles.

QUEEN OF HEARTS AND QUEENTECH: NEW SOVEREIGNS OF VIRTUAL SPACE

In the virtual Wonderland, two rulers vie for authority over data and disputes: the traditional nation-state, personified as the Queen of Hearts, and the powerful tech platforms, dubbed QueenTech. This dynamic represents a fundamental power struggle in the metaverse. Caught between them is Alice, the user. She might be sitting in New Delhi or Geneva, wearing VR goggles, wondering whose laws govern her digital life. The question is stark: whose head, whether of state or of Silicon Valley, will roll if the user steps out of line?

The Queen of Hearts, representing nation-state sovereignty, asserts its authority even when citizens interact in borderless virtual spaces. In India, the Queen of Hearts already claims far-reaching powers, and this stance is evident in the IT Act, particularly Section 69,[47] which grants the government broad powers to intercept, monitor, or decrypt information for national security or public order, among other grounds. These powers allow agencies to access digital communications and data flows, and non-compliance, such as refusal to assist with decryption, can result in criminal liability for corporate officers. This sovereignty-first stance recalls the real Queen of Hearts' dictatorial cry, 'Off with their heads!'—one might imagine her ordering a data centre executive into custody for stepping out of line. The anticipated DPDP Act further reinforces this by claiming authority over data and disputes wherever Indian users roam.

By contrast, Switzerland's Queen is a 'shrewder chess player,' prioritising privacy and fundamental rights through a framework of law and dialogue. The revised FADP was enacted to 'better protect privacy and fundamental rights'.[48] Switzerland actively welcomes blockchain and digital assets as economic opportunities, even calling Switzerland's position 'very positive' and an 'opportunity to take a global lead'.[49] As mentioned earlier, Swiss law is aligned with the EU's GDPR in many respects. Its FADP applies to any processing that 'has an effect in Switzerland, even if initiated abroad'. Foreign companies marketing to Swiss residents may be required to appoint a Swiss representative if their data-processing activities are extensive and involve high-risk operations.[50] In this way, the Queen's edict follows the data rather than being confined to physical devices or locations.

QueenTech represents the corporate sovereign of the metaverse, the invisible overlord setting rules through code and 'terms of use'. Tech platforms weave their codes and 'terms of use' that bind users by click or code, effectively setting their laws. For instance, parties in Decentraland's virtual bazaar might find that disputes are resolved under Panama's law by an ICC tribunal, simply because Decentraland's terms say so. Similarly, a game like Axie Infinity can impose Cayman Islands arbitration on its players by writing it into its fine print. Hence, tech companies prefer to set their castles apart, choose remote seats for arbitration, and, if possible, ignore foreign regulators. In theory, parties to a blockchain contract could encrypt their entire deal in code and let that code enforce itself, a fate entirely outside any human queen's grasp.

However, QueenTech also operates within the bounds of regulation. If metaverse platforms sell goods or services, they act as 'data fiduciaries' under India's anticipated DPDP Act (Chapter II, Sections 4–10) and must comply with all data obligations. In this sense, QueenTech wears a 'crown of regulation.' Yet, the potential for blockchain contracts to self-enforce entirely through code presents a scenario in which certain aspects of dispute resolution could exist outside the direct grasp of any human sovereign.

Ultimately, we see a tug of war. India's Queen of Hearts values territorial control above all; she wants data behind the borders, and Indian laws to apply. Switzerland's Queen emphasises individual consent, neutrality, and high data protection standards, seeking international cooperation. QueenTech's realm straddles both, being global yet often operating beyond traditional jurisdictional claims. This dynamic highlights that the struggle is not just about who governs, but how governance is achieved, through coercive state power (as seen in India's Section 69 of the IT Act) or market-driven compliance and self-regulation (as exemplified by Switzerland's representative requirements and platform terms). This suggests a future where legal authority is fragmented and negotiated, rather than centrally imposed, necessitating new models of collaboration or conflict resolution. Alice, with her Indian training and Swiss vantage point, must navigate these new sovereigns. She learns that no single crown rules unchecked in Wonderland: every claim to power meets resistance. The real question is whether (and how) these queens will ever sit at one table to govern their shared wonderland, or whether Alice will have to choose sides in an endless royal rivalry.

THROUGH THE LOOKING GLASS: THE ANOMALOUS ECONOMICS OF VIRTUAL DATA

Stepping through the looking glass into the Metaverse, Alice discovers that everything she thought she knew about value is upside-down and mirrored backwards. In Wonderland's economy, objects talk and chess pieces move themselves; similarly, the Metaverse's economy treats data as both treasure and traffic. Just as Alice found the Looking-Glass world full of nonsensical exchanges, scholars observe that modern platforms operate on a 'data as a payment model,' where users implicitly sacrifice their privacy to access 'free' services.[51] In practice, this means every click and gaze is now part of a trade. For example, free access to a virtual concert or NFT art exhibition often comes at the cost of behavioural profiling, creating a silent barter system where privacy is the price of entry. Platforms like Decentraland or Axie Infinity offer discounts or exclusive content in return for harvesting user behaviour, effectively embedding data collection into every transaction. This model echoes Shoshana Zuboff's concept of surveillance capitalism, where firms extract and monetise personal information without meaningful consent.[52] In other words, the currency isn't dollars at checkout but bytes in the back-end.

This web of data flows leads to strange new markets. Digital 'property' is bought and sold with real money. When Alice visits a virtual bazaar, she might pay cash (or crypto) for a Gucci handbag that exists only as pixels. Indeed, analysts report that a digital Gucci bag sold on Roblox for over US$4,000[53] has fetched record prices, around US$2.4 million in Decentraland and US$4.3 million in The Sandbox.[54] In Wonderland fashion, value isn't anchored to physical scarcity; data and digital scarcity can create price at the whim of community belief. One Swiss court might see such a transaction as a consumer goods trade, another as currency speculation, whereas an Indian court might demand data localisation proof before allowing money to leave the country.

Moreover, personal data itself can be rented, exchanged, or hoarded like a resource. Companies sell targeted ads or train AI on profiles, squeezing every euro and rupee of worth from each data point. Economists describe data as non-rivalrous; one person's data use doesn't diminish another's, so it resembles common goods like sunlight or air (albeit with price tags). Yet this virtue leads to skyrocketing returns: once accumulated, a big data cache can be sold again and again, fuelling economies of scale. Imagine a reverse Red Queen's race: platforms must constantly gather more data to keep their algorithms running, 'running' in place to deliver steady profits.

At the same time, states covet data in the name of welfare and security. India's draft policies have even discussed 'data colonialism', demanding that datasets be stored or mirrored on home soil for national interests. The DPDP Act will likely allow restrictions on transfers to certain countries, effectively treating data as critical infrastructure. Switzerland, conversely, emphasises adequacy agreements, allowing data to flow if the destination country offers a comparable level of data protection. The practical implication for companies is the need to replicate data across multiple jurisdictions or implement complex contractual safeguards to satisfy both tax collectors and regulators.

In this economic wonderland, wealth is measured not in coins but in clicks and metadata. Even ordinary citizens are treated as miniature information banks, their attention being leveraged as tokens to fuel global empires. For example, European regulations require organisations to systematically assess the risks associated with processing personal data profiles, particularly through Data Protection Impact Assessments (DPIAs).[55] Concurrently, there is a growing recognition among commentators and practitioners of the economic value and strategic importance of such data,[56] leading to its treatment as an asset necessitating protection and careful risk management. Platforms can monetise a single user's profile hundreds or thousands of times over (for marketing, training AI, and targeted virtual content). This has led to calls, even in academic literature, to treat data more like 'oil'[57] with special taxation regimes to curb its externalities and share its value[58] or as a 'national resource'[59] requiring bespoke licensing frameworks[60] or like the 'new oxygen'.[61] One study notes that in Web3, 'data has an evolved role; it is not only a valuable resource as understood in Web1 and Web2, but it is the infrastructure itself',[62] so that once every byte becomes a tradable product, the ideal of an open internet collapses. In short, the economics are maddening: virtual goods can be worth millions, but the platform still scolds Alice for sharing too much data about her dream vacation.

From an Indian perspective, the metaverse presents both immense opportunities and significant risks. India's startup scene is eager to enter the metaverse, but entrepreneurs fret about unpredictable rules. As colleagues often joke, 'local laws still govern everything in the metaverse'; this is a reminder to prepare to calculate and remit tax on crypto gains,[63] stay alert to evolving cross-border digital tax frameworks even after the equalisation levy's rollback,[64] and strengthen their privacy practices to comply with IT Act data security requirements and dodge penalties.[65]

Switzerland's innovators, by comparison, lean in more boldly, trusting that clear guidelines (like the Swiss DLT Act[66] (officially titled as Federal Act on the Adaptation of Federal Law to Developments in Distributed Electronic Register Technology) and FINMA (Swiss Financial Market Supervisory Authority) guidance[67] will shield their ventures. Both systems urge compliance: McKinsey suggests that companies proactively obtain user consent and implement security measures[68] well before any metaverse-specific regulations take effect.

In this topsy-turvy world, one lesson is clear: nothing is free. Alice cannot simply browse the Metaverse without cost; the balance sheet must always balance, whether paid in francs, rupees, or data traces. For the lawyer in her, the task is to figure out who owns the tokens, who can audit the ledger, and who will ultimately collect the rent in this brave new Wonderland economy.

JURISDICTIONAL COLLISIONS: A SOCIO-LEGAL AND ETHNOGRAPHIC PERSPECTIVE

Once Alice has learned to speak 'stream' and 'packet', she confronts another puzzle: law is usually defined by geography, but the Metaverse refuses borders. In Wonderland, Alice found that logic could twist absurdly; similarly, jurisdictional lines may become tangled when a contract is coded across continents. From a sociolegal viewpoint, we must ask: How do real-world courts meet these virtual spaces, and how do people in different cultures perceive the rules?

One approach is to observe the parties through a kind of legal ethnography. Consider two users in a VR world: one is in New Delhi, and the other is in Lausanne. They may transact on a Swiss-hosted platform. Who determines their dispute? If they later clash, PILA governs their international arbitration (Chapter 12, as revised as of January 1, 2021), since one party is non-Swiss (Article 176(2) of PILA even allows an opt-in to CPC Part 3). Swiss courts would first look to the parties' chosen seat and, in the absence of an express choice, to the tribunal's procedural rules under the Swiss Code of Civil Procedure (e.g., jurisdiction where the defendant is domiciled, CPC Articles 22–24). Indian courts, by contrast, assert jurisdiction under the Civil Procedure Code (Section 20 CPC), territorial jurisdiction based on where the defendant resides or the cause of action arises, and, where a consumer is involved, under the Consumer Protection Act 2019, rather than the IT Act. Procedurally, a Swiss civil-law judge (steeped in CPC/ZPO) might hesitate to examine whether the arbitration clause meets formal validity under Article 178 PILA before enforcing an arbitration clause embedded purely in smart-contract code, whereas an Indian tribunal would likely uphold it as a valid 'arbitration agreement' under Sections 7–8 of the Arbitration and Conciliation Act 1996 (as amended), provided it meets the 'in writing' requirement, which courts have interpreted flexibly in digital settings.

Another fault line emerges around evidence and procedure. Swiss domestic arbitration law (Part 3 of the Civil Procedure Code, effective 1 January 2021) is renowned for its efficiency, as it maximises party autonomy over procedure (CPC Article 373, as revised) and vests the arbitral tribunal with exclusive control over evidence gathering (CPC Article 375). There is no statutory default-disclosure catalogue under CPC Part 3; any production of documents or examination of witnesses occurs only to the extent the parties have expressly stipulated. By contrast, Indian tribunals operate under the Arbitration and Conciliation Act 1996, as amended in 2015 and 2019, with the full rigour of the Indian Evidence Act 1872. Suppose witnesses testify via avatars in a virtual hearing, their identities vouched for by blockchain-based digital signatures.

An Indian tribunal would likely pause to verify admissibility of any secondary copy of an electronic record under Section 65B(4) of the Indian Evidence Act 1872, which mandates a separate statutory certificate for each such copy (per *Arjun Panditrao v. Kishor* 2019), cannot be dispensed with when relying on secondary copies, and that non-compliance will render it inadmissible. This means that digital evidence, such as AI-generated transcripts or VR footprints, requires specific certification to be admissible in court. In contrast, a Swiss panel under the ZertES (Federal Act on Electronic Signatures) would readily admit a record bearing a qualified electronic signature, which Swiss law treats as equivalent to a handwritten signature (Article 14(2bis) of the Swiss Code of Obligations). These procedural divergences mirror deeper legal cultures: common law's emphasis on strict proof versus civil law's approach to electronic signatures and presumption of good faith.

A vivid illustration of jurisdictional friction is 'virtual property damage'. Suppose Alice's friend in India owns a collection of rare NFTs in a shared online gallery, and a Swedish acquaintance in Switzerland maliciously corrupts them. Is that vandalism? In India, the Information Technology Act supplies both civil and criminal remedies: Section 43 creates civil liability for unauthorised access, copying or data alteration; Section 66 penalises 'dishonest or fraudulent' access; and in egregious cases, Section 66D (cheating by personation using computer resources). In Switzerland, Article 144 SCC governs both tangible and digital property, including data, if its deletion causes economic harm, meaning that, if an NFT is characterised as data rather than property, its corruption may fall within the scope of this general damage to property offence. As digital assets proliferate, understanding which regime applies to a piece of corrupted code is no longer academic; it can mean the difference between a civil award, criminal sanctions, or no remedy at all. It's like Alice trying to choose between 'protect your holdings at all costs' and 'uphold the collective welfare of digital citizens'; two conflicting principles colliding in our borderless metaverse.

On the socio-legal plane, consider the roles of language and culture. A French-speaking Swiss arbitrator and an Hindi-speaking Indian claimant share the Metaverse's lingua franca (often English), but legal concepts can diverge. The idea of 'privacy' is constitutional in both contexts: Switzerland enshrines both informational and spatial privacy under Article 13(1) and Article 13(2) of its Federal Constitution of the Swiss Federation;[69] India's Supreme Court in Puttaswamy 2017 calls it 'sacrosanct' under Article 21. Yet, enforcement mechanisms differ. India currently relies on the IT Act 2000 and the 2011 IT-SPDI Rules framework until the DPDP Act 2023 is brought into force, whereas Switzerland enforces its revised FADP, which mandates lawful processing, which may be based on consent, legitimate interests, legal obligation, or contractual necessity. An Indian party might therefore assume all personal-data processing requires explicit consent, whereas Swiss counsel would remind them that, today, certain processing may lawfully proceed on legitimate-interest or legal-obligation grounds. Both systems now demand active consent for sensitive data while providing narrowly prescribed carve-outs for other lawful bases. From the ethnographer's desk, these are stories of adaptation.

Another point to note is the important concept of legal pluralism. On the ground, though, people often abide by community norms. Gamers and blockchain enthusiasts may follow community governance (e.g., Decentralised Autonomous Organisation (DAO)) or peer reputation rather than state law. A user might trust a Decentraland DAO to arbitrate disputes, even if that DAO has no formal legal status in Delhi or Lausanne. An ethnographic view would note that these users form subcultures: the Metaverse can cultivate its sense of fairness (e.g., against avatar 'swatting'), its own 'common law' of user agreements, and even rituals (such as communal validation of block transactions). These grassroots norms may conflict or coexist with state law. This suggests that harmonisation will not be about uniform rules but developing interoperable legal principles that respect these underlying cultural and philosophical divergences, fostering a 'legal pluralism' rather than a singular legal order. This implies that legal practitioners must be adept at navigating both formal state law and informal community governance.

We see Swiss companies introducing GDPR-inspired cookie banners into metaverse offices, educating Indian colleagues about cross-border data flows, and vice versa, with Indians advising Swiss colleagues on how to comply with Aadhaar or the Indian privacy board. We hear questions at trade fairs: 'Does this metaverse ID count as a passport in Delhi?' or 'If I set a smart contract in Switzerland, can Mumbai tax it?' Such collisions expose the gaps between the law on paper and the law in practice.

In sum, jurisdiction in the virtual is not just a technical puzzle but a human one. It depends on which norms the parties trust and which sword they choose to wield. Just as Alice realised there is 'no use going back to yesterday' because things have changed, cross-border litigants see that yesterday's jurisdictions need rethinking. Perhaps the answer lies in legal pluralism: accepting that different players bring different laws, or the coexistence of state law, platform norms, and user expectations, and trying to find harmony among them. Or perhaps, like Wonderland's final chess move, a surprising new order will emerge that treats the virtual and real as two halves of one game. Again, in this vast bazaar of code and custom, law will be written not just by parliaments, but also by programmers and every avatar's lived experience.

HYPOTHETICAL CASE

To bring these abstract ideas into focus, imagine the following scenario. Alice Raghav is a software developer from Bangalore, India, who is currently pursuing an LL.M. in Lausanne, Switzerland. She creates a unique avatar design and an animated 3D sculpture for the Swiss-based metaverse startup 'Wonderland Tech AG' (hereinafter 'Wonderland Tech'), which operates a global VR platform called 'Courtlandia'. Alice's contract stipulates that she will be paid in cryptocurrency (e.g., Ether (ETH)) for her work and includes an arbitration clause specifying that disputes will be resolved through ICC arbitration seated in Geneva under Swiss law. She had expressly retained all intellectual property rights, subject only to a licence granted to Wonderland Tech for operation on Courtlandia.

One day, Alice logs into Courtlandia to find her creations removed without notice and her digital wallet drained of funds. She suspects QueenTech Capital (hereinafter 'QTC'), another platform user in Courtlandia, who covertly misappropriated her NFT avatar and effectively stole her digital work. Alice decides to arbitrate. However, it remains unclear whether the rules of a sovereign state (Queen) or those of a private technology platform (QueenTech) will govern this dispute.

Under the engagement contract, Swiss law is the governing law, and Geneva is the seat of arbitration. By choosing Geneva, the parties agree that all procedural questions (e.g., tribunal constitution, interim relief, evidence admissibility) are governed by Swiss law (PILA Article 178(2)). A Swiss-seated arbitration is always under Swiss procedural rules unless the parties clearly agree otherwise (PILA Article 178(2)). Although the seat is Geneva, the actual venue for hearings is entirely virtual: Courtlandia's 'Hatter Hall'. Swiss practice (and the ICC's Guidance Note on Virtual Hearings) permits fully online hearings by agreement of the parties, but this does not relocate the seat itself. In other words, the seat (legal place) remains Geneva, even if every hearing happens 'inside' Courtlandia's virtual environment.

Under PILA Article 178(2), an arbitration clause is valid if it complies with Swiss law or the law chosen by the parties, even if covering future disputes. Moreover, Swiss practice treats multi-tier pre-arbitral steps (e.g., negotiation or mediation prerequisites) as enforceable if clearly drafted; failure to follow such steps normally leads to a stay, rather than outright dismissal. Swiss PILA Article 177(1) provides that any dispute involving an 'economic interest' is arbitrable. NFTs and other digital assets unquestionably fall within that scope when they carry monetary value. Under PILA Article 186(1), the tribunal has the authority to decide on its jurisdiction (competence-competence). A Swiss court, faced with a parallel court proceeding, must either stay or decline jurisdiction if a valid arbitration clause exists, unless that clause is plainly null or waived (PILA Article 7). Any statement on jurisdiction should reflect that Swiss courts will defer to the arbitration agreement rather than entertain parallel litigation. When both parties are Swiss, 'domestic' arbitrations fall under Article 353 of the Swiss Code of Civil Procedure (ZPO). However, parties may contractually elect to apply PILA (Ch. 12) even in a purely domestic context. In this case, because Wonderland Tech is Swiss and Alice is Indian, the arbitration is international, and PILA unquestionably applies.

Under Swiss CO (Schweizerisches Obligationenrecht, 'CO') Articles 1 et seq., a contract requires a mutual expression of intent by the parties and must be interpreted in accordance with general principles such as good faith and the parties' true and common intent. Although Switzerland does not yet specifically define 'NFTs', arbitral tribunals treat them as intangible property rights. Thus, Alice's NFT avatar will be regarded as an 'asset right' recorded on a permissioned ledger. Any deceitful misrepresentation (e.g., QTC impersonating Alice to drain her wallet) violates the duty of good faith. QTC's unauthorised transfer of Alice's NFT constitutes conversion under Swiss property law (akin to intangible property). If Wonderland Tech still controls a copy of the permissioned ledger showing the NFT, the tribunal could order specific restitution (i.e., restoration of the same NFT to Alice's wallet). If, instead, the token has been moved to a decentralised network outside Wonderland Tech's control, specific restitution is impossible. In that event, Article 62 CO permits Alice to claim monetary compensation equal to the NFT's fair market value at the time of theft. If QTC impersonated Alice or used deceit to gain access to her private key, that would amount to an abuse of rights. The tribunal will likely condemn such conduct as contrary to Swiss public policy on honest dealings. Had the parties embedded a smart-contract trigger in their agreement (e.g., 'If Alice's NFT is stolen, Wonderland Tech shall automatically transfer the equivalent ETH from escrow to Alice'), the tribunal's role would be largely supervisory, verifying the triggering event and ensuring the code executes correctly. In the absence of such a clause, however, the tribunal must craft relief through traditional legal mechanisms (e.g., monetary escrow) rather than mechanically effecting an on-chain transaction.

In addition to Swiss contract and property law, the Swiss Copyright Act (CopA/URG) also applies. Alice's avatar and 3D sculpture are protected under the CopA from the moment they are fixed in digital form as 'works' under Article 2(1)(d), which expressly includes 'three-dimensional representations', provided they exhibit the requisite 'individual character' in accordance with Article 3; a merely functional or trivial design would not suffice, whereas Alice's original creative output clearly does. Articles 9 to 11 then secure Alice's exclusive moral and economic rights: Article 9 confers the right to be recognised as author and to determine first publication, such that any removal of her attribution or unauthorised republication by Wonderland Tech or QueenTech Capital ('QTC') would infringe her moral rights; Article 10(2)(c) grants the exclusive right to 'make [her work] available … in such a way that persons may access it from a place and at a time individually chosen by them', thereby encompassing display, streaming or distribution on Courtlandia; and Article 11 protects the integrity of her work by prohibiting any alteration or distortion of the 3D model without her consent, meaning that QTC's unauthorised modifications (e.g., changing textures or embedding her avatar in another scene) would violate this provision. Under Article 16, Alice may grant Wonderland Tech a limited licence to host and display the NFT/avatar on Courtlandia, subject to any narrower restrictions specified in her contract, whereas Article 17, which governs only computer programmes created under employment contracts and vests usage rights in the employer, is inapplicable to her artistic works. Article 18 provides that once her work has been published with Alice's consent and the rights under Articles 10 and 11 have been exercised, those rights become subject to debt enforcement, meaning that any injunction or damages award can be enforced through Swiss debt-collection procedures if Wonderland Tech or QTC refuses to comply. CopA also contains intermediary exceptions under Article 24a, permitting transient copies integral to technological processes (such as caching or streaming), and under Article 39d, which obliges hosting providers, once duly notified of an infringement, to take reasonable technical and economic measures to prevent unlawful re-publication, thereby removing their safe-harbour protection if they fail to act upon notification. Finally, Article 67(1)(g bis) criminalises wilful and illegal acts such as making a work available 'from a place and at a time individually chosen by them', with penalties of up to one year's imprisonment or a fine; at the same time, civil remedies, interim injunctions, damages and recall of infringing copies, remain available under CopA's Title 4 provisions via ordinary civil-procedure proceedings.

The revised FADP aligns closely with the EU GDPR. For instance, consent is not the sole legal basis for processing (FADP Article 13), and data controllers (including Wonderland Tech) must comply with transparency requirements, breach notification obligations, and data-subject rights (rectification, erasure, access). The FDPIC (Federal Data Protection and Information Commissioner) now wields enhanced enforcement powers. Swiss law permits the transfer of personal data abroad only if the recipient jurisdiction ensures an 'adequate' level of protection, or if appropriate contractual or organisational safeguards are in place (analogous to GDPR). It is therefore inaccurate to state that FADP bans all transfers outside Switzerland. Moreover, FADP may apply extraterritorially if a Swiss data controller processes personal data abroad (e.g., if Wonderland Tech's Swiss headquarters manages data on servers located overseas). FADP applies to private actors and federal bodies; cantonal public authorities remain governed by their cantonal data-protection statutes, which typically mirror FADP but may differ in detail.

In Alice's case, her signature on the ICC arbitration clause counts as that ground (consent), because it implicitly authorises Wonderland Tech (and the tribunal) to process whatever personal data is strictly necessary to resolve the dispute. While consent can be a legal basis, under FADP (and GDPR), consent must be freely given, specific, informed, and unambiguous. Relying solely on an implicit authorisation from an arbitration clause might be challenged, especially for sensitive data. It would be more robust to also mention other potential legal bases for processing personal data in an arbitration context, such as 'legitimate interests' (e.g., for the administration of justice, ensuring due process) or 'legal obligation' (e.g., for record-keeping requirements of the arbitral institution or compliance with procedural rules), which are often more robust and less susceptible to withdrawal than implied consent in such scenarios.

But Alice's Indian background also plays a part. When she registered on Courtlandia, her account data (biometrics from her headset, metadata from interactions, etc.) was likely stored in Wonderland Tech's servers. Indian law claims authority over those records if Alice is considered an Indian 'data principal'. India's DPDP Act is not yet in force and has no binding effect. Instead, the IT Act, 2000, under Section 43A imposes civil liability on a 'body corporate' that fails to implement 'reasonable security practices and procedures' for sensitive personal data or information and thereby causes wrongful loss or gain. It does not cover ordinary personal data or government entities. Another point to consider is identity theft. Section 66C criminalises fraudulent or dishonest use of another individual's electronic signature, password, or 'unique identification feature,' specifically targeting identity theft. This section could apply if QTC stole Alice's private key and impersonated her.

Further, a Swiss tribunal cannot apply the unenforced DPDP Act directly, but may use it as 'persuasive authority', which is insightful. This would likely occur in the context of interpreting Swiss public policy (which is GDPR-aligned) or FADP's principles in light of evolving international data protection standards and the anticipated trajectory of Indian law, rather than a direct application of an unenforced foreign statute. The dual application of FADP and the anticipated DPDP Act (with the IT Act as current law) highlights the regulatory uncertainty and compliance burden faced by metaverse platforms operating globally. The need for a Swiss tribunal to consider an unenforced foreign law as 'persuasive authority' underscores the proactive role of international arbitration in anticipating and shaping legal norms in emerging tech spaces, even before formal legislation is fully operational.

Next comes evidence collection and enforcement in a metaverse context. Courtlandia maintains a permissioned blockchain that records all NFT transfers immutably across nodes located in Switzerland, India, and elsewhere.

These transaction hashes and timestamps, as digital evidence, are generally considered highly reliable, as altering a confirmed block requires a majority consensus. Under the ICC Rules 2021 (Rule 22(2), in conjunction with Appendix IV) and PILA Article 184(2), a Swiss-seated arbitral tribunal may order any party to produce 'all relevant documents in its possession, custody or control,' including digital records. If Wonderland Tech controls its network nodes, the tribunal can deem those logs 'accessible' and compel their production. However, if certain records reside on a permissionless portion of the blockchain beyond Wonderland Tech's control, the tribunal cannot force those remote nodes to comply without unanimous node consensus. Suppose the only evidence identifying QTC resides on an Indian node to which Wonderland Tech has no direct access. In that case, Alice may request that the Swiss court issue a letter rogatory under the Switzerland–India Mutual Legal Assistance Treaty. The rogatory should invoke Section 66C of India's IT Act (identity theft) to compel the Indian authorities to trace the individual behind QTC's wallet address. Swiss courts generally honour such MLAT requests; however, the procedural burden of obtaining and transmitting the letter rogatory lies with Alice (or her Swiss-seated tribunal, with Alice's consent). Even if QTC's wrongdoing is proven, blockchains are ordinarily immutable. A Swiss tribunal cannot compel a 'reversal' (i.e., a retroactive undoing of transactions), as blockchains require unanimous node consensus to reorganise. Where specific restitution is impossible, Article 62 CO can come into play.

Alice has dual avenues for interim measures: petitioning a Swiss court under PILA Article 183(1) for conservatory measures (e.g., preserving digital evidence on Swiss servers) or submitting an application for emergency relief to an ICC emergency arbitrator under Rule 29. Under Swiss PILA Article 183(1), Alice may petition a Swiss court (in this case, Tribunal cantonal de Genève) for interim or conservatory measures even before the arbitral tribunal has been constituted, requesting, for example, that Wonderland Tech preserve all digital evidence on Swiss-based servers. If Wonderland Tech fails to comply voluntarily, she may ask the court to apply Swiss law (Article 183(2)) and, if necessary, provide security (Article 183(3)). Such measures are limited to data and assets physically situated in Switzerland and do not prejudice the validity of her pending ICC arbitration. Under ICC Rule 29, Alice may also submit an application for emergency relief to an emergency arbitrator in accordance with Appendix V, provided her application reaches the Secretariat before the file is transmitted to the tribunal under Rule 16. The emergency arbitrator may issue provisional orders, such as directing Wonderland Tech to restore the NFT from escrow or to deposit an equivalent sum of ETH, although those orders are not binding on the eventual tribunal, which may modify or annul them per Rule 29(3). Importantly, ICC Rule 28(2) clarifies that seeking interim or conservatory relief from a judicial authority does not amount to a waiver of Alice's right to arbitrate. Any court orders obtained must be notified promptly to the ICC Secretariat, enabling parallel pursuit of both judicial and arbitral interim measures without jeopardising her arbitration rights.

Suppose QTC is initially just a 'user' on Courtlandia, Alice must first obtain QTC's real-world domicile or place of registration (e.g., via a procedural order against Wonderland Tech). Only once it is clear that QTC is, for instance, resident or incorporated in Lithuania, can Alice enforce the Geneva-seated ICC award under the 1958 New York Convention (hereinafter 'NYC'). A Lithuanian court should generally uphold a Geneva-seated ICC award, subject to the narrow grounds for refusal listed in NYC Article V and a check for conflicts with GDPR principles under EU public policy. For example, if the Swiss award requires disclosure of personal data (e.g., unredacted wallet-transaction logs or biometric records), the Lithuanian court will check for any conflict with GDPR principles. Because 'public policy' refusals under Article V(2)(b) are interpreted narrowly, Alice will need to demonstrate that the Swiss tribunal's redaction and minimisation measures comply with FADP and are thus aligned with GDPR, to avoid any GDPR-based refusal. Let's assume that the Geneva-seated award orders QTC to pay Alice in ETH or another foreign currency. In this case, Lithuanian courts allow enforcement either in the foreign currency specified by the award (e.g., ETH), in which case the judgment will direct QTC to deliver precisely that amount of ETH, or in the euro equivalent, calculated at the exchange rate on the date the judgment is registered under Lithuanian law. Alice must state her preference (ETH or euros) when she applies for enforcement.

In the end, Alice finds out that 'Metaverse Court' is just a patchwork of real-world laws. The complex interplay of blockchain immutability, national legal assistance treaties, and international arbitration enforcement highlights the multi-layered and fragmented nature of legal recourse in the metaverse. The fact that a Swiss tribunal cannot 'reverse' a blockchain transaction but must rely on traditional monetary remedies, coupled with the need for MLATs to access data across borders, demonstrates that even advanced legal mechanisms are still tethered to traditional state sovereignty and cooperation frameworks. She only wins by carefully juggling each of these legal layers. It's a good reminder that even in virtual space, you can't escape real-world legal systems. Just like Alice's trip through Wonderland, obtaining justice in Hatter Hall is fundamentally a hybrid process, requiring both technological understanding and mastery of conventional international law.

CONCLUSION

Looking ahead, it is clear that 'Metaverse law' will not emerge as a singular coherent system but as a fast-evolving patchwork of norms, jurisdictions, and experimental governance. Platforms such as Kleros and Aragon already illustrate how 'code as law' can automate on-chain dispute resolution. Yet they also underscore persistent concerns about due process, transparency, and accountability, since on-chain juries and smart contracts lack the procedural safeguards of traditional courts.

At the international level, bodies such as UNIDROIT[70] and UNESCO[71] have developed soft-law instruments and model frameworks that promote fairness, transparency, and human oversight, addressing areas involving digital assets, AI, and human rights in virtual environments. However, these instruments remain non-binding until individual states choose to incorporate them into domestic law. Concurrently, national regulators are taking incremental steps. India's anticipated DPDP Act, once fully in force, is expected to impose explicit consent requirements, data subject rights, and security standards on metaverse platforms that handle personal data. Through delegated rules or sectoral laws, it may also require onshore storage of critical or sensitive data, which could conflict with cross-border blockchain protocols. Switzerland, through its fintech sandbox and evolving cryptocurrency regulations, is carving out a permissive yet supervised environment for virtual asset innovation. While these regulatory sandboxes and community-led governance experiments (e.g., DAOs) can foster creativity and agility, they do not replace the need for enforceable state-backed frameworks when disputes cross borders or involve real-world assets. The idea of 'virtual jurisdictions', whether as formally recognised arbitration seats or as fledgling 'virtual republics', remains theoretical: unlike traditional states, purely digital entities cannot yet meet the international criteria for statehood[72] (territory, population, effective government, capacity for foreign relations). As history shows, new legal orders gain legitimacy only when existing sovereigns and courts acknowledge their authority.

Yet Alice's journey through this virtual Wonderland teaches us that traditional notions of territory, identity, and data control are turned inside out. In both India and Switzerland, data protection and arbitration law must now prepare to adapt to a realm without borders. But neither regime, in isolation, can govern the Metaverse. Instead, a hybrid approach will emerge, where international arbitration in virtual spaces may be seated in Geneva, but must still respect Indian data rights; enforcement may be coded into blockchain, yet ultimately depends on terrestrial courts. The Queen of Hearts and QueenTech alike may claim digital sovereignty, but Wonderland's lesson is one of pragmatic compromise. Parties can still choose an earthly law and a physical seat of arbitration, even as hearings occur in virtual reality. Meanwhile, businesses remain bound by existing privacy laws; consent, transparency, and accountability are no less essential through the looking glass. Law in the virtual age, then, is less about rigid national control and more about 'governance by design'. Hence, the fundamental transformation of the lawyer's role from a reactive dispute resolver to a proactive system designer is the need of the hour.

Having analysed both India's and Switzerland's emerging regimes, let us now envision how Alice Raghav might step outside existing legal binaries to co-create a fully party-driven dispute protocol. Building on her journey through divergent state and platform rules, she and her counterparty could co-design a bespoke tribunal that blends code, community, and complementary normative orders. Under this model, Courtlandia's platform charter would invoke a form of 'lex digitalis intermedia', whereby a smart-contract module automatically resolves routine escrow or payment disputes on-chain, reserving only novel, high-value, or fact-intensive matters for human review. Simultaneously, the tribunal would employ 'lex cryptographica', utilising immutable blockchain protocols to enforce critical evidentiary steps, such as identity verification, timestamping, and provenance, while granting a Swiss-law arbitral panel the authority to interpret or override on-chain findings when contextual nuances demand it. If QueenTech's anonymity or cross-border operations frustrate traditional enforcement, the tribunal could accommodate fragmented sovereignty by relying on token-holder consensus mechanisms and interoperable DAO charters to provide parallel redress pathways, all backed, if necessary, by mutual-recognition pacts among national courts.

In practice, this hybrid protocol would marry the rapid evidence-gathering and automated remedies of blockchain's 'White Rabbit' logic with the procedural safeguards and social legitimacy of human adjudication. Should due process or fairness concerns arise, Alice Raghav could appeal to a mixed tribunal combining on-chain jurors, specialised experts and ICC-appointed arbitrators. Thus, metaverse justice becomes a collaboratively governed protocol, code-enforced at the margins, interpreted by humans at its core, and underpinned by interoperable sovereignty pacts. Such a model transcends both 'code as law' and 'state as law', weaving a dynamic tapestry of governance in which fairness and consent remain unmistakable even as jurisdictional boundaries dissolve into the digital horizon. Of course, such a protocol introduces its challenges, including ensuring accessibility for non-technical parties and safeguarding against the centralisation of power within platform-specific tribunals.

As technology accelerates with AI avatars, neural-VR interfaces, and virtual courts, the boundaries between physical laws and digital realities become increasingly blurred, much like the shifting rules of Wonderland. In this evolving landscape, the Cheshire Cat's advice, 'If you don't know where you want to go, it doesn't matter which path you take,' rings true for those unprepared. But for legal professionals, uncertainty is no excuse for inaction. Like Alice, we must negotiate each turn with care, and lawyers must become architects of digital governance rather than mere interpreters of existing statutes. This calls for active engagement, including participation in multidisciplinary dialogue to shape future treaties, clarification of jurisdictional rules, and establishment of mechanisms for cross-border cooperation. Drawing on Switzerland's tradition of comparative law and India's vibrant constitutional democracy, we are uniquely positioned to advocate for a governance framework that protects both innovation and fundamental rights.

Ultimately, the law of the virtual era may not be dictated by a single imperious Queen, but by a collaborative council, human and digital, whose authority is rooted in consent and shared stewardship. As Wonderland teaches us, the challenge is to strike a balance between creativity and order. Even in the most fantastical realms, justice and the rule of law must remain our guiding stars. The Metaverse is not a lawless kingdom, but an evolving space where every actor, whether sovereign or code, must remain accountable. Just as Alice learned to question Wonderland's logic, legal practitioners must interrogate the governance models of the digital realm. Only by adopting an interdisciplinary, international perspective and speaking up when the Mad Hatter blurs the line between chaos and law can we help build a world where the rule of law continues to guide us. Through this lens, Alice's adventures become more than fantasy; they are a call to legal imagination in which Indian and Swiss voices, human and machine actors alike, find a rightful place at the table.

NOTES

1. McKinsey & Company, "What Is the Metaverse—and What Does It Mean for Business?" McKinsey & Company, accessed 2 April 2025, https://www.mckinsey.com/capabilities/mckinsey-digital/our-insights/what-is-the-Metaverse-and-what-does-it-mean-for-business.
2. International Trademark Association, "Trademarks in the Metaverse White Paper," International Trademark Association, published 12 April 2023, https://www.inta.org/perspectives/inta-research/trademarks-in-the-metaverse-white-paper/.
3. Christine Lagorio-Chafkin, "An Entrepreneur's Guide to Finding New Business Opportunities in the Metaverse," *Inc*, 15 April 2022, https://www.inc.com/christine-lagorio-chafkin/metaverse-virtual-world-layers.html.
4. Ministry of Law and Justice, "The Digital Personal Data Protection Act, 2023," *Gazette of India*, 11 August 2023, https://www.meity.gov.in/static/uploads/2024/06/2bf1f0e9f04e6fb4f8fef35e82c42aa5.pdf.
5. Quick note on the legal status of the DPDP Act: Although the Indian Parliament has enacted the DPDP Act, its provisions have not yet been notified for enforcement as of May 2025. The analysis in this article is based on the text of the enacted act and relevant draft rules and is intended to reflect the anticipated regulatory framework once fully operationalised. References to the DPDP Act should be understood as forward-looking projections of its expected legal effect.

6. *K.S. Puttaswamy (Retd.) v. Union of India*, 10 SCC 1 (Supreme Court of India 2017).
7 SME Portal, "New Federal Act on Data Protection (nFADP)," accessed 3 April 2025, https://www.kmu.admin.ch/kmu/en/home/fakten-und-trends/digitalisierung/datenschutz/neues-datenschutzgesetz-revdsg.html.
8 Vahid Rezadoost and Pragya Choudhary, "Arbitration Tech Toolbox: Applicable Law, Choice of Courts and Enforcement Issues in Metaverse Disputes," *Kluwer Arbitration Blog*, 27 September 2023, https://arbitrationblog.kluwerarbitration.com/2023/09/27/arbitration-tech-toolbox-applicable-law-choice-of-courts-and-enforcement-issues-in-metaverse-disputes/; Candidus Dougherty, "Bragg v. Linden: Virtual Property Rights Litigation," *SSRN Scholarly Paper* no. 1092284 (Social Science Research Network, n.d.), accessed 28 April 2025, https://papers.ssrn.com/sol3/papers.cfm?abstract_id=1092284.
9. Pratyush Panjwani and Emily Hay, "Metaverse Dispute Resolution Colloquium," presentation, Digital Law Center, 24 March 2023, https://www.digitallawcenter.ch/sites/default/files/inline-files/metaverse-dispute-resolution-colloquium-presentation-pratyush-panjwani-and-emily-hay-24-mar-2023.pdf; Clement Lesaege, Federico Ast, and William George, "Kleros," white paper, September 2019, https://kleros.io/whitepaper.pdf.
10. "Metaverse Industry and Companies Analysis Report 2025–2030," *GlobeNewswire* press release, 25 April 2025, accessed 21 May 2025, https://www.globenewswire.com/news-release/2025/04/25/3068346/28124/en/Metaverse-Industry-and-Companies-Analysis-Report-2025-2030-Are-We-Ready-to-Shift-from-WFH-to-WFM-Revenues-Set-to-Reach-US-1-1-Trillion-by-2030.html.
11. "Peace of Westphalia | Definition, Map, Results, & Significance | Britannica," *Encyclopaedia Britannica*, 22 March 2025, https://www.britannica.com/event/Peace-of-Westphalia. For a critique, see Heinz Duchhardt, "The Peace of Westphalia as a Place of Memory in Germany and Europe," *Pedralbes Journal of Modern History* 19 (December 1999): 147–55, https://revistes.ub.edu/index.php/pedralbes/article/view/36866.
12. William M. Richman and William L. Reynolds, *Understanding Conflict of Laws*, 4th edn (LexisNexis 2013).
13. "American Banana Co. v. United Fruit Co., 213 U.S. 347 (1909)," *Justia Law*, accessed 5 April 2025, https://supreme.justia.com/cases/federal/us/213/347/.
14. Antonio Cassese, *International Criminal Law*, ed. Paola Gaeta, 3rd edn (Oxford University Press 2013).
15. Gary B. Born, *International Commercial Arbitration*, 3rd edn (Kluwer Law International 2021).
16. Jean-Marc Rickli and Federico Mantellassi, *Our Digital Future: The Security Implications of Metaverses*, Issue 24 (Geneva Centre for Security Policy 2022).
17. Vahid Rezadoost and Pragya Choudhary, "Arbitration Tech Toolbox: Applicable Law, Choice of Courts and Enforcement Issues in Metaverse

Disputes," *Kluwer Arbitration Blog*, 27 September 2023, https://arbitration-blog.kluwerarbitration.com/2023/09/27/arbitration-tech-toolbox-applicable-law-choice-of-courts-and-enforcement-issues-in-metaverse-disputes/.
18. "Section 75 in The Information Technology Act, 2000," accessed 5 April 2025, https://indiankanoon.org/doc/576992/.
19. "India Code: Section Details," accessed 17 May 2025, https://www.indiacode.nic.in/show-data?actid=AC_CEN_3_46_00004_199626_1517807323919&orderno=20.
20. "India Code: Section Details," accessed 17 May 2025, https://www.indiacode.nic.in/show-data?actid=AC_CEN_3_46_00004_199626_1517807323919&orderno=21.
21. "India Code: Section Details," accessed 17 May 2025, https://www.indiacode.nic.in/show-data?actid=AC_CEN_3_46_00004_199626_1517807323919&sectionId=24525&sectionno=24&orderno=25.
22. "India Code: Section Details," accessed 17 May 2025, https://www.indiacode.nic.in/show-data?actid=AC_CEN_3_46_00004_199626_1517807323919&orderno=32.
23. Delhi High Court, "Video Conferencing Rules, 2020," High Court of Delhi, accessed 6 March 2026, https://delhihighcourt.nic.in/files/Notifications%20and%20Practice%20Directions/notificationfile_uldc4uvqwz9.pdf.
24. "Section 3 in THE DIGITAL PERSONAL DATA PROTECTION ACT, 2023," accessed 5 April 2025, https://indiankanoon.org/doc/84660522/.
25. "Section 18 in THE DIGITAL PERSONAL DATA PROTECTION ACT, 2023," accessed 5 April 2025, https://indiankanoon.org/doc/146786225/.
26. "SR 235.1 – Federal Act of 25 September 2020 on Data Protection," Fedlex, accessed 5 May 2025, https://www.fedlex.admin.ch/eli/cc/2022/491/en.
27. "SR 235.11 – Ordinance of 31 August 2022 on Data Protection," Fedlex, accessed 18 May 2025, https://www.fedlex.admin.ch/eli/cc/2022/568/en.
28. "SR 235.13 – Ordinance of 31 August 2022 on Data Protection," Fedlex, accessed 18 May 2025, https://www.fedlex.admin.ch/eli/cc/2022/569/en.
29. DLA Piper, "Data Protection Laws in Switzerland – Data Protection Laws of the World," DLA Piper Data Protection, accessed 7 May 2025, https://www.dlapiperdataprotection.com/?c=CH.
30. "SR 291 – Federal Act on Private International Law (PILA)," Fedlex, accessed 7 April 2025, https://www.fedlex.admin.ch/eli/cc/1988/1776_1776_1776/en.
31. Swiss Arbitration Association, "Swiss Rules 2021," Swiss Arbitration Association, accessed 7 April 2025, https://www.swissarbitration.org/resources/swiss-rules-2021/.
32. "SR 235.1 – Federal Act of 25 September 2020 on Data Protection," Fedlex, accessed 3 April 2025, https://www.fedlex.admin.ch/eli/cc/2022/491/en.
33. "Section 27 in THE DIGITAL PERSONAL DATA PROTECTION ACT, 2023," accessed 3 April 2025, https://indiankanoon.org/doc/192991000/.
34. "Data Protection Laws in Switzerland – Data Protection Laws of the World," accessed 7 May 2025, https://www.dlapiperdataprotection.com/?c=CH.

35. Carnegie Endowment for International Peace, "Understanding India's New Data Protection Law," accessed 18 May 2025, https://carnegieendowment.org/research/2023/10/understanding-indias-new-data-protection-law.
36. GDPR.Eu, "Everything You Need to Know about the 'Right to Be Forgotten'," GDPR Overview, 5 November 2018, https://gdpr.eu/right-to-be-forgotten/.
37. Organisation for Economic Co-Operation and Development (OECD), *A Preliminary Mapping of Data Localisation Measures*, OECD Trade Policy Papers, no. 262 (Paris: OECD Publishing 2022), https://www.oecd.org/en/publications/a-preliminary-mapping-of-data-localisation-measures_c5ca3fed-en.html.
38. Organisation for Economic Co-Operation and Development (OECD), *The Nature, Evolution and Potential Implications of Data Localisation Measures*, OECD Trade Policy Papers, no. 294 (Paris: OECD Publishing 2023), https://www.oecd.org/en/publications/the-nature-evolution-and-potential-implications-of-data-localisation-measures_179f718a-en.html.
39. Digital Agency, "Data Free Flow with Trust (DFFT) | Digital Agency," 16 October 2024, https://www.digital.go.jp/en/policies/dfft; World Economic Forum, "Data Free Flow with Trust, Now Entering Implementation Phase," World Economic Forum, 20 May 2022, https://www.weforum.org/stories/2022/05/cross-border-data-regulation-dfft/.
40. G7 Digital Ministers, "Annex 1: G7 Action Plan for Promoting Data Free Flow with Trust," in *Ministerial Declaration G7 Digital Ministers' Meeting*, 2021, 1–2, https://www.bundesregierung.de/resource/blob/998440/2038510/e8ce1d2f3b08477eeb2933bf2f14424a/2022-05-11-g7-ministerial-declaration-digital-ministers-meeting-en-data.pdf.
41. National Board of Trade Sweden, *Navigating Cross-Border Data Flows: Trade Policy Recommendations for the Digital Economy* (Stockholm: National Board of Trade Sweden, 2025), https://www.kommerskollegium.se/globalassets/publikationer/rapporter/2025/navigating-cross-border-data-flows.pdf.
42. World Economic Forum, "Here's Why We Need to Secure Trusted Cross Border Data Flows," World Economic Forum, 27 April 2023, https://www.weforum.org/stories/2023/04/how-and-why-data-must-flow-freely-and-responsibly-across-borders/.
43. World Economic Forum, *From Fragmentation to Coordination: The Case for an Institutional Mechanism for Cross-Border Data Flows* (Geneva: World Economic Forum, 2023), https://www.weforum.org/publications/from-fragmentation-to-coordination-the-case-for-an-institutional-mechanism-for-cross-border-data-flows/.
44. World Economic Forum, "Here's Why We Need to Secure Trusted Cross Border Data Flows," World Economic Forum, 27 April 2023, https://www.weforum.org/stories/2023/04/how-and-why-data-must-flow-freely-and-responsibly-across-borders/.
45. "Section 16 in THE DIGITAL PERSONAL DATA PROTECTION ACT, 2023," accessed 6 May 2025, https://indiankanoon.org/doc/172647580/.

46. "SR 235.1 – Federal Act of 25 September 2020 on Data Protection," Fedlex, accessed 17 July 2025, https://www.fedlex.admin.ch/eli/cc/2022/491/en.
47. "Section 69 in The Information Technology Act, 2000," accessed 19 May 2025, https://indiankanoon.org/doc/1439440/.
48. Federal Data Protection and Information Commissioner (EDOEB), "The New Data Protection Act in Figures," accessed 19 May 2025, https://www.edoeb.admin.ch/en/18112024-the-new-data-protection-act-in-figures.
49. Global Legal Insights (GLI), "Blockchain & Cryptocurrency Laws 2025 | Switzerland," GLI, n.d., accessed 19 May 2025, https://www.globallegalinsights.com/practice-areas/blockchain-cryptocurrency-laws-and-regulations/switzerland/.
50. 'DLA Piper, "Data Protection Laws in Switzerland – Data Protection Laws of the World," DLA Piper Data Protection, accessed 19 May 2025, https://www.dlapiperdataprotection.com/?t=law&c=CH.
51. Leon Anidjar, Nizan Geslevich Packin, and Argyri Panezi, "The Matrix of Privacy: Data Infrastructure in the AI-Powered Metaverse," *Harvard Law & Policy Review* 18, no. 1 (2024): 61–114, https://journals.law.harvard.edu/lpr/wp-content/uploads/sites/89/2024/08/18.1-Matrix-of-Privacy.pdf.
52. Brookings, "The Partial Data Barter Trades of the Digital Economy," Brookings, n.d., accessed 20 May 2025, https://www.brookings.edu/articles/the-partial-data-barter-trades-of-the-digital-economy/.
53. Margaux MacColl, "After a Virtual Gucci Bag Sold for over $4,000, More than a Real One, VC Alexis Ohanian Predicts Virtual Fashion Will Be Huge. Gucci and Atari Agree," *Business Insider*, accessed 20 May 2025, https://www.businessinsider.com/virtual-gucci-bag-sale-sign-digital-fashion-is-a-trend-2021-5.
54. Letícia Melo, "Most Expensive Land in the Metaverse," *DappRadar*, 17 April 2023, https://dappradar.com/blog/most-expensive-land-in-the-metaverse.
55. European Commission, "Guidelines on Data Protection Impact Assessment (DPIA) (WP248rev.01)," Article 29 Working Party, accessed 21 May 2025, https://ec.europa.eu/newsroom/article29/items/611236/en.
56. Gianclaudio Malgieri and Bart Custers, "Pricing Privacy – The Right to Know the Value of Your Personal Data," *SSRN Scholarly Paper* no. 3047257 (Social Science Research Network, n.d.), accessed 21 May 2025, https://papers.ssrn.com/sol3/papers.cfm?abstract_id=3047257.
57. University of Sheffield, "Humby, Clive," accessed 27 October 2021, https://www.sheffield.ac.uk/cs/people/academic-visitors/clive-humby.
58. Amanda Parsons, "Defining the Goal of a Data Tax," *European Law Open*, Cambridge Core, 2024, https://doi.org/10.1017/elo.2024.38.
59. World Economic Forum, "We Should Treat Data as a Natural Resource. Here's Why," World Economic Forum, March 2020, accessed 21 May 2025, https://www.weforum.org/stories/2020/03/we-should-treat-data-as-a-natural-resource-heres-why/.

60. Thomson Reuters, "Data Licensing: Taking into Account Data Ownership," Thomson Reuters, accessed 23 May 2025, https://legal.thomsonreuters.com/en/insights/articles/data-licensing-taking-into-account-data-ownership.
61. IE Edu, "Data Is More than the New Oil – It's Oxygen," IE Edu, accessed 21 May 2025, https://www.ie.edu/blue-talks/data-is-more-than-the-new-oil-its-oxygen/.
62. Leon Anidjar, Nizan Geslevich Packin, and Argyri Panezi, "The Matrix of Privacy: Data Infrastructure in the AI-Powered Metaverse," *Harvard Law & Policy Review* 18, no. 1 (2024): 61–114, https://journals.law.harvard.edu/lpr/wp-content/uploads/sites/89/2024/08/18.1-Matrix-of-Privacy.pdf.
63. "Section 115BBH in The Income Tax Act, 1961," accessed 23 May 2025, https://indiankanoon.org/doc/4837707/.
64. Business Standard, "India to Scrap 6% Equalisation Levy on Digital Ads, Leading to Revenue Loss," *Business Standard*, 1 April 2025, https://www.business-standard.com/industry/news/india-equalisation-levy-removed-tax-impact-2025-125040100810_1.html.
65. "India Code: Section Details (Order No. 95)," accessed 23 May 2025, https://www.indiacode.nic.in/show-data?actid=AC_CEN_45_76_00001_200021_1517807324077&orderno=95; "India Code: Section Details (Order No. 49)," accessed 23 May 2025, https://www.indiacode.nic.in/show-data?actid=AC_CEN_45_76_00001_200021_1517807324077&orderno=49.
66. State Secretariat for International Finance (SIF), Information Technology Act, 2000, §§43A and 72, India Code, accessed 23 May 2025, https://www.indiacode.nic.in.
67. Eidgenössische Finanzmarktaufsicht FINMA (FINMA), "La FINMA Pubblica Una Guida Pratica Sulle ICO," accessed 23 May 2025, https://www.finma.ch/en/news/2018/02/20180216-mm-ico-wegleitung/.
68. McKinsey & Company, "The Power of Language: Navigating Global Legal Practice," accessed 23 May 2025, https://www.mckinsey.com/featured-insights/in-the-balance/the-power-of-language-navigating-global-legal-practice.
69. Fedlex, "SR 272 – Swiss Civil Procedure Code of 19 December 2008," accessed 29 May 2025, https://www.fedlex.admin.ch/eli/cc/2010/262/en.
70. UNIDROIT, "Principles on Digital Assets and Private Law," January 2024, https://www.unidroit.org/wp-content/uploads/2024/01/Principles-on-Digital-Assets-and-Private-Law-linked-1.pdf.
71. UNESCO, "Ethics of Artificial Intelligence," accessed 26 June 2025, https://www.unesco.org/en/artificial-intelligence/recommendation-ethics.
72. ILSA, "Montevideo Convention," accessed 17 July 2025, https://www.ilsa.org/Jessup/Jessup15/Montevideo%20Convention.pdf.

11. Are we at risk of Alice in Wonderland syndrome?

Mark Findlay

In thinking about governance and personhood in the metaverse, are we suffering distorted perceptions – seeing some things bigger or smaller than they are; nearer to us or farther away? After consuming the 'Drink me' bottle or eating a small piece of mushroom, our world seems different, and we become larger or smaller than life-size. The same could be said of how we wrestle with the possibility of entirely new thinking or instead return to the comfort of what we know, even if this changes us irrevocably.

Alice expresses a deep desire to break free of how she sees herself, is seen by others, and is positioned in life experiences. 'If I had a world of my own, everything would be nonsense.' This aspiration is not to be confused with a wish for chaos or disorder; it is a recognition that our words and their external meanings may not match. *Nonsense*, as Alice would have it, is when and where the parameters of our reasoning (often external and imposed) go topsy-turvy – so that sense is sensitised, not sensible.

Respecting the metaphor that underpins all these contributions, it is necessary not to reconcile Wonderland with realspace but rather to engage imagination and, in so doing, navigate the unpredictable and sometimes absurd. Thereby we can be at ease with the paradox of Wonderland and its inversion of what we thought was reality. Otherwise, it is impossible to see the meaning in the Dodo Caucus race. Like the Dodo in searching for governance solutions to profound challenges undermining identity and personhood, our objective is to help the animals dry off after falling into the pool of tears. So, we construct a race with no start or finish, no rules, a circular track – and everyone is declared the winner in the end. Are our contributors (and we as editors) at risk of advocating any and all potentialities and being left with more uncertainty than we sought to diminish? Not so. Remember, the caucus race ends after the animals have been running for half an hour, when the Dodo suddenly calls out, 'The race is over!'[1] Is this nonsense, as Alice preferred, or an example of external power determining rules without rules? In some respects, the race has no beginning and no end. The animals run in whatever way they choose, and everybody wins, so why would definitive conclusions be required?

Taking the metaphor back to the content and structure of this collection, it should be realised that each contributor starts and concludes as they see the governance challenges as constituted, and the best governance outcomes as achieved. It is about the energy of innovation and fresh thinking, not predetermined rules or right answers.

Reverting back to rational reasoning, the race could be understood as an allegory for living with a lack of direction, in a state of purposelessness. Seen through a Wonderland lens, it is not the players we criticise in their chaos but rather the meaninglessness of searching for the single solution, beating all others, determined by capricious authority.

How does this translate into innovative governance as addressed by our contributors? Three ways emerge in running the race to find governance that ensures personhood:

- where the metaverse challenges our thinking about pre-existing governance regimes, while seeking to have these regimes transition from realspace but with modified or restructured core features;
- where technology offers new governance tools and settings, and pre-existing governance devices are adapted and incorporated even if sometimes distorted; and
- where the governance action must leave realspace and find form in new ways of social bonding and with new values and stakeholders.

Which is to be preferred? That is for the reader to determine, having identified how she sees her personhood and how its governance is challenged in the virtual life experience she would want to enjoy. And in so doing, the reader should share Alice's courage and be *curiouser and curiouser.* This interaction between the young voices and the readers is intended to create ongoing conversations about governing in the virtual, wherein ideas can grow and be fertilised in future Wonderland encounters.

In seeking a better future for life in the virtual, one offering freedom and integrity, not discrimination and enclosure, we look to ways of governance in which we can be represented and participate. Too often, young voices have had little or no say in governance crafting. As the mission of this collection, the voices of our contributors in their own reasoning are asserting that innovative governance requires recognition of fresh minds and new understandings.

Of course, there is the risk that other interpretations which do not sit well with the governance options as currently determined will be dismissed as Wonderland nonsense. To counter this possibility, we return to the metaphor not as a place to hide out but from which to assemble new governance energies.

Alice rejected the King of Hearts' attempt at governance through rule 42, that '[a]ll persons more than a mile high leave the court'[2] – not so much as nonsense but rather as a fake rule invented to get rid of her (as the rationale for the dismissing of young voices might be). She turns the King's interpretation of established authority back on him. If it was a real rule, it would be number 1 and not number 42, she retorts. The best defence he can muster is that it is the oldest rule in the book. For Alice, 'Then it ought to be number 1.'[3]

Was that her actual reasoning? Unlikely. By confronting and calling out the bluster of unreasonable dominion, young Alice ridicules pernicious power as stuff and nonsense. Alice finally diffuses the illusion by declaring that the King, Queen and their court are nothing but a pack of cards.

Does this destroy Wonderland? Never. Rather it reveals Wonderland is a critical context in which those not burdened with the nonsense of convention can challenge what to everyone seems meaningless, but where only the few have the courage to say so.

Even when the White Rabbit presents as damning evidence a letter with no address, no identifiable handwriting and no signature, the King still holds it to be proof of the Knave's guilt because an honest man would have signed his name. 'If any of them can explain it,' said Alice[,] 'I'll give him sixpence. I don't believe there is an atom of meaning in it.' 'If there is no meaning in it,' said the King, 'that saves a world of trouble, you know, as we needn't try to find any.'[4] Putting risks to safety and freedom in the digital universe against novel approaches to governance in the virtual, both the risk and the response should be understood in terms of the problematic and unfulfilled meanings in realspace. Instead, if Wonderland teaches us anything, it is that the individuality and identity of our thinking is not to be valued or confirmed through conformity with the Dodo's arbitrary intervention, or the King's illogical and confused rules.

The trial of the Knave of Hearts is also profoundly revealing for the contributors to this collection. Up until this point, Alice had been an observer, a bystander, as chaos and confusion evolved around her. Finally, as an eager witness overturning the jury box in her haste to tell it as she saw it, Alice inserts herself and takes control of the snowballing governance madness that culminates in a call for sentence before verdict.

To get young voices heard is, as with Alice's contestation, a battle against powerful regressive forces. AI is the Queen of Hearts, demanding only one dominant logic to be followed, no matter whether this is with or without accountability. The Dodo is big info tech, determining who can race and when all things must come to an end. Individuality and personhood are claimed by young voices in revealing an ability to navigate the weird and unpredictable world of Wonderland as an alternative mind power that tackles new life experiences and their challenges in digital space for fresh thinking.

The voices in this collection approach governance down their chosen paths that move away from governance as we know it at different speeds, using different vehicles but each with a common intent. Like Alice's sister, they dream of sharing her dream and living her Wonderland.

> So she sat on, with closed eyes, and half believed herself in Wonderland, though she knew she had but to open them again, and all would change to dull reality—the grass would be only rustling in the wind, and the pool rippling to the waving of the reeds—the rattling teacups would change to tinkling sheep-bells, and the Queen's shrill cries to the voice of the shepherd boy—and the sneeze of the baby, the shriek of the Gryphon, and all the other queer noises would change (she knew) to the confused clamour of the busy farm-yard—while the lowing of the cattle in the distance would take the place of the Mock Turtle's heavy sobs.[5]

It is for the reader to determine how far they want to stray from what they know. It is for the reader to decide whether they wish to be drawn back to dull reality. As the unauthorised downloading revolution became a symbol of mass mundane resistance against the commodification of ideas and creativity at the end of the last century, governance of virtual futures cannot be contained by compromised hierarchy structures, illogical logic, rigid rules and arbitrary authority. Alice walked through Wonderland on a journey of self-discovery, in which shifting identity and perceptions did not see her run from imagination, but instead to answer the Caterpillar's 'Who are you?'[6] question. While initially she doesn't really know (it is alright not to have all the answers), and then she does not feel herself (it is okay not to live within your comfort zone), Alice finds the answer in her ever-changing personhood. 'I could tell you my adventures—beginning from this morning,' said Alice a little timidly; 'but it's no use going back to yesterday, because I was a different person then.'[7]

NOTES

1. *Alice's Adventures in Wonderland*, Chapter 3. https://www.gutenberg.org/files/11/11-h/11-h.htm#chap03
2. *Alice's Adventures in Wonderland*, Chapter 12. https://www.gutenberg.org/files/11/11-h/11-h.htm#chap12
3. *Alice's Adventures in Wonderland*, Chapter 12. https://www.gutenberg.org/files/11/11-h/11-h.htm#chap12
4. *Alice's Adventures in Wonderland*, Chapter 12. https://www.gutenberg.org/files/11/11-h/11-h.htm#chap12

5. *Alice's Adventures in Wonderland*, Chapter 12. https://www.gutenberg.org/files/11/11-h/11-h.htm#chap12
6. *Alice's Adventures in Wonderland*, Chapter 5. https://www.gutenberg.org/files/11/11-h/11-h.htm#chap05
7. *Alice's Adventures in Wonderland*, Chapter 5. https://www.gutenberg.org/files/11/11-h/11-h.htm#chap05

PART IV

Technologies of possibility: emancipation and embodiment

Introduction to Part IV

Noha Lea Halim and Sofie Schönborn

When speaking about the metaverse, we are not referring to a single technology or platform, nor to a clearly defined destination. The metaverse is an evolving convergence of technical, social, and economic developments: an open-ended project shaped by continuous experimentation, negotiation, and design. As new technologies intersect and mature, they create novel experiences and new spaces of governance, interaction, and human possibility.

This evolving space forces us to consider and reconsider how we experience presence, agency, and interaction in digital worlds. As interfaces expand beyond screens to include touch, gesture, and immersive interfaces, the boundary between body and system starts to shift. Technologies like haptics, brain–computer interfaces, and spatial computing suggest that embodiment itself may become increasingly programmable. This brings new possibilities for learning, creativity, and emotional connection. However, also new questions arise about consent, privacy, and who controls access to these extended forms of experience.

Concurrently, we see shifts in how rules, rights, and responsibilities are constructed with new technologies. The rise of decentralized systems, blockchain networks, smart contracts, and autonomous governance models offers new ways to structure agreements and resolve disputes without traditional intermediaries. These architectures promise transparency and autonomy, yet also challenge long-standing legal and ethical assumptions. How do we ensure fairness in automated systems? What constitutes justice when decision-making is distributed across code, algorithms, and global communities? And how do we maintain accountability in systems designed to operate beyond conventional jurisdiction?

Beyond these specific technologies lie further frontiers still coming into view. Synthetic realities, where physical, virtual, and augmented spaces increasingly overlap, invite us to rethink how we inhabit space and time themselves. As these developments converge, the metaverse becomes less a parallel world and more an integrated layer across multiple dimensions of human experience.

For younger voices engaging with these possibilities, the horizon remains open. These technologies do not arrive with fixed trajectories. Instead, they invite active reflection on which futures we might wish to build.

What forms of freedom or constraint will emerge? How might new forms of identity expression and collaboration take shape? And how can we ensure that these expanding digital environments serve as spaces of emancipation rather than exclusion?

This Part opens a conversation about these shifting possibilities. It cautions us to remain attentive to evolving contours of the metaverse, where technological design, embodiment, and governance converge to shape not only how we interact, but who we might become.

Source: Generated using DALL-E, building on the original illustrations from *Alice's Adventures in Wonderland*, drawn by John Tenniel, https://www.alice-in-wonderland.net/resources/pictures/alices-adventures-in-wonderland/

Figure IV.1 Digital futures of Wonderland

12. The chaos of blockchain-based dispute resolution mechanisms: lessons learnt from the Queen's croquet in Wonderland

Narges Keshavarz Bahadori

INTRODUCTION

> "I don't think they play at all fairly," Alice began, in rather a complaining tone, "and they all quarrel so dreadfully one can't hear oneself speak—and they don't seem to have any rules in particular; at least, if there are, nobody attends to them—and you've no idea how confusing it is all the things being alive; for instance, there's the arch I've got to go through next walking about at the other end of the ground—and I should have croqueted the Queen's hedgehog just now, only it ran away when it saw mine coming!"
>
> The players all played at once without waiting for turns, quarrelling all the while, and fighting for the hedgehogs; and in a very short time the Queen was in a furious passion, and went stamping about, and shouting "Off with his head!" or "Off with her head!" about once in a minute!

In Lewis Carroll's Alice's Adventures in Wonderland[1], the Queen's croquet game is a place of chaos and confusion, where the rules are arbitrary, and the players are at the mercy of the Queen's impulsive orders. This metaphor properly describes the current state of blockchain-based dispute resolution mechanisms.

Since Bitcoin's invention in 2008 as a "peer to peer electronic cash system"[2] by the pseudonymous Satoshi Nakamoto, smart contracts, i.e., self-executing computer protocols designed to automatically enforce the terms of agreements,[3] complement this AI-automated financial engagement. Blockchain developers have promised decentralized, distributed, transparent, and efficient venues for smart transactions beyond human and natural commercial worlds' shortcomings and which are therefore free from conflict and disputes.

In data-driven and AI-enhanced transactions arranged in virtual market spaces, it is impractical to expect that parties can address all potential challenges and disputes that may arise during their contractual relationship. Therefore, an inventor's promise of a dispute-free domain is not realistic as disputes are inevitable in on-chain transactions, as with any other lucrative activity.[4]

Can blockchain-based off- and on-chain disputes be resolved by blockchain-based systems? "The very technology that made traditional dispute resolution processes inaccessible, could also provide the basis for developing new, innovative and accessible avenues of redress".[5]

Blockchain-based dispute resolution platforms emerged and are structured in ways similar to off-chain arbitration. These platforms, by adopting game theory considerations and crowdsourcing methods, seek to resolve disputes in a rapid and decentralized manner.[6]

As on-chain dispute resolutions produce final and binding awards, respecting the due process requirements such as the parties' right to present their case before a fair and impartial tribunal that treats them equally, is mandatory. In my analysis to follow, much like the Queen's croquet game, I assert that blockchain-based platforms are not without challenges. Even offering potential for efficiency in dispute resolution, the decentralization of blockchain-based structures and the lack of regulatory frameworks or clear procedural guarantees raises important questions about their fairness and justice.

My reflections explore the complexities of blockchain-based dispute resolution, drawing parallels to the chaotic world of Wonderland. First, I delve into the historical development of blockchain technology and the role of smart contracts in facilitating transactions. This background is offered to familiarize readers with the language and imaginings of blockchain.

Further, the types of disputes that arise within blockchain ecosystems, both on-chain and off-chain, and the mechanisms available for their resolution are critically reviewed.

Using perspectives from law, sociology, and philosophy, I unpack the procedural guarantees necessary for ensuring on-chain fairness and justice, to provide a comprehensive understanding of the current contentious landscape and the potential for future regulatory approaches to decentralized distributed platforms in the context of on-chain and virtual dispute resolution. From here we can anticipate new challenges to dispute resolution in the virtual.

Finally, I examine existing regulatory approaches and propose a theoretically grounded strategy for ensuring all stakeholders' interests, from developers and policymakers to their most important users, i.e., disputants and adjudicators.

BLOCKCHAIN ECOSYSTEM: A WONDERLAND OR A PLAYING FIELD IN THE WONDERLAND OF DIFFERENT JURISDICTIONS?

The foundation for blockchain was laid in the 1960s. Paul Baran developed two main categories of networks, "centralized" and "distributed", constituting the underlying features of today's blockchains.[7] Meanwhile, a group of young computer scientists called "Cypherpunks" saw the centralized surveillance of governments as unjust, coercive, and a threat to privacy.[8] Seeking resilience against these threats, they came up with a "crypto-anarchy" ideology, "using encrypted communication and electronic money to smash the state"[9] centralization. Between 2007 and 2009, the world faced its worst financial crisis since the Great Depression. As global banking systems faltered,[10] Nakamoto published the Bitcoin whitepaper on the Cypherpunk mailing list, presenting it as a "peer-to-peer electronic cash system."[11] Free from failing banking system protocols, Bitcoin emerged as a proposed solution, replacing the need for a trusted third party with a proof-of-work system, "using a set of cryptographic hash functions called SHA-256 designed by the US National Security Agency".[12]

In 1994, the concept of "Smart Contracts" was introduced,[13] defined as "a set of promises, including protocols within which the parties perform on [sic] the other promises" implemented via computer programs—making them "smarter" than traditional contracts.[14]

These arrangements are enforceable, automated agreements residing in blockchains.[15] They can be triggered when a user initiates a transaction, allowing non-trusting parties to interact without a centralized intermediary.[16]

This fusion of enforceable, self-executing contracts with decentralized, immutable blockchains creates a powerful new agreement paradigm.

HOW BLOCKCHAINS FUNCTION

> "... and you've no idea how confusing it is all the things being alive."
>
> Chapter VIII: The Queen's Croquet-Ground

Among the several attempts to define blockchain technology, Mik's 2018 definition stands out: "Blockchain is often described as a decentralized, peer-validated ledger providing a publicly visible, chronological and permanent record of all prior transaction".[17] Despite traditional transactions that require an intermediary, an escrow agent, a bank, or even online "server–client architecture", blockchain operates on a decentralized peer-to-peer network.[18] They are distributed and encrypted.[19] Participants in a blockchain network, known as nodes, can be any device or individual, anonymous or pseudonymous, connected to others.[20] Centralized systems are more vulnerable to manipulation and hacking, making data security a critical concern in digital transactions.

Blockchain's cryptographic encryption and consensus mechanisms offer built-in security, removing the need for external firewalls or third-party oversight. Once broadcast, data becomes immutable and resistant to tampering. At first glance, blockchain technology appears to offer an ideal solution to systemic issues that complicate financial arrangements and may promote disputation. There is no centralized external authority, so no politically enacted regulation. No failing centralized banking and financial system. Its decentralized and immutable nature is often praised for enhancing security and reducing cyber vulnerabilities. In this light, blockchain appears to be a trustworthy and autonomous digital ally. Yet, such optimism warrants scrutiny. If the system were truly flawless, would dispute resolution still be necessary? Can technology alone resolve the legal and political complexities of human interaction? The next section explores the dispute types likely to arise in blockchains and the mechanisms best suited to resolve them.

BLOCKCHAIN DISPUTES: FROM MATHEMATICAL VULNERABILITIES TO ACTUAL LEGAL SHORTCOMINGS

Blockchain-related disputes can be categorized into off- and on-chain disputes.[21] Despite the blockchain inventor's promises of a dispute-free domain, disputes are inevitable in on-chain transactions. It is unrealistic to assume that parties can address all potential challenges that may arise during their contractual relationship either in a traditional or a smart contract.[22] Disputes can also arise beyond contracts and transactions—in the blockchain's technical layers like data, communication, hardware, storage, and code, due to their complex, math-heavy nature.

On-chain Disputes

On-chain disputes, occurring at the foundational layer of blockchain architecture, primarily concern governance among participants—developers, miners, token holders, etc.

Keeping the focus on on-chain management, the "governance" issue refers to mechanisms that are built directly into the data layer of a distributed ledger system. The goal is to establish a formalized decision-making process, increasing legitimacy and reducing the risk of network splits caused by controversial or uncoordinated protocol changes.[23]

Governance is critical in blockchain's adversarial environment where malicious actors exploit system vulnerabilities.[24] Blockchain-based systems can be a fertile ground for malicious attempts profiting from vulnerabilities of the code or exploiting consensus mechanisms and rules of transferring the crypto assets or any other attempt to disrupt the network.

Governance disputes in blockchain involve disagreements over the network's direction, rules, upgrades, or decision-making processes. As Finck observed, "power structures very much persist in respect of distributed ledgers".[25] Governance disputes can result in a fork, and in the case of a hard or continuous hard fork, the entire ecosystem of the blockchain is affected and may split.[26]

Smart contracts can also spark disputes. If poorly coded or flawed in logic, they are vulnerable to attacks or failure, risking users' assets—especially in Solidity-based systems like Ethereum.[27]

Smart contracts' on-chain shortcomings can be sorted into different categories of vulnerabilities. One of the most severe vulnerabilities of Ethereum Smart Contract is "Reentrancy" or "External Calls". This vulnerability relies on the interaction between two smart contracts.[28] Any public function in a smart contract can be "called" by any other contract. This means a malicious user could take advantage of this openness to exploit vulnerable functions.[29] In other words, if a contract makes an external call before updating its internal state, attackers can repeatedly withdraw funds before the balance is updated.[30]

Phishing can happen through "Tx.origin" or "Transaction Origin" vulnerability. Tx.origin would set the attacker address as the contract owner, giving the attacker full access to trick contracts into unauthorized actions, making it possible to instantly drain all the funds.[31]

Another precarious function of smart contracts on Ethereum is the "Self-destruct" or "Deprecated" function, used to delete contracts and lock funds.[32] If users do not update to a new contract address, they may send funds to the old one and lose them, something attackers can exploit by force-sending funds to manipulate balances.[33]

Even though the list of vulnerabilities is long, the final shortcoming introduced here is the aptly named "Timestamp Dependence".[34] This vulnerability occurs when "using the block timestamp as a condition to trigger and execute a transaction".[35] In Ethereum, miners create blocks and have some flexibility in setting a block's timestamp during the mining process. Since timestamps are often used as a seed for generating random numbers, attackers can manipulate them to influence a smart contract's behaviour in their favour.[36]

Each of these—from governance disputes to smart contract flaws—can cause real harm, often financial, to parties. When illicit acts, causation, and damage align, disputes inevitably follow. These disputes aren't limited to the codes or contracts; they can extend even beyond the chain into the real world. Known as off-chain disputes, they require further elaboration.

Off-chain Disputes

At first impression, off-chain blockchain-related disputes may seem similar to traditional legal conflicts. However, they possess distinct features that set them apart from conventional commercial disputes.[37]

Crypto economy is ridden with fraud, hack problems, and intellectual property infringement issues.[38] With the growing adoption of virtual assets, their role in the global economy has become significant. A 2024 review highlighted major growth in this sector, driven by favourable policies and macroeconomic trends.[39] As of writing, the total market capitalization of cryptocurrencies is valued at $2.73 trillion.[40] Yet, this rapid expansion brings legal challenges—especially around ownership, transaction validity, and rights security. The *Bybit* hack in February 2025, involving $1.5 billion in Ethereum, underscores the risks tied to custodial wallets.[41]

The lack of clear legislation, slow policy development, and regulatory ambiguity mean many disputes are inevitable. These may involve investors and exchanges, corporate transactions like mergers, or public sector regulations affecting crypto businesses.[42]

In 2022, over 200 individual and class action lawsuits, ranging from fraud and securities violations to consumer protection breaches, had been filed only in US courts, marking a 50% increase since the beginning of 2020.[43]

Blockchains and smart contracts' potentials and implications can be further explored within the context of the Metaverse. The Metaverse, as a parallel commercial realm to realspace, can also host transactions, title transfers, and any other legal and economic activities, provided these currently link back to realspace legal arrangements. It may operate as a digital marketplace where people interact, buy, sell, and conclude any type of contracts. Therefore, massive amounts of heterogeneous data will be acquired (just like banks or credit agencies do in realspace), generated, and stored.[44] The decentralized nature of blockchains will reduce the time necessary to identify parties[45] and their solvability and authenticate transactions.

Moreover, the use of blockchain technology will improve the flexibility and adaptability of the metaverse data and their storage.[46] Use of blockchain technology in Metaverse by blockchain-based platforms and cryptocurrencies will bring on-chain and off-chain disputes to the surface. The borderless nature of the Metaverse raises fundamental legal questions regarding applicable law and competent jurisdictions for the disputes. As such, the nature and scope of legal regulation in the virtual, intervening in blockchain disputes is far from settled.

Another concern for the governance of such disputes in the virtual is that smart contracts are rigid by design—unlike traditional contracts, they can't adapt to events like *force majeure* or changing circumstances. Once deployed on platforms like Ethereum, they run automatically, even if flawed.[47] To address this, "Upgradable Smart Contracts" were introduced, allowing changes to the contract's logic while preserving its state. However, this flexibility compromises immutability and predictability, and may reintroduce centralization into a decentralized system.[48]

Moreover, it is difficult, if not impossible, to incorporate the intent of the parties as such into a smart contract. Subjective concepts like reasonableness, fairness, etc. cannot be translated into mathematical codes.[49] In many respects this is a microcosm of the problems in transitioning law's essential normative foundations into digital governance.

In realspace, smart contracts also produce real-world effects, such as title transfers or payments.[50] While automated systems like decentralized autonomous organizations (DAOs) may seem dispute-proof, this is not always the case. For example, while creditors may not worry about collection, debtors must ensure payments aren't reclaimed—otherwise, disputes may arise.[51]

HOW TO DEAL WITH BLOCKCHAIN-BASED DISPUTES IN REAL WORLD AND VIRTUAL REALITY?

As discussed, blockchain-related disputes—whether on-chain, off-chain, in the real world, or in virtual reality—are pressing issues in digital commerce. Finding the most efficient, accessible, fair, and prompt answer to them is crucial not only for maintaining the flow of digital commerce but for upholding due process and fundamental human rights.[52]

As per William E. Gladstone, "Justice delayed is justice denied". It is an accepted adage in dispute resolution, especially when justifying the priority of alternative dispute resolution mechanisms in comparison to litigation.

Blockchain transactions, like those on Ethereum, occur in "real time", often within 12 to 15 seconds.[53] How "rapid" can the mechanisms for disputes based on Ethereum be? How long can be considered a delay? The effect of real-time technology makes us rethink the notions of justice and due process in temporal terms.

Traditionally, disputes arising from complex, tech-driven environments have required rapid, efficient, and often extra-legal mechanisms tailored to the nature of the conflict. Arbitration, with its flexibility, enforceability, and adaptability, has long been considered the most suitable alternative dispute resolution (ADR) method.[54]

With the emergence of E-Commerce Online Dispute Resolution (ODR) mechanisms, the technology in ODR is known as the "fourth party"[55] by not replacing the conventional third party, i.e., the arbitrators and mediators, but rather functions like an ally or collaborator.[56] ODR platforms are used by intermediaries like e-commerce sites, credit card companies, and startups to resolve claims ranging from consumer disputes to personal injury.[57]

As blockchain technology gains momentum, scholars believe that—being free from human limitations—ODRs are more efficient mechanisms than, say, litigation when it comes to blockchain-based disputes.[58]

The next section discusses blockchain-based Dispute Resolution (BDR) mechanisms, followed by a closer look at one of the most prominent platforms in this space: Kleros. The provision of this detail will offer a basis for reflecting on the wider possibilities for automated dispute resolution in the virtual, beyond financial contesting.

Blockchain-based Dispute Resolution: What Game Is Being Played?

Blockchain technology can provide a fertile ground to facilitate the dispute resolution procedure. Disputes can both arise in relation to blockchains or be settled through them.[59] To resort to any ADRs instead of resorting to litigation, parties should give their prior consent either in the main contract through a dispute resolution clause or afterwards through a separate agreement.[60]

On-chain transactions are conducted via self-enforcing smart contracts residing in a block.[61] To resort to the BDR process, smart contracts must contain an arbitration clause. A party wishing to activate the BDR process triggers the smart contract by directing a transaction to it.[62]

BDR platforms use blockchain's key traits—pseudonymity, decentralization, and immutability—and combine them with legal and economic imperatives and understandings to resolve smart contract disputes.

In this form of ADR, automation means a semi-automated process where human input remains essential as settlements rely on crowdsourcing and the idea that people act rationally in a democratic context, both assumptions being problematic in practice. Crowdsourcing is a decision-making process in the BDRs, mainly relying on putting disputes to a public vote, or "using the wisdom of the crowd".[63] This purely economic assumption implies that each juror will vote for the decision they anticipate the majority will favour.[64] Game theory and the Schelling focal point are among the main economic theories that platforms use to provide "an automatically available dispute resolution mechanism that can be encoded directly into the contract".[65]

Economists contentiously claim that in the absence of communication, individuals will naturally arrive at a consensual logical result. In addition to the rational assumption, consensual decision is reinforced in BDRs by the arbitrators' economic incentives, i.e., the distribution of the arbitration fee.[66] The system of reputation debits and credits, associated with the jurors' answers, is another motivation to vote in conformity with the majority position. In this way, jurors who vote in line with the majority gain reputation, while others face reputation deductions.[67] The reputation system entices the jurors to vote in consensus to augment their chances for the next random selection rounds.

Kleros, as the most prominent platform offering decentralized justice, relies heavily in practice on these theories.

Constructing a decision-making frame on assumptions of rationality, further influenced by financial incentives to conform, can be criticized for producing the impression of communal consensus, which instead is a way to diffuse disputes for the benefit of a preferred majority of stakeholders. The outcomes of such resolutions may not conform with principled notions of fairness and due process. The rationale is justice being seen to be done.

Kleros

Kleros is a token-based business built on the Ethereum blockchain network. Using game theory and rationality assumption, it provides smart contractual disputes with a series of on-chain courts.[68] Its system is powered by blockchain's inherent features and a crowdsourced jury model. Kleros developers believe that the anonymous nodes of a blockchain, in the absence of communication, can reach a consensus; this is the illustration of the Schelling focal point theory, whereby solutions are derived that seem natural or prominent due to shared expectations or cultural norms, allowing individuals to coordinate their actions without explicit agreement.

Kleros operates as a decentralized randomizer: jurors are selected randomly from among holders of its native token, PNK, who voluntarily nominate themselves. The selection process uses a random number generator based on the most recent block hash, which is repeatedly hashed to prevent prediction and manipulation. This ensures juror anonymity and reduces the risk of strategic interference.[69]

Kleros operates on Ethereum, requiring users to spend ETH on gas fees and purchase PNK tokens to participate.[70] PNK is used to either initiate disputes or enter the jury pool.[71] Jury selection is influenced by the amount of PNK staked, so more tokens mean a higher chance of being chosen.[72] Selected jurors have a portion of their tokens temporarily locked, while non-selected users have their full stake returned.[73]

Parties can submit evidence within a set timeframe.[74] Jurors vote by submitting a hashed vote containing their decision and a random "salt" value, ensuring vote secrecy.[75] The votes are not alterable. After the voting period, each juror should reveal their vote.[76] Those aligning with the majority receive arbitration fees; those who don't may lose part of their deposit.[77] A refusal to reveal a vote will result in a double penalty.[78] Consequently, the smart contract will be executed upon the voting.

An on-chain appeal mechanism is envisaged before the execution, allowing cases to be judged by small juries and avoiding "unnecessary duplication of effort".[79] Each appeal adds one juror to the previous panel, discouraging repeated appeals by increasing costs and complexity.[80]

It can be seen in this atmosphere of constructed consensus how the appearance of unanimity and democratic majority could be little more than the Queen's croquet game and her assertions of result above due process.

How Fair Is This Game?

On blockchain-based platforms, the outcome of decentralized justice is binding and can even surpass traditional rulings, since it is automatically enforced. Even if theoretically, it is still possible to appeal to a court, as the subject matter of the dispute is already transferred in an irreversible on-chain transaction to the opposing party, the court's decision on appeal does not have any practical effect on the appellant's legal sphere.[81]

This highlights the necessity of having a dispute resolution procedure that guarantees parties' procedural rights to a fair process, one even stronger than litigation and arbitration, to ensure access to justice. De Oliviera asserts that access to justice is not spending a day in a court or an arbitration institution, but to have a "sentiment of fairness" while a dispute is being settled.[82] Does the strict observance of due process requirements on-chain or during a proceeding in the virtual world result in a sentiment of fairness as well, and even so can this sentiment be translated into accountable procedural justice?

Due process consists of the minimum mandatory requirements in each proceeding that cannot be derogated by parties' agreements.[83] It first appeared in state court criminal procedure to guarantee the fundamental rights of defendants.[84] Additionally, these requirements are also mandatory in civil procedure as well as before extrajudicial arbitration tribunals.[85] Such mandatory requirements include ensuring that parties are given proper notice of the case and an adequate opportunity to present their case before an independent and impartial tribunal that treats them equally.[86]

These guarantees are incorporated in international instruments and institutional rules. For instance, Art. 17(1) UNCITRAL arbitration rules states that, "subject to these Rules, the arbitral tribunal may conduct the arbitration in such manner as it considers appropriate, provided that the parties are treated with equality and that at any stage of the proceedings each party is given a full opportunity of presenting his case …".

The New York Convention, adopting a permissive language in its Art. V(1)(b), affirms that the recognition and enforcement of awards "*may*" be refused when "the party against whom the award is invoked was not given proper notice of the appointment of the arbitrator or of the arbitration proceedings or was otherwise unable to present his case".[87] Article 34(2)(a)(ii) of the UNCITRAL Model Law reaffirms the same approach as grounds to set aside an award. These provisions have been adopted by many countries in their national arbitration laws.[88]

Blockchain-based platforms, while innovative, are not without their technological and legal limitations. One key issue is the potential bias in the impartiality of the decision-making panel. Jurors, influenced by game theory and financial incentives, may prioritize their economic interests over making a fair and just decision. Additionally, the right to present a case in an on-chain dispute is limited due to the one-time submission of documents, with arbitrators having no power to compel discovery.[89] This limitation can lead to adverse inferences and result in decisions that do not accurately reflect the complexities of the case. To address these challenges, some have suggested allowing state courts to intervene to assist the jurors or review the award post-hearing. However, this solution could undermine the decentralized nature of blockchain, which is designed to remove the need for a centralized authority to act as an intermediary.[90]

In practice, there is a delicate balance between the fear of violation of one's procedural rights and abuse of rights. Thus, tribunals are hesitant when dealing with allegations of due process violations, and rarely is an award set aside based on such allegations.[91] However, the fear of abuse of rights is not a sufficient justification to disregard the mandatory due process requirement.[92] Interestingly, while disregarding due process requirements is a big no-go zone, they have undergone several revisions and reinterpretations to align better with constitutional principles of procedural fairness.[93] This re-evaluation is particularly evident in arbitration, where adaptations have been made to better address their complex and high-stakes disputes.

In blockchain-based disputes, however, one doesn't necessarily face a high-stakes dispute; at least the majority of the time, they deal with small claims.[94] The complication here is not the dispute but the on-chain environment in which disputes occur and in which they are going to be resolved, which at this stage, as illustrated by Ortolani, is a terra incognita.[95]

The issue for assuring procedural fairness in a "decentralized justice" environment is whether another round of re-evaluation of the due process requirements is inevitable to align it with the constitutional rights of parties' access to justice and prerequisites of the New York convention for their recognition and enforcement. If so, how is this possible? Is regulating this environment by comparison with realspace ADR requirements and expectations practicable in the blockchain environment, and who is competent to achieve any such governance objective, the developers or the policymakers?

On-chain Sentiment of Justice

As mentioned, if access to justice is satisfied through recognizing a "sentiment of fairness" while a dispute is being settled,[96] is this sufficient to equate with how a fair procedure is perceived?

Fairness can be considered a "Decision Heuristic", replacing "a full exploration of the implications and possible motives of each directive from an authority".[97] Moreover, the "fairness-heuristic theory" suggests that people evaluate not only the process of a dispute settlement but also its outcome to form an overall impression of whether an authority is fair or not, and consequently whether they will comply with that outcome or not.[98]

The "fair procedure effect" is a phenomenon enabling parties to accept the outcome even if it is less favorable than they had anticipated or desired.[99] This effect is grounded in "self-interest theories". Accordingly, people's acceptance of decisions they receive depends on how they personally feel about it, whether it is evaluated objectively or subjectively.[100] Also, people's feelings about an outcome can be affected by their "egocentric bias" regarding what they define as "fair". Is this to be considered a problematic approach if justice is to mean more than impressions?

"Justice" is the most important value associated with law.[101] John Rawls in his "The Sense of Justice" paper draws inspiration from Rousseau's assertion that this sense "is no mere moral conception formed by the understanding alone, but a true sentiment of the heart enlightened by reason".[102] He illustrates the questions of justice and fairness with an example. In his view, those notions arise when individuals, all equal in status, come together to establish guiding principles of their institution and to ensure their observance.[103] Thus, an institution is fair when its principles are those that all its participants could agree upon freely and equally. It can be concluded that the foundation of the notions of "fairness" and "justice" can be traced back to the shared values and ethical considerations of the societies. Given that different societies and individuals hold different values, there is no single, absolute system of justice.[104]

As any system of justice is grounded in values that are not universally fixed or objectively determined but rather adopted based on cultural, historical, or philosophical perspectives of a given society, it is often argued that the foundations of justice are to some extent arbitrary.[105] This clarifies why no single, universal system of justice exists and why justice takes on different forms, degrees, and nuances in different societies.

Nowadays, the concept of justice has become more subjective and relative, losing its strong moral or ethical foundation and increasingly being viewed as derived from social agreements, hypothetical contracts, or personal experiences and emotions.[106] The relativity of justice means that its communal location and understanding is essential, and this is very much so with virtual communities.

Subjective and relative considerations of justice can evolve general understanding of procedural justice. It is commonly believed that the procedural justice judgments primarily originate from prosocial motives, including "social norms, moral values, and principles that dictate equality and impartiality".[107]

Van Prooijen assessed the possibility that procedural justice judgments are shaped by egocentric motives.[108] To that effect, when individuals have a personal stake in a complex moral dilemma, their fairness reasoning may be unconsciously influenced by self-oriented motives or egocentrism.[109] Egocentrism can be composed of a need to endorse fair procedures to achieve a satisfactory outcome for oneself, both tangible, such as monetary outcomes, and nontangible, such as social status.[110] One's need for structure in an uncertain world is also considered a component of Egocentrism.[111] He concluded that egocentric motives are of pivotal importance to understand an individual's fairness-based reactions to decision-making procedures and, in general, to procedural justice.[112]

Based on above-mentioned minimum procedural guarantees incorporated in law and provisions of different jurisdictions and confirmed in international conventions on the one hand, and the more subjective manifestation of justice and fairness on the other hand, one can conclude that procedural justice is not an absolute notion. That's why the phrase "procedural guarantees" in due process is always accompanied by the word "minimum". They can be nuanced from one society to another and can be to some extent even arbitrary. That may be why allegations of due process infringements are always looked at with circumspection in ADR contexts.[113] And that's why the degree of justice required in litigation is not the same as in arbitration. For instance, for the accepted value of "impartiality and independence", the requirement is slightly less strict in the former as compared to the latter.[114] Article 4 of the IBA Guidelines on Conflicts of Interest in International Arbitration provides for an *ex post* waiver of bias by parties wholly aware of potential conflicts and with a certain degree of decision-making power.[115]

Based on the arguments mentioned here, one can expect that the procedural guarantees in blockchain-based dispute resolution proceedings can also be re-evaluated to fit best with the peculiarities of this innovative technology. As long as the minimum due process can be ensured in such an environment and parties can have a sense of justice, BDR platforms will argue they provide another satisfactory means of access to justice to those wishing to resort to decentralized justice for their on-chain and off-chain disputes.

But when the issue is reduced to decentralized justice, participants and stakeholders might well be skeptical about how even "the minimums" will be guaranteed. BDR platforms are largely ungoverned creatures, not familiar with having external regulation imposed on them. The final section examines this issue.

From "Off With Their Head" To More Civilized Regulations?

I have earlier argued that maintaining justice and fairness in dispute resolution requires minimum mandatory rules, blockchain-based platforms being no exception. Enacting these rules on decentralized data structures is, however, a delicate topic.

From a computer scientist's point of view, the idea of regulating blockchains always provokes criticisms, as it seems to negate the "decentralization" characteristic.[116] Procedural law scholars, however, argued that the protocol-based decentralized communities, not exhibiting formal organization, need regulation to ensure accountability and safeguard the legitimacy of procedures.[117] Therefore, determining where to draw the line between legitimate regulation and the suppression of innovation in BDRs requires resolution if this emerging form of dispute resolution is to avoid producing substandard justice situations, particularly in the digital/virtual.

"Autopoietic Systems Theory" appears to be a compelling approach for resolving the regulation/autonomy dialectic. "Systems theory", as developed by Luhmann, sees modern society as consisting of distinct communication-based systems.[118] Each of them operates independently through "Autopoiesis", where any system creates and maintains itself through its own internal processes.[119] Systems are "cognitively open" processing external information, but "normatively or operationally closed", operating according to internal rules and logic.[120] Blockchain-based structures, it could be similarly argued, present the same characteristics in their governance and interactions as those described in systems theory for modern societies.

Regulation can be understood as "the use of legal instruments to implement social and economic policy objectives".[121] Applying regulation to an autopoietic system, the cognitively open and normatively closed aspects should be analyzed as distinct dimensions. Reflecting that "We tend to overestimate the effect of a technology in the short run and underestimate the effect in the long run",[122] those advocating for under-regulated technology highlight their positive aspects in reducing transaction costs and enhancing efficiency, which could be retarded if externally governed.[123] Conversely, techno-sceptics are concerned about the internal inflexibility of technology, and consequent social vulnerabilities in their application.[124]

While using blockchain technology in dispute resolution may seem like just adapting a tool for linking transactions and bridging on-chain and off-chain disputes, its impact runs deeper.

Reducing blockchain to a mere technological tool overlooks its distinctly decentralized and democratic nature. The "terra incognita" of blockchain technology is, however, too nascent and internally complex for legal scholars and policymakers to readily engage with. Uncertainty about how blockchains are created, operate, or their future impacts on one hand—and their dynamic and fast-evolving technological reach on the other hand—makes them seem intimidating subjects, too confounding to govern.

Framing blockchain merely as a tool risks oversimplifying the regulatory challenges it poses. If seen as a means to serve justice, it may be treated as just another "part" of the adjudicatory system—subject to external control. In democratic contexts, this location within the wider adjudicatory frame opens space to expand access to justice; yet in authoritarian regimes, external regulation can become a tool for surveillance and control.[125]

This holistic adjudicatory view may seem straightforward but reduces blockchain uniqueness by ignoring its core feature—decentralized, distributed data. Treating it merely as a tool for existing dispute resolution methods overlooks its original nature and leads to flawed, incomplete expectations. So, what would be the most suitable and grounded approach when applying this technology in on-chain and virtual worlds where its dispute-generating/resolving potential needs resolving?

One might draw a lesson from the Queen's croquet game in Alice in Wonderland, using it as an allegorical lens to illustrate the underlying complexities of the issue and to reach potential responses through an analogy. Balls, mallets, and hoops are simple "means" or "tools" to play a croquet game in any location. Take them to Wonderland, and mallets are live flamingos, balls are live hedgehogs, and croquet hoops are soldiers bent over in arches. Being alive and having autonomous willpower equipped them with characteristics that made a basic croquet game an arduous task for players, with a chaotic process and severe outcomes: "off with their heads!" The Queen cares more about asserting dominance in regulating this game by making up rules on the spot and changing them at will. The result is the infamously chaotic Queen's croquet game!

This vivid metaphor highlights the dangers of unaccountable, arbitrary rule-making in systems that lack mechanisms for normative challenge and cognitive engagement. It also warns against being mystified by representations and languages that belie what is really going on with the essential technologies of the game. Just as the Queen's game descends into absurdity due to her unchecked authority and sudden rule changes, regulating the blockchain environment without its "cognitively open" and "normatively closed" system will risk being arbitrary, unpredictable, and control-oriented, consequently resulting in chaos. That being said, as with the croquet game, failing to expose the internal irrationality and misperceived order within the game as the Queen would have it leaves the players at risk of exploitation and disempowerment.

Justice in such systems cannot be merely left to the decisions of internal logic, without the ability to challenge normative closure and without cognitive openness that connects to external reasoning. It requires openness to reason, fairness, and the realities of the disputants resorting to decentralized justice even in the virtual world.

To achieve this, one solution can be adopted and inspired by existing successful practices. For instance, the existing idea of "self-regulation" through protocols, governance structures, or consensus mechanisms, inspired by commerce and industry seems appealing. It is a win–win game for both developers and policymakers.

For developers, first, it will maintain the promised decentralization as the innovative and main characteristic of blockchain-based structures. By self-regulation of the dispute resolution procedure to respect minimum guarantees, they will stay away from potential legal liabilities, avoid the threat of more heavy-handed government regulation, and finally boost their reputation.[126] All in all, this will result in a viable and economically rewarding business for them, and for policymakers, who might "lack the necessary expertise or resources to run a successful regulatory program themselve*s*".[127] Interestingly, this is also a win for the on-chain disputant: instead of submitting their disputes to an unregulated platform-based procedure, they experience transparent and reliable dispute resolution ensuring respect for their procedural rights. At the end, blockchain-based disputants will experience a sense of justice and fairness, even in an on-chain virtual world.

CONCLUSION

The journey through the Wonderland of blockchain-based dispute resolution is accompanied by both promise and peril. On the one hand, the decentralized nature of blockchains offers a revolutionary approach to resolving disputes, free from the constraints of traditional legal systems. On the other hand, the absence of standardized procedural guarantees and regulatory oversight poses significant challenges to ensuring fairness and justice.

In human life today, in the era of intelligent automation and virtual systems, this technology continues to mature. Therefore, it is imperative that developers, legal scholars, policymakers, and users collaborate to establish a tailor-made framework that delicately balances innovation with the protection of fundamental rights.

Using the allegorical perspective of the Queen's croquet game serves as a metaphoric case example, reminding us that without clear rules and safeguards, the pursuit of justice can quickly descend into chaos. Finally, the success of blockchain-based dispute resolution will depend on the ability of stakeholders to navigate this complex terrain with a commitment to fairness, transparency, and accountability. Using social and philosophical theories, this study aimed to embrace the particularities of the underlying technology with both the potential and the pitfalls for dispute resolution mechanisms to rethink the notion of decentralized justice and sentiment of on-chain fairness in the digital age.

Moreover, the present study sought to find the most suitable regulatory approach to decentralized distributed platforms in the context of on-chain and virtual dispute resolution mechanisms. It advocates a win–win strategy of regulation for all stakeholders, i.e., developers, policymakers, and users (disputants or jurors), that recognizes the transformative potential of decentralized systems while remaining mindful of their characteristics, technical limitations, rapid evolutions, legal complexities, and formalities of the policymaking process for their regulation. So far, "self-regulation" strategies, like those being used by industry and corporations for decades, offer a compelling approach, comprehensive to all mentioned concerns. That said, the dangers inherent in self-regulation without some level of cooperation between internal compliance and external accountability, particularly when the governance terrain is novel and closed in its understanding, cannot be overlooked, and that is where managing cognitive openness in responsible and explicable ways is essential.

NOTES

1. Lewis Carroll, *Alice in Wonderland*, https://www.gutenberg.org/files/11/11-h/11-h.htm
2. Satoshi Nakamoto, "Bitcoin: A Peer-to-Peer Electronic Cash System", 2008, https://assets.pubpub.org/d8wct41f/31611263538139.pdf.
3. Nick Szabo, "Smart Contracts", unpublished manuscript, 1994.
4. Orna Rabinovich-Einy and Ethan Katsh, "Blockchain and the Inevitability of Disputes: The Role for Online Dispute Resolution", *Journal of Dispute Resolution* 2 (2019): 55.
5. Rabinovich-Einy and Katsh, 57.
6. Federico Ast and Clément Lesaege, "Kleros, a Protocol for Decentralized Justice", in *Dispute Revolution – The Kleros Handbook of Decentralized Justice* (Kleros.IO, 2017).
7. Kelsie Nabben, "Resilience as 'Political Decentralization': An Alternate History of the Cypherpunks Origins of Decentralised Technology", available at SSRN 3938626, 2021, 3, https://papers.ssrn.com/sol3/papers.cfm?abstract_id=3938626.
8. Nabben, "Resilience as 'Political Decentralization'", 1.
9. Rob Myers, "Blockchain Poetics", *Artists Re: Thinking the Blockchain* (1st edn, Torque Editions & Furtherfield, 2017), 239.
10. Alex Hughes et al., "Beyond Bitcoin: What Blockchain and Distributed Ledger Technologies Mean for Firms", *Business Horizons* 62, no. 3 (2019): 274.
11. Nakamoto, "Bitcoin".

12. Martín Nadal and César Escudero Andaluz, "Critical Mining: Blockchain and Bitcoin in Contemporary Art", *Artists Re: Thinking the Blockchain* (2017): 73.
13. Emanuel Palm, "Architectures for Automated Contractual Cooperation" (PhD Thesis, Luleå University of Technology, 2021), 22, https://www.diva-portal.org/smash/record.jsf?pid=diva2:1553738.
14. Nick Szabo, "Formalizing and Securing Relationships on Public Networks", *First Monday* (1997), http://firstmonday.org/ojs/index.php/fm/article/view/548; Konstantinos Christidis and Michael Devetsikiotis, "Blockchains and Smart Contracts for the Internet of Things", *IEEE Access* 4 (2016): 2296; Christian Sillaber and Bernhard Waltl, "Life Cycle of Smart Contracts in Blockchain Ecosystems", *Datenschutz und Datensicherheit-DuD* 41, no. 8 (2017): 498.
15. Christopher D. Clack, Vikram A. Bakshi, and Lee Braine, "Smart Contract Templates: Foundations, Design Landscape and Research Directions", arXiv Preprint arXiv:1608.00771, 2016, 2.
16. Christidis and Devetsikiotis, "Blockchains and Smart Contracts for the Internet of Things", 2297.
17. Eliza Mik, "Blockchains: A Technology for Decentralized Marketplaces?" *Impact of Technology on International Contract Law: Smart Contracts and Blockchain Technologies, Forthcoming*, 2018, 162, https://papers.ssrn.com/sol3/papers.cfm?abstract_id=3264565.
18. Christian Schönfeld, "Smart Contracts under Swiss Law", *Fintech Hub, London* (2018): 4, https://www.prager-dreifuss.com/en/news/smart-contracts-under-swiss-law-296.
19. Schönfeld, 4.
20. Wang, Lumineau, and Schilke, 5.
21. Katarzyna Szczudlik, "'On-Chain' and 'Off-Chain' Arbitration: Using Smart Contracts to Amicably Resolve Disputes", *Newtech.Law* (blog), June 4, 2019, https://newtech.law/en/articles/on-chain-and-off-chain-arbitration-using-smart-contracts-to-amicably-resolve-disputes.
22. Nino Sievi and Viola Donzelli, "Chapter 1: Crypto Arbitration – Is It Really a Thing?" in *Transforming Arbitration: Exploring the Impact of AI, Blockchain, Metaverse and Web3*, ed. Sean McCarthy (Radboud University Press, 2025), 23, https://library.oapen.org/handle/20.500.12657/98058.
23. Michel Rauchs et al., "Distributed Ledger Technology Systems: A Conceptual Framework", available at SSRN 3230013, 2018, 56, https://papers.ssrn.com/sol3/papers.cfm?abstract_id=3230013.
24. Rauchs et al., 22.
25. Bianca Kremer, "Blockchains, Smart Contracts, and International Arbitration: The Emergence of a Crypto Autonomous Legal Order" (Switzerland, St. Gallen 2022), 127, https://www.alexandria.unisg.ch/entities/publication/18e1f2df-829b-4f42-b788-3e682b00930b.
26. Kremer, 124.

27. "Solidity and Smart Contract Vulnerabilities on Ethereum I QuickNode Guides".
28. Ardit Dika and Mariusz Nowostawski, "Security Vulnerabilities in Ethereum Smart Contracts", in *2018 IEEE International Conference on Internet of Things (iThings) and IEEE Green Computing and Communications (GreenCom) and IEEE Cyber, Physical and Social Computing (CPSCom) and IEEE Smart Data (SmartData)* (IEEE, 2018), https://ieeexplore.ieee.org/abstract/document/8726833/.
29. Sendner et al., "Smarter Contracts", 3.
30. Zhou, Milani Fard, and Makanju, "The State of Ethereum Smart Contracts Security", 365.
31. Alexander Mense and Markus Flatscher, "Security Vulnerabilities in Ethereum Smart Contracts", in *Proceedings of the 20th International Conference on Information Integration and Web-Based Applications & Services* (iiWAS2018: 20th International Conference on Information Integration and Web-based Applications & Services, Yogyakarta Indonesia: ACM 2018), 369, https://doi.org/10.1145/3282373.3282419; Zhou, Milani Fard, and Makanju, "The State of Ethereum Smart Contracts Security"; Dika and Nowostawski, "Security Vulnerabilities in Ethereum Smart Contracts".
32. "Solidity and Smart Contract Vulnerabilities on Ethereum I QuickNode Guides".
33. Zhou, Milani Fard, and Makanju, "The State of Ethereum Smart Contracts Security", 367.
34. Mense and Flatscher.
35. Mense and Flatscher.
36. Dika and Nowostawski, "Security Vulnerabilities in Ethereum Smart Contracts"; Mense and Flatscher, "Security Vulnerabilities in Ethereum Smart Contracts"; Perez and Livshits, "Smart Contract Vulnerabilities", 9.
37. Sievi and Donzelli, "Transforming Arbitration", 24.
38. Kremer, "Blockchains, Smart Contracts, and International Arbitration", 119.
39. "Virtual Assets 2024 Review and 2025 Outlook – KPMG China", KPMG, December 19, 2024, https://kpmg.com/cn/en/home/insights/2024/12/virtual-assets-2024-review-and-2025-outlook.html.
40. "Cryptocurrency Prices, Charts And Market Capitalizations", CoinMarketCap, accessed April 1, 2025, https://coinmarketcap.com/.
41. Faarea Masud, "Cryptocurrency Theft of $1.1bn Could Be Biggest Ever, Says Bybit", *BBC*, February 22, 2025, https://www.bbc.com/news/articles/cx2844nvwx8o.
42. Sievi and Donzelli, "Transforming Arbitration", 24.
43. Elizabeth Chan, Nicole Tang, and Edward Taylor, "Crypto Disputes: The Valuation Challenge", *Dispute Resolution International* 17 (2023): 28.
44. Pasika Ranaweera et al., "Blockchain for the Metaverse: A Review", *Future Generation Computer Systems* 143 (2023): 407–8.
45. Ranaweera et al., 408.
46. Ranaweera et al., 409.

47. Governatori et al., "On Legal Contracts, Imperative and Declarative Smart Contracts, and Blockchain Systems".
48. Xiaofan Li et al., "Characterizing Ethereum Upgradable Smart Contracts and Their Security Implications", in *Proceedings of the ACM Web Conference 2024* (WWW '24: The ACM Web Conference 2024, Singapore: ACM 2024), 1884, https://doi.org/10.1145/3589334.3645640.
49. Schönfeld, "Smart Contract under Swiss Law", 9.
50. Schönfeld, "Smart Contract under Swiss Law", 11, 15.
51. Sievi and Donzelli, "Transforming Arbitration", 24.
52. Sebastiano Nessi, "Arbitration, Human Rights and Due Process: Recent Developments in Switzerland", *Arbitration Blog*, July 19, 2016, http://arbitrationblog.practicallaw.com/arbitration-human-rights-and-due-process-recent-developments-in-switzerland/.
53. Seungmin Jeon, "Future of Ethereum (1): Beam Chain", *Medium* (blog), January 6, 2025, https://medium.com/@organmo/future-of-ethereum-1-beam-chain-52492e39af62.
54. Gary Born, *International Commercial Arbitration*, vol. 1 (Kluwer Law International, 2009), 250–55.
55. Daniel Rainey, "Glimmers on the Horizon: Unique Ethical Issues Created by ODR", *Dispute Resolution Magazine* 21 (2014): 40.
56. Janet Rifkin, "Online Dispute Resolution: Theory and Practice of the Fourth Party", *Conflict Resolution Quarterly* 19, no. 1 (2001): 121.
57. Cindy Shearrer, "Library Guides: Online Dispute Resolution: Companies Implementing ODR", 2020, https://libraryguides.missouri.edu/c.php?g=557240&p=3832247.
58. Rabinovich-Einy and Katsh, "Blockchain and the Inevitability of Disputes", 57.
59. Orna Rabinovich-Einy and Ethan Katsh, "Access to Digital Justice: Fair and Efficient Processes for the Modern Age", *Cardozo Journal of Conflict Resolution* 18 (2016): 57.
60. Bernhard Berger and Franz Kellerhals, *International and Domestic Arbitration in Switzerland* (Bloomsbury, 2015), 94; Born, *International Commercial Arbitration*, 1:3.
61. Clack, Bakshi, and Braine, "Smart Contract Templates", 2.
62. Narges Keshavarz Bahadori, "Due Process Requirements in Blockchain-Based Arbitration", in *Yearbook of Private International Law Vol. XXIV–2022/2023*, ed. Andrea Bonomi, Ilaria Pretelli, and Gian Paolo Romano (Verlag Dr Otto Schmidt, 2023), 168.
63. Ast and Lesaege, "Kleros, a Protocol for Decentralized Justice".
64. Ast and Lesaege.
65. Clément Lesaege, "Long Paper v2. 0.2 Clément Lesaege, William George, and Federico Ast July 2021", 2021, https://kleros.io/static/yellowpaper_en-8ac96b06f39f19a6a28106cf624e3342.pdf; James Metzger, "The Current Landscape of Blockchain-Based, Crowdsourced Arbitration", *Macquarie Law Journal* 19 (2019): 87.

66. Narges Keshavarz Bahadori, "Due Process Requirements in Blockchain-Based Arbitration", in *Yearbook of Private International Law Vol. XXIV – 2022/2023*, ed. Andrea Bonomi, Ilaria Pretelli, and Gian Paolo Romano (Verlag Dr Otto Schmidt, 2023), 179, https://doi.org/10.9785/9783504388454.
67. Metzger, "The Current Landscape of Blockchain-Based, Crowdsourced Arbitration", 94.
68. See Kleros board in: http://klerosboard.com/ last accessed on 15 November 2024.
69. William George, "Why Kleros Needs a Native Token?" *Medium*, 11 July, 2018, 136, https://medium.com/kleros/why-kleros-needs-a-native-token-5c6c6e39cdfe.
70. Luis Bergolla, Karen Seif, and Can Eken, "Kleros: A Socio-Legal Case Study of Decentralized Justice & Blockchain Arbitration", *Ohio State Journal on Dispute Resolution* 37 (2022): 58.
71. Bergolla, Seif, and Eken, 58.
72. Keshavarz Bahadori, "Due Process Requirements in Blockchain-Based Arbitration", 179.
73. Clément Lesaege and Federico Ast, "Short Paper v1. 0.7 Clément Lesaege, Federico Ast, and William George September 2019", 2019, 34, https://kleros.io/whitepaper.pdf.
74. Michael Buchwald, "Smart Contract Dispute Resolution: The Inescapable Flaws of Blockchain-Based Arbitration", *University of Pennsylvania Law Review* 168 (2019): 1395.
75. Buchwald, 1395.
76. Lesaege, "Long Paper v2. 0.2 Clément Lesaege, William George, and Federico Ast July 2021", 14.
77. Lesaege, 14.
78. Buchwald, "Smart Contract Dispute Resolution", 1390.
79. George, "Why Kleros Needs a Native Token?" 111.
80. Lesaege and Ast, "Short Paper v1. 0.7 Clément Lesaege, Federico Ast, and William George September 2019".
81. Cemre Ç. Kadıoğlu Kumtepe, "Chapter 2 – Defining Boundaries of Due Process in Blockchain Arbitration", in *Transforming Arbitration: Exploring the Impact of AI, Blockchain, Metaverse and Web3*, ed. Sean McCarthy (Radboud University Press, 2025), 61.
82. Leonardo V.P. de Oliveira, "To What Degree Should Access to Justice Be Secured in Arbitration", in *Access to Justice in Arbitration: Concept, Context and Practice*, ed. L. V. P de Oliveira and Sara Hourani (Wolters Kluwer, 2021), 12.
83. Huseyin Alper Tosun, "Public Policy Concepts in International Arbitration" (PhD Thesis, UC Berkeley, 2019), 48.
84. Lucy Reed, "Ab(Use) of Due Process: Sword vs Shield", *Arbitration International* 33, no. 3 (2017): 366.
85. Reed, 367.
86. Reed, 366.

87. Bernard Hanotiau and Olivier Caprasse, "Arbitrability, Due Process, and Public Policy under Article V of the New York Convention-Belgian and French Perspectives", *Journal of International Arbitration* 25 (2008): 727.
88. Zoran Jordanoski, "Due Process as Minimal Procedural Safeguard in International Commercial Arbitration", *Iustinianus Primus Law Review* 8 (2017): 6.
89. Keshavarz Bahadori, "Due Process Requirements in Blockchain-Based Arbitration", 190.
90. Keshavarz Bahadori, 191.
91. Benjamin Ainsley Gill, "Due Process Paranoia: Need We Be Cruel to Be Kind", *Journal of International Arbitration* 34, no. 6 (2017): 936.
92. Gill, 936.
93. Keshavarz Bahadori, "Due Process Requirements in Blockchain-Based Arbitration", 190.
94. Alessandro Palombo, Raffaele Battaglini, and Luigi Cantisani, "A Blockchain-Based Smart Dispute Resolution Method", n.d., 549.
95. Ortolani, "The Impact of Blockchain Technologies and Smart Contracts on Dispute Resolution", 243.
96. de Oliveira, "To What Degree Should Access to Justice Be Secured in Arbitration", 12.
97. E. Allan Lind et al., "Individual and Corporate Dispute Resolution: Using Procedural Fairness as a Decision Heuristic", *Administrative Science Quarterly* (1993): 225.
98. Lind et al., 226.
99. Leo Montada and Jürgen Maes, "Justice and Self-Interest", in *Handbook of Social Justice Theory and Research*, ed. Clara Sabbagh and Manfred Schmitt (New York, NY: Springer New York, 2016), 120, https://doi.org/10.1007/978-1-4939-3216-0_6.
100. Lind et al., "Individual and Corporate Dispute Resolution", 227.
101. Wojciech Dziedziak, "Thoughts on the Notion of Justice", *Studia Iuridica Lublinensia* 30, no. 2 (2021): 140. And the references therein.
102. John Rawls, "The Sense of Justice", *The Philosophical Review* 72, no. 3 (1963): 281.
103. Rawls, 282.
104. Dziedziak, "Thoughts on the Notion of Justice", 141.
105. Dziedziak, 141.
106. Dziedziak, 140.
107. Jan-Willem van Prooijen, "Egocentrism in Procedural Justice Effects", *Justice* (2008): 31.
108. van Prooijen, 31.
109. van Prooijen, 49.
110. van Prooijen, 50.
111. van Prooijen, 50.
112. van Prooijen, 46 and 50.
113. Gill, "Due Process Paranoia", 936.

114. Keshavarz Bahadori, "Due Process Requirements in Blockchain-Based Arbitration", 186.
115. Matti Kurkela and Santtu Turunen, *Due Process in International Commercial Arbitration* (Oxford University Press, USA, 2010), 127.
116. Buchwald, "Smart Contract Dispute Resolution", 1404.
117. Primavera De Filippi and Benjamin Loveluck, "The Invisible Politics of Bitcoin: Governance Crisis of a Decentralized Infrastructure", *Internet Policy Review* 5, no. 4 (2016): 14, https://papers.ssrn.com/sol3/papers.cfm?abstract_id=2852691.
118. John Paterson, "Decentralised Finance, Regulation, and Systems Theory", *Oñati Socio-Legal Series* 14, no. 5 (2024): 1301.
119. Paterson, 1301.
120. John Paterson and Gunther Teubner, "Changing Maps: Empirical Legal Autopoiesis", *Social & Legal Studies* 7, no. 4 (December 1998): 459, https://doi.org/10.1177/096466399800700401.
121. Molly Cohen and Arun Sundararajan, "Self-Regulation and Innovation in the Peer-to-Peer Sharing Economy", *University of Chicago Law Review Dialogue* 82 (2015): 119.
122. Christian Crews, "How Far to Look Ahead?" *Research-Technology Management* 62, no. 5 (September 3, 2019): 59, https://doi.org/10.1080/08956308.2019.1638487.
123. Ortolani, "The Impact of Blockchain Technologies and Smart Contracts on Dispute Resolution", 431.
124. Schönfeld, "Smart Contract under Swiss Law"; Christidis and Devetsikiotis, "Blockchains and Smart Contracts for the Internet of Things", 9.
125. Paterson, "Decentralised Finance, Regulation, and Systems Theory", 1311.
126. Daniel E. Walters and Hannah J. Wiseman, "Self-Regulation in Emerging and Innovative Industries", *Houston Law Review* 62 (2024): 555.
127. Walters and Wiseman, 555.

13. Touching wonderland: the emancipatory power of haptics in the Metaverse

Jonathan Fiene and Philipp Müller

INTRODUCTION

In Lewis Carroll's Alice's Adventures in Wonderland, one of the most striking scenes unfolds when Alice participates in the Queen of Hearts' croquet game. Instead of mallets and balls, she is given a live flamingo and a hedgehog. As she attempts to play, the flamingo wriggles and twists in her hands, refusing to remain rigid, while the hedgehog scampers about, making it nearly impossible to align her shot. Although this episode is full of Carroll's trademark absurdity, it also speaks to a deeper truth about physical interaction: we rely on both tactile and proprioceptive feedback to manage objects and anticipate how they will respond to our touch. In Wonderland, this feedback loop is comically disrupted, just as it often is in contemporary digital environments, where we can see and hear elaborate virtual worlds but remain deprived of convincing tactile cues.

Such disjunction between sight, sound, and touch is especially pronounced in today's instantiation of the Metaverse. Over the past few decades, video and audio technologies have advanced dramatically: graphical resolutions now approach photorealism, and spatial audio systems allow us to locate sounds with uncanny accuracy. Yet haptics—the science and application of touch—continues to lag far behind. While rudimentary force-feedback joysticks and vibration motors were introduced in the 1980s, widespread adoption and refinement of haptic technologies have not kept pace with the exponential growth seen in the audiovisual domain. As a result, the Metaverse, despite its promise of full immersion, often reproduces the limiting conditions of earlier digital spaces—enchanting to the eyes and ears, but strangely mute to the sense of touch.

To understand why this matters, it helps to distinguish between tactile and proprioceptive feedback. Tactile input involves the sensations our skin detects—pressure, vibration, and texture—while proprioception informs us of our body's position, the tension in our muscles, and the forces we exert to move or hold something still. Together, these senses underpin a continuum of embodied experience, from mundane tasks such as handling utensils to more complex activities like playing a musical instrument or, in Alice's case, maneuvering a live flamingo mallet to strike a hedgehog. Depriving digital environments of these vital cues can render virtual interactions awkward, imprecise, or outright disorienting.

Beyond mere convenience or "enhanced realism," haptic technologies carry an emancipatory potential. Human beings, evolutionarily disposed to seek efficiency, often find themselves passively entertained by screen-based media. True embodied engagement, however, can awaken untapped reserves of skill, curiosity, and creativity. By integrating tactile and proprioceptive elements into virtual contexts, the Metaverse could evolve into a space that invites meaningful exploration and personal growth, rather than just offering another avenue for passive consumption. Indeed, just as Alice's adventures in Wonderland compel her to adapt and innovate in a world of shifting sizes and unpredictable inhabitants, robust haptic feedback can challenge and refine our motor and cognitive capabilities, enabling us to become more active participants in constructing and understanding our digital experiences.

Yet how can haptic technologies unlock this emancipatory potential in digital environments, and what challenges—technical, ethical, and economic—stand in the way of their broader integration? These questions animate the central inquiry of this chapter. By examining the current state of haptic research, contextualizing its slower trajectory relative to audio and video innovation, and exploring real-world barriers, we will uncover both the promise and the pitfalls of designing for touch. In so doing, we seek to establish that a more tactile Metaverse is not merely an aesthetic upgrade but a fundamental shift in how we engage with digital spaces.

To address these issues, the chapter proceeds in four parts. First, it frames haptics by exploring its scientific foundations and illustrating its relevance to everyday human experience. Second, it outlines the evolutionary arc of audiovisual technologies, offering a comparison that highlights why haptics remains relatively undeveloped. Third, it details the upsides of haptic integration, revealing how touch can amplify immersion, enhance learning, and foster unique synergies. Finally, it confronts the ethical and practical challenges of implementing haptics at scale, paying particular attention to questions of cost, access, and the potential for tactile illusions to undermine rather than enhance user experience. By weaving these threads together, the chapter argues that haptic innovation is essential to creating a Metaverse that is not only visually stunning or aurally rich, but also capable of stimulating the full breadth of our perceptual and cognitive faculties—leading us, like Alice, toward a world where wonder and embodied engagement go hand in hand.

I. EMANCIPATION, EMBODIMENT, AND HAPTICS: A CONCEPTUAL FRAMEWORK

Technology, for all its promise as a force of emancipation, has repeatedly revealed a paradoxical nature. The printing press democratized literacy while consolidating editorial power in certain hands; the internet enabled instantaneous global communication yet entrenched new forms of digital inequality. True emancipation therefore demands more than eradicating barriers—it requires enabling individuals to fully act, create, and engage. Haptic technologies hold remarkable promise in this regard because they address a dimension of human experience that has been all but excluded from traditional digital domains: the complex interplay of body, movement, and touch.

Central to haptics' potential is the principle of embodiment, a core theme in fields ranging from phenomenology to cognitive science. Embodied cognition theory suggests that our minds and bodies form an integrated system; the sensory feedback we receive from our muscles, skin, and joints directly shapes how we perceive and interact with the world. In most digital interfaces, however, visual displays and auditory cues overshadow this embodied aspect, leaving us to operate in a disembodied, purely representational mode. Haptic technologies reverse this marginalization of the body. By incorporating tactile sensations and proprioceptive feedback, they anchor users in virtual spaces, allowing them to feel grounded, exert force, and sense resistance in ways that mirror real-world interaction.

At least three primary levels of haptic engagement illustrate how such technologies can serve an emancipatory function. First, enhanced proprioception supports more intuitive navigation and interaction within virtual environments. When a user can feel resistance or pressure, movement in digital spaces becomes less abstract and more akin to physical action. Second, tactile communication leverages vibrations, forces, and other stimuli to convey meaning, emotion, or urgency, moving beyond purely visual or auditory signals. This opens the door to subtler, more immediate forms of interpersonal expression and information transfer—much like a reassuring hand on a shoulder in the physical world. Third, adaptive feedback loops foster learning and skill acquisition by providing real-time, touch-based cues calibrated to the user's actions. This immediate feedback can expedite the development of fine motor skills or professional proficiencies that would be difficult to master through screens and sounds alone.

Together, these facets of haptic technology set the stage for a digital landscape that is not only more immersive but also more aligned with human sensory–motor systems. By bringing the body back into the equation, haptics counters the disembodied drift common to earlier digital innovations. In doing so, it allows individuals to engage with virtual environments as fully embodied agents—an experience that can catalyze creativity, agency, and personal growth. From this vantage point, haptics does more than simply add "realism" to the Metaverse; it has the potential to emancipate users from the passive consumption models that have long dominated screen-based interactions, nudging them instead toward more active, imaginative, and holistic modes of participation.

II. THE ARC OF DEVELOPMENT: FROM RUDIMENTARY TO HYPER-REALISTIC

Technology evolves in waves, with each new generation often surpassing the last in scope, scale, and finesse. This pattern is readily observable in audiovisual technologies. In the 1970s, digital audio systems were limited to rudimentary beeps and monophonic outputs; by the turn of the millennium, innovations such as Dolby Surround and sophisticated compression algorithms had revolutionized sound quality, immersing audiences in multi-dimensional audio landscapes. A similar leap can be seen in video: from grainy, monochrome displays to 8K ultra-high-definition screens that render minute details with astonishing clarity. Each developmental arc reflects a concerted, multi-decade effort by engineers, researchers, and commercial enterprises to push the frontiers of fidelity and accessibility.

In contrast, haptic technology has lagged behind these rapid advances. Its current state of development is roughly where digital audio stood in the early 1980s—awareness of its importance exists, but wide-scale, high-fidelity solutions remain elusive. While a variety of haptic devices has been introduced, most offer only basic forms of tactile or force feedback: simple vibrations (as in gaming controllers), simplistic force feedback (as with early flight simulators), or motion-tracking gloves that deliver rudimentary touch cues. Such systems can be effective under certain conditions but often sacrifice realism for cost and convenience. Consequently, they can require users to develop a mental "translation" layer—mapping the device's limited haptic output onto the far more nuanced sensations they would expect in a real-world scenario. This cognitive effort not only dampens immersion but also underscores the infancy of haptics relative to other sensory technologies.

The Interface: Distance and Intimacy in Haptic Design

One reason haptic development has remained comparatively stalled lies in the intimate nature of touch. Audio and video engage senses at a perceptual "distance"—sound waves reach our ears without physical contact, and light reaches our eyes similarly. In contrast, touch is fundamentally close-range and requires specialized interfaces to make virtual contact feel real. Unlike wearing headphones or gazing at a screen, integrating tactile feedback often involves wearables, specialized gloves, or full-body suits—introducing layers of cost, complexity, and practical inconvenience that can deter mainstream adoption. Indeed, the more realistic and encompassing the system aims to be, the bulkier or more expensive it often becomes, creating a significant barrier to entry for everyday users.

Additionally, it is critical to distinguish tactile (skin-based) from proprioceptive (muscle and joint-based) feedback. Tactile technology focuses on simulating surface sensations like texture or pressure on the skin, while proprioceptive systems aim to replicate force and resistance, helping the user sense where their limbs are in space. Achieving both forms of feedback with precision requires diverse technological strategies.[1] For instance, localized vibration feedback can simulate a textured surface, but simulating the weight of an object or the rigidity of a surface demands more complex force-feedback mechanisms.

The Challenge of Realistic Haptic Integration

While there are commercially available products—such as "rumble packs," vibration-enabled XR controllers, and cyber gloves—that can provide limited forms of feedback, these solutions have drawbacks. They may offer only a "one-size-fits-all" vibration, so users must mentally interpret the haptic signals rather than perceive them as naturally corresponding to the virtual stimulus. Alternatively, systems that attempt more realistic force feedback (through exoskeleton rigs, suspended cables, or complex mechanical linkages) often prove cumbersome and prohibitively expensive, limiting their application to specialized industrial or research contexts.

Researchers have advanced numerous creative solutions to tackle these issues, experimenting with ultrasonic levitation, electro-tactile stimulation, pneumatic actuation, and more. Each approach attempts to replicate aspects of real-world touch—texture, pressure, temperature, weight, or resistance—yet each faces engineering and design challenges. Even the most promising prototypes must reckon with comfort, safety, power consumption, and cost-effectiveness. Moreover, inconsistent feedback or mechanical glitches can break the immersive illusion, throwing the user into what has been termed the "uncanny valley of haptics,"[2] where partially convincing sensations feel more unsettling than no haptic feedback at all.

Consequently, the haptics domain remains in a state analogous to audio technology before the widespread adoption of compact discs or the MP3 format—tangible progress, but still lacking a defining breakthrough or standard that can propel it into the mainstream. Until such a leap occurs, the average user's experience of the Metaverse will likely continue to be a largely visual and auditory affair—dazzling to the eyes and ears, but muted in terms of embodied engagement. In the next section, we explore how emerging haptic innovations and design strategies are poised to overcome these barriers, and why doing so may prove essential for realizing the full emancipatory potential of the Metaverse.

III. FROM DISEMBODIMENT TO EMPOWERMENT: THE UPSIDES OF HAPTIC INTEGRATION

In one of her more bewildering encounters, Alice finds herself at a never-ending tea party, unable to fully grasp the social dynamics or the objects around her. The teacups shift in size, the chairs move on their own, and the table settings refuse to stay in place. It is a scene of perpetual disarray—yet Alice's frustrations are as much about her uncertain, disembodied role in this nonsense as they are about the nonsense itself. She can see the teacups and hear the rapid-fire chatter of the Mad Hatter and March Hare, but she cannot confidently maneuver or control her surroundings. In much the same way, users in digital environments often glimpse impressive virtual vistas, hear immersive soundscapes, and even move an avatar through simulated spaces—yet the absence of any true sense of touch leaves them similarly unmoored. This disconnect speaks directly to the critical role haptic feedback can play in anchoring us within virtual domains, turning what might otherwise be an extended state of confusion into a more concrete and empowering experience.

The key lies in translating passive observation into active participation. When users can feel texture, pressure, or resistance, they are no longer mere spectators; they become embodied agents capable of real-world-like interactions. Such tactile grounding makes it easier to develop muscle memory, fine-tune motor control, and react spontaneously to changes in the environment. This heightened immersion can be especially useful in educational or professional simulations, where real-time tactile cues expedite learning. The aspiring surgeon, for example, who practices suturing on a haptically enabled simulator gains an intuitive grasp of force and precision that purely visual interfaces simply cannot deliver.[3] Athletes refining their technique with haptic feedback gain an embodied understanding of posture and balance, while musicians practicing intricate finger placements on a virtual instrument receive immediate, localized corrections that accelerate skill acquisition. Through these direct, tangible interactions, individuals are not only learning tasks faster but also cultivating a deeper sense of self-efficacy—a hallmark of emancipatory experience that moves technology from a passive medium to an active catalyst of personal growth.

Such gains in personal agency extend beyond formal learning contexts to encompass broader social and emotional dimensions as well. Touch has long been understood as one of the most intimate and immediate forms of communication—capable of conveying reassurance, empathy, and urgency in ways speech or images cannot. In a digitally mediated world, haptics can bring this intimacy back into interpersonal connections. Tele-haptic systems, for instance, allow remote users to share a handshake, a reassuring pat on the shoulder, or even an embrace. These tactile exchanges can bridge emotional distance far more effectively than video chats or text messages alone, fostering a sense of presence and trust. Similarly, collaborative efforts—whether they are in creative design, gaming, or remote teamwork—become more seamless when participants can co-manipulate objects and feel each other's contributions. This shared sense of touch encourages collective problem-solving and mutual attentiveness, generating a more cohesive group dynamic that is otherwise difficult to achieve through screen-based interfaces.

Beyond these social and skill-based benefits, haptic feedback holds potential for genuinely novel experiences that merge or even transcend conventional sensory boundaries. Researchers in human–computer interaction have begun to experiment with synesthetic applications of haptics, where tactile signals are purposefully mapped onto non-tactile data. A data visualization might, for example, use subtle vibrations to represent temperature changes or textural patterns to signify different data streams. Such cross-sensory designs can deepen comprehension, making abstract concepts more accessible by turning them into something one can literally feel. These exploratory projects hint at a horizon of creative possibility in which haptics acts not merely as an extension of existing senses, but as a gateway to new modes of perception, a form of emancipation that expands the contours of what it means to learn, communicate, and experience.

However, just as Alice discovers that Wonderland's eccentricities can also harbor hidden perils, the benefits of haptics come with caveats. The data collected by haptic devices—ranging from heartbeat rhythms to patterns of pressure exerted—can be sensitive, demanding thoughtful privacy protections and user consent protocols. And although sophisticated systems promise near-seamless immersion, high costs and specialized equipment can reinforce existing inequalities, relegating advanced haptics to privileged contexts. Striking a balance between innovation and accessibility, protection and exploration, is crucial if we are to ensure that haptics truly empowers individuals, rather than reinforcing existing barriers or creating new ones. Even so, the core takeaway remains: by reintegrating the sense of touch into digital interaction, haptic technologies have the power to move users from a state of disembodied detachment to one of active, creative engagement. This shift from passive witness to embodied participant underscores haptics' immense potential for emancipation—helping people learn faster, collaborate more effectively, and expand their sensory horizons in ways that were once inconceivable.

IV. ETHICAL DIMENSIONS OF HAPTICS IN THE METAVERSE: ENSURING EMBODIED EMPOWERMENT

Lewis Carroll's Alice's Adventures in Wonderland often underscores the allure and risk of powerful illusions. Although Wonderland shimmers with opportunity, its inhabitants wield arbitrary rules and perplexing transformations that can overwhelm Alice's sense of agency. A parallel risk emerges in haptically enabled Metaverse experiences, where ever-more convincing tactile illusions may either expand human freedom or undermine it, depending on how these systems are designed, governed, and commercialized. As haptic technology advances beyond simple vibrations toward full-body, lifelike sensations, questions of privacy, autonomy, and equitable access demand urgent attention.

One of the foremost ethical considerations arises from the intimate data haptic devices collect. Unlike purely visual or auditory media, tactile interfaces glean real-time information about a user's body, including muscle movements, pressure patterns, and even physiological responses indicative of stress or excitement. This depth of insight can enhance user experiences—adapting tasks to one's skill level or monitoring fatigue during rehabilitation—but it also raises concerns about bodily integrity. Without rigorous data protection standards, sensitive biometric signals might be commodified, exploited, or weaponized, creating unprecedented invasions of privacy. Establishing clear boundaries for data collection, storage, and sharing becomes essential, as does informing users—beyond boilerplate consent forms—about the scope and implications of what is tracked.

On the commercial side, haptics holds the potential to enrich digital engagements and open revenue streams for businesses specializing in immersive entertainment, education, or communication. Yet this very potential can lead to exploitative practices if developers design haptic feedback loops to influence purchasing decisions, prolong screen time, or shape user behavior through micro-manipulations of force and pressure. A core principle of ethical haptics is thus user autonomy. Individuals need transparent, user-friendly ways to calibrate or disable haptic features, ensuring that tactile cues operate as forms of empowerment rather than covert persuasion. Research institutions and industry leaders share a responsibility to establish community-driven guidelines or review boards that evaluate haptic applications for psychological manipulation or intrusion.

Beyond privacy and autonomy, there is the challenge of ensuring that haptic technology does not exacerbate existing inequities. Advanced hardware such as full-body exoskeletons or sophisticated force-feedback rigs can be prohibitively expensive, limiting access to well-funded institutions or affluent consumers. If the most immersive and realistic haptic experiences remain out of reach for many, new social and economic divides may emerge. Equitable access to haptic devices and platforms becomes particularly pressing when these tools are deployed in critical areas like medical simulation, physical therapy, or educational programs where their benefits could be transformative. Businesses can mitigate such disparities by adopting modular designs that allow gradual, affordable upgrades or by open-sourcing core aspects of their technology to encourage broader innovation. Governments and funding agencies can foster pilot projects in underserved communities, ensuring that haptic opportunities for learning or healthcare do not become the exclusive domain of the privileged.

The question of governance cuts across all these concerns. In order to develop haptic systems that genuinely expand human capacities rather than restrict them, policymakers, technology companies, and academic researchers must cooperate. Shared ethical standards—potentially modeled on existing frameworks for medical devices or data protection—can set baselines for transparency, fairness, and accountability. Public–private partnerships might support large-scale studies that gather empirical data on user safety and well-being, informing regulations grounded in actual practice. Researchers can play a pivotal role by publishing open data on device efficacy, privacy protocols, and unintended side effects, thereby fostering a spirit of scientific exchange and replicable evaluation.

Crucially, ethical frameworks must regard haptics not merely as an adjunct to audiovisual media but as a domain in which the human body becomes an integral interface with technology. In Carroll's Wonderland, encounters unfold through a series of physical transformations—changes in size, battles with animate objects—that unsettle Alice's understanding of her own body and environment. Likewise, haptic systems can reshape how users perceive and inhabit the Metaverse. If these systems are designed and governed ethically, such transformations can be liberating, allowing people to cultivate new skills, deepen emotional bonds, and explore creative horizons. However, if developers prioritize profit over user welfare, or if regulations fail to keep pace with innovation, the same tactile capabilities could facilitate surveillance, social control, or commodification of intimate biological signals.

Ensuring that haptics fulfills its emancipatory promise thus entails a complex interplay of technological ingenuity, business responsibility, and public oversight. Together, these stakeholders can forge a landscape in which users benefit from heightened immersion, personal growth, and meaningful social connections—free from manipulative or exploitative practices. In Carroll's tale, Alice eventually confronts Wonderland's arbitrariness and reclaims her autonomy by challenging the capricious authority around her. In a similar spirit, a collective commitment to ethical design and governance can steer haptic technology toward true embodied empowerment, enabling immersive and transformative digital experiences that remain respectful of individual rights, societal equity, and human dignity.

CONCLUSION

From Alice's tangled adventures on the croquet field to the emerging frontiers of the Metaverse, this exploration has illustrated how vital touch is to human experience—and, by extension, how pivotal haptics can be for the future of digital interaction. At its core, haptic technology tackles a fundamental shortcoming in our virtual worlds: the absence of meaningful, embodied contact that undergirds so much of our perception, cognition, and emotional life. Rather than relying solely on visuals and sound, integrating tactile and proprioceptive feedback can profoundly increase the sense of immersion, skill development, and interpersonal connection we derive from virtual spaces. In so doing, haptics raises the possibility of transforming passive consumers into active participants, furthering the emancipatory potential that technology so often promises but rarely delivers.

Yet realizing this vision is no straightforward endeavor. While audio and video have enjoyed decades of exponential growth in fidelity, haptics lags behind, challenged by engineering hurdles, economic pressures, and the inherent complexity of recreating a distributed sensory system across the entire human body. Moreover, as the technology matures, it brings with it weighty ethical concerns that echo the paradoxes of Wonderland: if haptics endows us with unprecedented immersion, it also opens new avenues for data collection, behavioral manipulation, and social inequality. Ensuring that these capabilities enhance rather than erode personal agency will require concerted efforts from researchers, businesses, and governments. Only through collaborative governance, community-driven standards, and careful attention to equitable access can haptic systems evolve as tools of genuine empowerment.

Alice's journey ultimately underscores how disorienting yet transformative it can be to enter a realm where the usual rules of interaction are upended. Similarly, as the Metaverse expands and haptic technologies become more prevalent, our digital encounters will demand fresh adaptations and new ways of thinking about embodiment. The reward for meeting these challenges, however, could be extraordinary: a more inclusive, dynamic, and richly textured digital world that respects human dignity and expands our capacity to learn, create, and connect. By forging haptic solutions that marry technical ingenuity with ethical foresight, we stand poised to usher in a chapter of digital development that not only enthralls the eyes and ears but also, and perhaps more importantly, reclaims the human body's place at the center of the virtual stage.

Taken together, the contributions offer more than thematic insight; they form a methodological exercise in rethinking governance and personhood through the lens of the Metaverse. Rather than offering answers, they explore tensions and paradoxes that resist resolution: the coexistence of property and sharing, control and openness, presence and absence, linear and fragmented time. Questions of value, public interest, and responsibility are traced not as fixed coordinates, but as evolving negotiations within these immersive environments. In this way, the Metaverse is not treated as a destination, but as a moving framework, a conceptual space where known concepts are reconsidered and reimagination takes place.

NOTES

1. Katherine J. Kuchenbecker, "Haptics and haptic interfaces," in *Encyclopedia of Robotics* (Springer, Berlin, Heidelberg, 2018, pp 1–9). https://link.springer.com/rwe/10.1007/978-3-642-41610-1_19-1
2. Christopher C. Berger, Mar Gonzalez-Franco, Eyal Ofek, and Ken Hinckley, "The uncanny valley of haptics," *Science Robotics* 3, no. 17 (2018): eaar7010.
3. Jacinto Colan, Ana Davila, and Yasuhisa Hasegawa, "Tactile Feedback in Robot-Assisted Minimally Invasive Surgery: A Systematic Review," *The International Journal of Medical Robotics and Computer Assisted Surgery* 20, no. 6 (2024): e70019.

PART V

Back up the digital rabbit hole

Introduction to Part V

Noha Lea Halim and Sofie Schönborn

Turning back toward realspace, we carry what we learned in virtual wonderlands into our everyday lives. This last section begins with a final reflection on power, personhood, and governance, an echo of the book's central thread that authority in the metaverse both inverts and intensifies real-world asymmetries, and that meaningful governance requires finding a voice, contesting nonsense, and securing human integrity in digital spaces.

We then offer a glossary-like kaleidoscope of perspectives. We call it a kaleidoscope because shifting vantage points, terms, and experiences produce new patterns rather than a single, fixed picture about "the metaverse." The entries, curated from our contributors, map multiple imaginaries, facets, and logics of virtual worlds.

Together they serve as a reader's guide and interpretive toolkit: prompts to question assumptions, compare frames, and rethink how virtual worlds are governed by law and norms, code and markets, communities and platforms. Stepping "back up" the rabbit hole, we invite you to look again at familiar realities with refracted insight and to keep turning the tube.

Source: Generated using DALL-E, building on the original illustrations from Alice's Adventures in Wonderland, drawn by John Tenniel, https://www.alice-in-wonderland.net/resources/pictures/alices-adventures-in-wonderland/

Figure V.1 Back up the digital rabbit hole

14. Dreaming on the riverbank – governance and power?

Mark Findlay[1]

Alice in Wonderland is a story of power and its negotiation. It locates power in vibrant contexts of change and crisis. Metaphorically, Alice's journey of personal discovery mirrors the challenges to personhood that pepper a digital universe. The characters she encounters represent and live out many of the reasons why realspace power relations are inverted in digital space. At the same time, oppressive power asymmetries traverse realspace into the virtual and can be exacerbated if governance counter-movements are not fit for purpose in transformative environments.

As a child, Alice enters Wonderland structurally and situationally disempowered. She was used to the dominion of hierarchical authority, whether that was parents, teachers or the myriads of rules and conformities that governed her inferior status and limited autonomy. In Wonderland she comes up against similar frames of power/governance, but they do not operate in ways she has been programmed to expect from ordered society. The more she reacts against the illogicality of these frames, the more the legitimacy of their realspace parallels can be questioned.

Initially, Alice confronts power plays with her wits. She recalls what she has learned in the past that has given her comfort, identity and positive responses from her elders. When she is dealing with the Caterpillar's hectoring, she tries to recite a poem she would have memorised, but fails to satisfy her critic. Interestingly, the poem is a conversation between a youth who is confused not by aging but by the ability to laugh at it, and an elderly male who turns aging on its head. The poem ends with the old man asserting his power by threatening force – the exercise of blunt authority unable to contend criticism. It is only when she seems to gain some control over her expanding and diminishing physical presence by a measured acceptance of the Caterpillar's fantastical advice, rather than reaching back to what would have gained approval (the faultless recitation of a poem), that Alice conjures up a plan to get into the beautiful garden.

In her encounter with the Caterpillar, her mushroom eating and the sulky pigeon, Alice came to accept the possibilities presented through radical change. The Caterpillar presented itself as an authority figure but in the end offered the solution to her concerns about changing too often, as resting in her own measured ingestion of the mushroom. As for the pigeon, a stronger, more assertive Alice sees it off with a more convincing argument about a little girl's preference for eggs.

When she meets the absurd and unchecked authority of the King and Queen of Hearts, exhibiting all the arbitrariness on which the misuse of power often relies, Alice finds her own voice. She settles the questions about executing the Cheshire Cat's head by removing the authority from the King, the Queen and the Executioner and reverting to the cat's rightful owner. This is not only wise; it is crafty. And to draw out the madness of the Knave's trial (and indeed Wonderland for the present), Alice, in regaining her full size, has the confidence to unmask all around her – '"Who cares for you? … You are nothing but a pack of cards!"'[2]

In confronting power, gaining a voice, managing change, finding an identity and most of all embracing imagination, Wonderland would always be for Alice a wonderful dream. As a metaphorical tool for the contributors and their readers, Wonderland offers three questions concerning governance, personhood and the virtual:

What is governance?

What should be governed?

How can governance secure power in the virtual?

Relying on the metaphorical experience, I will unpack each of these in turn.

WHAT IS GOVERNANCE?

In Wonderland, governance is a process of individual and collective empowerment to confront abusive power. For instance, the Jabberwock is a tyrannical creature causing fear and threatening chaos through a destructive use of its physical power. It is overcome using a vorpal sword – the power of language and reason above violence. But the underlying lesson in the poem is the need to be vigilant against abusive power in all its forms and to take action that does not exert the same form of power through fear and cruelty.

The conventional styles of governance that might in realspace be relied upon to confront abusive power, such as rules, justice and law, are sometimes revealed in Wonderland as little more than abuses in themselves, exhibitting nonsensical logic and language. Thus, if law is to be invoked in the virtual it may need to be transformed so that its normative values overcome its paradoxical practices.

Yet, as a governance frame, it could be said that law as we know it has not been as innovative or malleable as the technological and digital advances that formulate the digital universe. If this is so, how can those who believe that law should be relevant in the virtual enliven thinking about and acting out law so it offers more than an aspirational normative language for governance in the virtual?[3]

Perhaps the legal system can be seen as being in a co-evolutionary relationship with frontier technology. In other words, while law by default emphasises the application of existing norms when new phenomena such as disruptive technologies emerge – a functional response rooted in the idea of the 'rule of law' itself and a mechanism to help stabilise societies confronted with change – there are moments of change in the law that can be tied to technological advancement.

The interesting question, then, is under what conditions such 'evolutionary' advancements occur? Typically, this occurs as a blend of legal tradition, cultural attitudes, and – above all – matters of political economy and, increasingly, geopolitical considerations that shape whether and when the 'law' evolves in one direction or another.

Another question is how the law evolves in such moments? Different patterns emerge, ranging from gradual adjustments (e.g., where a court borrows a doctrine from patent law and applies it in copyright law – the inducement theory in secondary liability where consciousness of another's wrongdoing transfers, being a case in point) to more radical 'innovations,' which typically involve legislators (the EU AI Act might fall into this category). Taken together, these 'responses' of the legal system – including instances of insisting on existing rules being complied with, gradual upgrades or more fundamental change across rights, processes, institutions and methods – are aimed at providing stability on the one hand (recognising too much legal change typically signals revolution) and facilitating socio-technical transformation on the other. It's a delicate, complex dance – particularly because it's decentralised with no single conductor orchestrating it with foresight or anticipation.

Given the law's default posture as a regulatory language in realspace, it should not be surprising if the application of existing legal norms within familiar procedural and institutional frameworks is currently the dominant pattern when arguing that present governance frames can translate into the virtual – particularly in areas such as IP (intellectual property) rights and consumer protection (as some of these traditional frameworks are now being activated in 'metaverse' courts, such as recently in Colombia). Perhaps there are also early traces of gradual innovation – for instance, in the context of digital assets and NFTs, or in the realm of governance and DAOs (decentralised autonomous organisations). Presumably, some of the gaps in law's transition will eventually be addressed by gradually expanding existing doctrines or even enacting new laws.

The notion of co-evolution, no doubt, has great historical substance, particularly considering legal systems and applications, as well as reflecting on how law responds to the interfacing of humans and technology. In public law, the development of state police, particularly in the US with the task of regulating a disciplined and predictable workforce at the time of industrialisation in the 1800s, is such an example. The radical repositioning of capitalist obligation through the Factories Acts in the UK gave birth to the expansive judicial and administrative organs responsible for industrial health and safety; likewise the explosion of telecommunications legislation and their judicial positioning as the telephone lines branched out across the world. The advance of national security legal paraphernalia and policing, as the technologies of pervasive surveillance bloomed during the Covid pandemic, is closer to our experience.

But does a preference for revolution over co-evolution rest in the novelty of this new technological era and its propensity foe seismic change, making the law/tech tension different this time around? These differences can be manifested in four realms. The first is structural, where jurisdictional distinction is melting away due to globalisation, the rise of the corporate megaliths, and the information economy – meaning that much of international law and its frames are eroded or disempowered. The second is a deeper tension that emerges as a consequence of the fragility of the neoliberal global economic order. Whether it is the shaken institutions of world trade or more broadly the inability of law to secure property rights as it once could, law's marketability is less profitable. The third is the collapse of the public/private divide. This can be seen in how public and private data sources merge in mass data sharing through the online delivery of multiple social services and associated datification. Finally, populist politics has profoundly undermined the teleology of the rule of law, as it blames legal regulation for every failing of social, commercial and material ordering. In its discourse, law is a plaything of elites or something to be sidelined in preference for authoritarian dealmaking and power supremacy above rules-based international relations. The impact of such representations of law and law enforcement on popular wisdom should not be underestimated. Therefore, this era of the law/tech tension is significantly different from other times when law and tech adjusted to each other, if not in a symbiosis, but rather through occasions of pragmatic reformulation.

A central governance challenge posed by AI-assisted technology and, more essentially, its voracious manipulation and consumption of data is the disenfranchising of human decision-making. Like other regulatory languages, law has not crafted modern answers to this beyond adjusting its traditional remedies and protections to pressing commercial threats, somewhat on the run.

Administrative frames like personal data protection regimes focusing on individual rights and privacy violations are not providing global coverage, nor are they adapting to data re-use situations.

No doubt, there are emerging examples of where legal systems, institutions and processes are adjusting to and accommodating digital technology, but these are too localised and specific to represent a wave of repositioning. Along with such examples there are many other situations of mimicking or distorting legal/juridical mechanisms to achieve dispute resolutions in digital contexts. As with the preference for regulation through ethical compliance, the advocates of unencumbered or self-regulated tech appear to be endorsing and adopting 'soft' legal processes and principles. An example is the questionable application of 'juries' by Kleros and others in marketing their version of blockchain dispute resolution (BDR) – 'juries' that are paid to come up with the right answer and punished if they don't.

Returning to the suggestion that law and tech are co-evolving with (or within) the digital universe is under-explored or plagued by missed opportunities, perhaps any answer rests in how we perceive law and the metaverse. When concentrating on how law is delivered via legal systems (and associated systems of technology), the contributors to this book do evidence specific interests in system-based engagement (like legal personhood for AI creations, legal protections for gender endangerment, legal containment of frontier tech, etc.). However, more than this, the contributors often sideline law as some lesser governance paradigm when thinking about managing the power asymmetries between humans and tech. Facing this, one missed opportunity is the chance to argue more broadly for the value of governing AI in a manner respectful of proactive and responsible innovation, and particularly to say law (and its systems) are relevant in doing so. Too often it is assumed that governance is good, and law has a place in it. Such cannot be assumed in the metaverse. The argument for law's broad relevance as a governance frame will not be convincing enough by selectively identifying instances in metaverse commerce, or social, political and economic human activity where law as we know it can be adapted to provide some governance potential. This approach means that we will be fighting fires as they emerge rather than transforming the place of law within digital space. You can find many examples in the contributions to the book where law could be adapted to have governance impact. It is not too difficult to construct legal remedies against avatar harassment that might result in the award of damages to the image maker or impose some broad sanction against perpetrators. But each of these falls back to whether courts, police and the institutions of law enforcement can or should have a place in the virtual.^

Moving away from missed opportunities towards a more fundamental conception of under-exploration of what law should and will look like in the virtual, there cannot be any holistic co-evolution of law and frontier tech without a fundamental rethink of two essential understandings of realspace law. The first focuses on law as form. Much of what law does and is valued for in realspace relates to the commodification of private property. In this role, law can become a commodity in itself. Should this role continue in the virtual, then there needs to be much more critical consideration given to the nature of markets in the metaverse, the nature of property in the virtual (and data's alliance with property) and how law can ensure commercial valuing in spaces and arrangements where technology and human use do not reach consensus that conventional property rights should be respected as they are presumed to be in realspace. For the advocates of transiting law and markets and property into the metaverse, this fundamental thinking needs much more energy. The second understanding is law as a social fact. If, as Ehrlich wanted, lawyers should supplement their technical knowledge bases with observations about local social regulation, then the law needs to recognise the contextual differences of any digital universe and apply this understanding to help craft institutions, processes and outcomes to which it can contribute. An example is Intellectual Property. Many of the 'creations' that currently employ AI-assisted technology are made not to financially benefit exclusive licence holders. Instead, they may be 'valued' in the way they create celebrity, identity, community location, enjoyment, art-for-art's sake. If law is only employed to protect 'rent' for the use of these creations, then it remains confined in its own language of ownership and alienation. In practical terms, the missed opportunity is developing law and its systems to help identify and enhance new ways and forms of social valuing. This sounds revolutionary, but, as we have seen from the commercial wash-up of the unauthorised downloading generation, it may be located in quite mundane market and social relations.

If the metaverse is the product of social construction and not just commercial opportunism, then whether the 'social' employs technology to create the digital universe does not define the transcendental space beyond indicating how it can be entered and maintained. If living in a digital realm involves a collective sensemaking process, the metaverse is like any other social space that employs the makings of humans to create a dynamic social experience – thus it is a space more than it is a thing or a place that can be owned or marketed. The missed opportunity for law within this interpretation is through behaving like a regressive agent reproducing systems from the past, rather than acting as a world-making tool.

Technological transformation introduces multiple legal life-worlds, being unique and different spaces for the existence and operation of the law. In this context, new domains (and terrains) of digital technology create a pluralist legal universe that takes on original shapes and relationships under conditions of globalisation. As such, the globalising of markets and the development of multi-national commerce and the creation of non-state dependent digital currencies have been pressuring private law particularly to adjust even without the transition into the virtual.

WHAT SHOULD BE GOVERNED?

Living in the virtual is the growing experience of those who share the demographic of our young voices. This life experience can range from occasional gaming and sharing through digital communities and advance on to using the potentials of frontier technology to broadcast creativity or in establishing multiple identities. Whatever the purpose for transiting into the virtual, people want both freedom and safety, and these should not be seen as mutually exclusive aspirations.

In *The Machine Question: Critical perspectives on AI, robots and ethics*[4] David Gunkel takes up the issue of who or what deserves ethical consideration. Initially limited to 'other men', gradually moral philosophy came to consider foreigners, women, animals and even the environment. Today autonomous, intelligent machines of our own making are called upon to be ethical. There is an emerging fear that, like Hal in Stanley Kubrick's *2001: A Space Odyssey* or Mary Shelley's *Frankenstein*, frontier technology could turn on its human creators unless we somehow invest it with moral agency. Gunkel considers the genuineness of this endeavour as deciding who is and who is not a legitimate moral agent by asking whether technology exists within or outside a community of moral subjects. The place of AI-assisted technology embedded in its recipient communities cannot be established merely by placing ethical requirements on the ecosystems that produce it. More than this, there is a need to empirically establish that AI can work for the benefit of communities and not only for the few who might have commercial or political power over its placement and proliferation.

With AI-assisted information technology currently acting as the gateway into and sustainer of life for human moral subjects in the digital universe, the focus of governance endeavours in large part over this powerful function should be to ensure that human life experiences in the virtual are safe and liberating. To achieve this, governance strategies that stop with general ethical frameworks or particular rights protections like privacy may not provide a sufficiently communitarian approach that is required for governing the conditions under which human flourishing is ensured. Whether they prefer external or internal regulatory tools, some having their origins in realspace and others innovated for the virtual environment, our contributors all argue for governance that enlivens personhood when existing in digital social spaces.

So, the answer to what should be governed is both universal and context specific, but it is rooted in how we want personhood to have integrity in the unique environment of a digital universe. An example may make this assertion clearer. One of our contributors is a songwriter and performer. He has chosen to market his music to a community of followers and admirers using digital pathways and AI-assisted communication technology. Employing these pathways and technologies, he can create and record his music on his own if he wishes and then manage its marketing, distribution and valuing. In terms of the latter, he can enjoy a mix of personal satisfaction, celebrity and material reward without having to share these with an exclusive licence holder or some intervening agent. Before these digital technologies became available and affordable, he would have been contracted to a recording company and tied to all the phases of their commercial and legal governance over his creation. Therefore, in many senses, technology has enabled him to create and participate in a community audience that brings him much closer to his personhood as a musician than could have been possible without digitising and technological pathways. It would appear that his transit into the virtual provides him with autonomy, liberty and a sense of safety to enjoy how he prefers to value creativity.

However, there are questions of moral agency that intervene at vital stages in this apparent freedom. For his music to reach his audience, he needs to engage a distributor. This involves finding a commercial entity that has access to the major digital sharing platforms and signing a contract of service. In selecting such an entity, he reads reviews from communities of users and confirms to his satisfaction that the *ethical direction* of this entity seems to suit his aspirations. At this point, he has used the views of a community to select a community use platform (all in realspace) to reach his virtual community. What perhaps he has not considered in detail is who benefits most from the terms of the contract of service he has signed, and the extent to which the royalty dimension of the distributor and the digital sharing platform could possibly infringe his autonomy and personhood. Up until this point, the external governance features involve a web of contracts and any uncertain claims of intellectual property. The internal governance features are more consensual, appearing as download measures, audience reception, and transactable rewards back to the creator. What remains unclear are the market imperatives driving the distributor and the sharing platform, and the nature of moral agency they assume in providing the technology. No doubt these stakeholders in our creator's community would see the limits of their moral agency set out in the contract of use.

Assume for the sake of this example that our creator later receives email correspondence from the distributor that his music has been removed from the sharing platform due to what they refer to as having detected a significant amount of artificial streams on his music loaded on the sharing platform. The distributor justifies their action with the suggestion that these artificial streams amounted to fraudulent activity, although it does not allege who is responsible for the fraud. This notification is the first that our creator has heard of any artificial streaming, and he responds firmly to the distributor, warning that they should not interfere with his copyright, and that as he has no knowledge of the streaming, he cannot be involved. He demands that the tracks be reinstated.

Here we have what the creator sees as disarming governance challenges. With his music removed from the sharing platform he cannot reach his audience or his community – or enjoy his rewards. The artificial streaming occurred in the virtual and as the creator has no way of knowing the details of this activity, he can do little to challenge the details of the distributor's invocation.

This is a telling example of how the context may change but the commodification of music remains the same. Access to the digital realm gives you what seems to be freedom to circulate your music, reach your wider, like-minded audience, improve your notoriety with that audience, and allows you to take over many of the roles that once were only available through a recording contract. However, in reality you are controlled by the terms of mega streaming platforms, their distribution arms and their royalty agencies. As in this case, they can shut off your access and broadcasting based on unproven allegations and reverse the onus of proof. You are forced to deny activity about which you are not in a position to know sufficient detail, because you are innocent of the allegations. In fact, only if you were associated with what they say is unauthorised streaming (whatever that may be) would you know the details that they allege you need to deny.

From a governance perspective, the scenario shows how impotent external regulation through recourse to IP is to protect the creator's personhood. The creator can assert copyright and creative ownership over the songs that have been removed, but in so doing, the distributor and the sharing platform would respond that in this action they are not breaching those 'rights' but instead accusing actors unknown of fraud in manipulating the downloads that will advantage the creator's royalties. More than this, the distributor is acting as the streaming platform's agent to protect their control over streaming and their customer measures of popularity. The creator is not in a position to refute their allegations beyond asserting his prior good behaviour, and the risks posed by anonymous unauthorised streaming, against which he can do little to protect his creations. The alleged fraudulent activity could only occur through the use of digital technology and virtual space. The reason that the distributor and streamer have reacted so harshly is that the legitimacy of their consumer response measures is crucial to the commercial valuing of their activities.

Often, when it comes to governing these huge digital monopolies, they are not concerned about IP protections in realspace because they were born out of its violation. As for other realspace legal remedies, there are few or none that apply, and it is likely that the contract terms to which the creator signed up with the platform and the distributor contain a variety of conditional clauses that protect their total discretion in these situations. As an occasion of power asymmetry, the contract terms would rarely be negotiated with individual users, who either sign or forgo the provision of service. In such situations, consent offered by the user is anything but free.

What innovative governance strategies are on offer? How can the creator contest the reversal of proof obligations like these and answer the fraud implications? He cannot, and thus in realspace thinking the contract and the nature of unauthorised streaming give the distributor and the sharing platform an unassailable position of power. So much for liberty and dignity in the creator's digital life experience and that of his audience and community.

What to do? The one thing that hurts these information distribution giants, and particularly their smaller feeder firms, is an attack on reputation and undermining consumer and collaborator confidence. Examining the reviews of the distributor's service, which drew the creator to sign up with them, their business viability relies on the confidence of individual contracting parties in the integrity of their service. Understanding the commercial value of community approval and trust in their virtual trading gives the creator a governance tool that he and his audience community can activate and participate in its impact. They can threaten and enact reputational damage that can, by employing social media and other digital communication avenues, force the distributor to re-evaluate its exercise of discretion.

This case study shows that the appearance of moral agency may be valued by stakeholders. But appearance is not sufficient to ensure fair treatment procedurally if powerful commercial players think their market status is at risk. In this situation, moral agency needs to be given teeth through community resistance and reaction. The creator cannot rely on external institutional governance backup but instead can call upon integrated and representative governance intervention that takes the form of bargaining community trust.

HOW CAN GOVERNANCE SECURE POWER IN THE VIRTUAL?

Returning to the broad statement that governance is a process of levelling abusive power asymmetries, governance in the digital universe needs to first identify the nature, extent and location of any such asymmetries and then innovate remedies that benefit human stakeholders and their communities. Our contributors identified many specific power asymmetries that regularly arise in realspace and transit into the virtual. Where and how these asymmetries originate and how they are sustained will determine whether they can be governed by already existing regulatory regimes in realspace (in part or completely) and if on transiting into the virtual they assume new forms requiring novel governance interventions.

As the case study in the section above demonstrates, the use contract was settled between the distributor and the creator under realspace legal provisions and, as such, its enforcement will rely on realspace legal institutions and processes. However, the contract is for services that are digital and expand into virtual environments, affecting virtual communities. If the clauses in such a contract could be seen as unconscionable or even abusive, they might be challenged under realspace law, but if they only create a power imbalance that does not allow for legal action, but seriously impacts the enjoyment of the creator and his audience community in the virtual, then other forms of governance need to be devised.

Digital transformation has produced revolutionary challenges to established governance frames in realspace and in the virtual. An area of human endeavour that is particularly relevant to our young voices, embarking on careers now and in the future, is employment. Promoters of platform economies that rely on what they refer to as franchised (or independent contract labour) have asserted that they offer disruptive employment arrangements and relationships that shake off the confines of conventional employment regulation. They argue that the platform is not an employer but merely provides a communication frame through which contract service providers and customers can transact. As such, the workers should not expect from the platforms the type of benefits and guarantees that the law often determines and enforces over parties in traditional employment arrangements. There is no doubt that these labour forms have radically reshaped private hire vehicle services and food delivery networks. But even in these less-skilled labour fields, the courts in many jurisdictions have rejected the laissez-faire claims from platform operators and instead determined these to be employment relationships that, while disruptive, still necessitate employer/employee regulation of more conventional forms.

Our contributors are likely to progress into employment situations with more professional connotations. Even so, they will work in worlds where the previously understood conditions governing capitalist wage labour are changing fast. While they will not have to struggle against the mythical assertions of the platforms regarding the disruption of itinerant labour, they will still face challenges regarding the rewards of work, the conditions of employment, and the extent to which the incursion of AI and frontier technologies are reformulating working demographics and environments.

AI, information technology and digital transformation are adding to the waning neoliberal reliance on wage labour, due to the disengagement of capital from labour as the means of production. In the current age of info capitalism, AI applications and AI-assisted technology purport to replace human labour not just in mundane and repetitive work, but more and more in situations of data management and associated decision-making, which would have once been the province of young professionals. The interests and marketability of tertiary education are shifting radically to accommodate work futures that are heavily AI-reliant. Higher up the labour chain, the lure of innovation (and the fascination with start-ups as a trajectory for new ideas to make millionaires) is seeing what once was professional labour (lawyers, doctors, architects, etc.) being incorporated by AI (and its dependencies), via workplace cultures of convenience, and this is creating entirely new calibrations of labour value. Through this, the promoters of AI can reach well beyond itinerant and low-skilled labour in their advance on reshaping capitalism in the image of AI. The dependencies evolving in this new world of work will be fertile opportunities for abusive power asymmetries. Take as an example what is expected of young law graduates entering law firm structures. There has been a recent rush to technologise almost every aspect of data analysis and document evaluation in professional legal service delivery. Contracts are being drafted by ChatGPT, algorithms are doing discovery, and due diligence compliance is determined through AI. Some larger firms have enormously expanded their case-load portfolio using AI because those time-consuming information and data analysis tasks that once made the risky costs involved in running more problematic cases prohibitive have been contained through automation. As positive as this all sounds, if it leads to greater legal representation and lower charges to clients (neither perhaps necessarily the firms' primary reason for digitising), there are downsides to this trend. The demographic of legal firms has changed radically. Legal secretaries, paralegals and junior lawyers have become expendable labour as technology can perform their routine functions quicker, cheaper and without the ancillary obligations. What impact this transition has had on the reality of in-house legal training is yet to be fully evaluated. Young lawyers are expected also to be coders and responsible for the analysis and decisions offered by AI-assisted applications. Ironically, the young lawyer is in charge of overseeing the accuracy and probity of the technology that is eating away at her job security. Professional responsibility (and liability perhaps) is being passed down from the technologically unskilled senior partners to younger lawyers who may not be able to convince their seniors of their employment value or promotion prospects, who are more interested in AI-assisted profit outcomes than how these efficiencies are achieved.

Move all this into the young professional operating in employment and market environments that are predominantly virtual, and the risks of unprotected exploitation through abusive power asymmetries and absent governance frames are exacerbated. What can be done to protect the integrity and liberty of their personhood in the workplace?

Let's return to Alice's journey, which could be seen as losing and regaining control over her personhood. Whether it be through shocking physical changes, confronting belligerent and idiosyncratic characters, losing her capacity for language or facing down oppressive authority and its foolish rules, every aspect of the identity she knew, the life experiences she was comfortable with and her reliance on the predictable, evidenced power asymmetries that were abusive. In clawing back a personhood that would eventually allow her to return from the virtual and wake up happy to enjoy the dream, she employed a strategy that was governance over power. Initially, it was essential that she harnessed her curiosity to see power for what it was, rather than being subdued by it. This required seeking out as many meanings in the face of meaninglessness that her limited capacity to reason allowed. For a traveller in the virtual, this requires tackling information deficits and constantly and critically seeing governance challenges in terms of personhood and betterment. Next, she questioned the assertion of oppressive authority at every turn. The traveller in the virtual similarly needs not to be fooled by what presents as authority that is beyond critique. From here, she had to find her voice, and such a central requirement in personhood, for young travellers, is a driving motivation behind this collection. Put together, such encounters resulted in Alice finding a stronger identity and using it to draw on a countervailing personal power that, at the very least, could be the foundation for collective resistance and retaliation if a community of Alices came together with a common purpose. In working to ensure integrated and representative governance options in a digital space, human participants should question where AI and technology sit within their communities, what moral agency can be expected of them, and how to articulate what is desired for a safe and enlivening interaction.

As an elderly American white male evangelist, who might otherwise be seen as a voice of oppressive authority, serendipitously observes:

> That brings us back to Humpty Dumpty's claim that when he uses a word, it means just what he chooses it to mean, neither more or less. When Alice protests, asking how words can mean so many different things, Humpty Dumpty pulls the power card …
>
> "The question is," said Humpty Dumpty, "which is to be master? That's all."
>
> That is the real question. Who gets to be the master of the language? Who determines, as master, what the language will be? Who determines what words must be used and how those words will be understood? …
>
> But remember that in the literary tale, Alice is presented as the one who speaks sense and Humpty Dumpty as the one who speaks nonsense. But we're now living in an age determined to turn that story upside down.[5]

Governance is about rebalancing power differentials. In achieving this aim, part of the struggle is the mastery of language. Many of the power imbalances that produce abuse grow from the titles given to stakeholders. As with our young voices, it has been common for hierarchical authority to exclude young people from governance planning and action. In part, that has been due to equating *young* with inexperienced, incapable and requiring guidance. None of these diminutives holds in the digital universe, where the younger traveller is likely to be more skilled in the technology and, as such, more capable of understanding its dangers, more experienced in forming virtual identities and communities, and, as such, a better guide when it comes to identifying risks and formulating solutions. To reposition young voices in the governance frame is not achieved by simply restructuring titles, but language is powerful in creating and challenging the meanings that give strength to an argument for repositioning governance power. In this way, our young voices have made nonsense out of popular governance wisdom and, in so doing, speak sense when they are given the room in digital space to control their virtual life experiences by contesting authority.

NOTES

1. The views expressed in this brief reflection concerning the nature of governance are those of the author and may not necessarily be shared by the other editors, contributors or dialogue partners.
2. *Alice's Adventures in Wonderland*, Chapter 12. https://www.gutenberg.org/files/11/11-h/11-h.htm#chap12
3. The discussion that follows to the end of this section is a summary of a discussion about the question posed, between Urs Gasser and Mark Findlay.
4. David Gunkel, *The Machine Question: Critical perspectives on AI, robots and ethics* (Cambridge, Mass.: MIT Press, 2012)
5. Albert Mohler, 'Alice in Wonderland, Humpty Dumpty, and the Masters who Control Language' (2019), https://albertmohler.com/2019/08/02/humpty-dumpty-alice-in-wonderland-and-the-masters-who-control-the-language/.

15. A kaleidoscope of ideas and perspectives about the Metaverse

The metaverse is a concept as expansive and dynamic as the digital landscapes it promises to encompass. Each of us brings our own experiences, assumptions, and hopes to this idea, shaped by personal backgrounds, cultural contexts, and technological fluency. This glossary captures these diverse perspectives and provides a snapshot of how we, as contributors of this project, understand and engage with the notion of the metaverse and virtual worlds.

> **What characteristics define virtual worlds and the metaverse? How do you relate to the concept of virtual worlds? Are they spaces of opportunity, creativity, escapism, or critical engagement?**

This is not a traditional glossary. Rather than offering fixed definitions, it presents a mosaic of ideas, expectations, and visions that reflect the many ways the metaverse is imagined and approached by young voices. It is a collection of personal interpretations, emerging concepts, and critical questions.

As a reader, you can use this section in different ways: as a starting point for exploring what virtual worlds mean to you, as a reference for discussions about digital environments, or as a selection of interpretive lenses to apply to this evolving space.

Our contributors reflect on what fundamentally comprises the metaverse: from its technical foundations and infrastructures, to the social experiences it enables, the identities it shapes, and the underlying market and platform dynamics that influence its direction. Through their entries, they invite you to question, imagine, and co-create what this emerging space could (and should) be.

WHAT IS THE METAVERSE (TO YOU)?

> The metaverse represents an expansive virtual world that both emulates and reimagines our ("real") physical world. It is characterized by increasing levels of immersion through virtual reality (VR) technology and, to a lesser degree, augmented reality (AR). (…) Contrary to depictions in novels such as *Snow Crash* or films like *Ready Player One*, it seems improbable that a single, monolithic Metaverse (with a

capital "M") will emerge. Rather, we already see – and will increasingly encounter – a multiplicity of metaverses, a multi-metaverse, designed for different areas of focus and tailored to specific use cases.

– David T.

Technologies in the ownership of large commercial entities will offer a basis for the metaverse. The smallest entity of such will be data. Data sources of users and companies will merge until they become inseparable, as the metaverse will acquire characteristics of a self-sustaining system. The boundaries between the metaverse and the offline world will blur, as the access to the metaverse will be established in daily activities: education, work, or doing the groceries. The easy access to the metaverse will probably be offered through mobile phone apps or browser extensions.

– Nikola S.

(…) The metaverse's essence transcends mere technology; it fundamentally comprises a radical redefinition of "place" and "value." It establishes a borderless digital domain where traditional territorial jurisdiction often dissolves into a "jurisdictional rabbit hole," with authority increasingly embedded in code or platform terms. The underlying market dynamics are equally transformative, moving beyond conventional economic models to treat personal data as a direct form of payment or a perpetually tradable asset. This reconfigures not only our understanding of property, consent, and accountability but also challenges existing regulatory oversight in a realm where digital interactions directly drive real-world value, foreshadowing a multi-trillion-dollar "avatar economy" fueled by novel concepts of digital real estate, NFTs, and cryptocurrencies.

– Somya S.

In my view, the metaverse can be defined as a new cultural logic that redefines how knowledge, experience, and the interaction between humans and usable environments are constructed. More than a purely technological product, it represents a system of hybrid thinking, where human cognitive structures and digital infrastructures – such as augmented reality, extended reality, and artificial intelligence – merge, creating combined environments in which humans act, learn, and communicate in new ways. (…) This emerging cultural logic is inspired by the interactive architectures of gaming, where space, interaction, and narrative work together to shape immersive worlds. In these worlds, experience occurs through avatars, digital projections of the self, in graphically generated environments that refer to a "digital twin" of physical reality. (…) In this perspective, the metaverse is not merely a technological interface or the sum of immersive technologies, but becomes a new epistemological and symbolic dimension that redefines the organic unity between man and machine, between natural and digital cognition. In other words, it introduces a new organization of knowledge and communication, forming a new cultural horizon where people act and think according to profoundly transformed logics. Therefore, in my opinion, it functions as a new cognitive and cultural system, reorganizing communicative and cognitive practices through synergetic and trans-media modalities.

– Ivan D.

WHAT DOES THE METAVERSE MEAN TO YOU, TO YOUR SENSE OF SELF, TO YOUR SENSE OF BELONGING? WHICH OPPORTUNITIES DO YOU SEE?

The Metaverse is not merely a virtual destination; it is an experiential landscape where identity is shaped, challenged, and sometimes reclaimed. (…) I understand the Metaverse as a space where **users don't just act; they become**. Through avatars, sensory cues, and narrative choices, users embody digital personhood, bringing with them histories, hopes, traumas, and dreams. These are not cosmetic layers. They are psychological extensions of self. This sense of embodied presence: flinching when danger approaches, feeling joy in synchrony with a digital character, reacting with real emotion to virtual rejection, reminds us that immersive experiences have a real impact. But feeling "present" is not the same as feeling safe or welcome. That is where belonging becomes critical. When design defaults, erases diverse bodies, identities, and stories, the promise of freedom becomes a performance of exclusion. And yet, there is power here, too. The Metaverse, at its best, can act as a space of identity exploration, fluidity, and creative defiance. (…) However, identity play is not neutral. It is structured by systems, tools, economics, moderation, and narrative frames that can liberate or limit. We must recognize the Metaversal Mirror: these environments reflect our social values, and if we do not actively challenge their defaults, they will simply reproduce the hierarchies of the physical world.

– Auxane B.

For me, the metaverse currently represents a fiction of imagined futures of new social constellations. It includes the overcoming of spatial boundaries for a certain population, which will consist of the users who can afford to access the metaverse. Right now, the metaverse profits off its potential to re-invent the social. However, the metaverse at the same time is based on the technological foundation offered by primarily commercial entities: platform companies. The potential of revolutionary social orders is carefully built on certain companies' desire to profit off our imaginations and personal data. This is why next to its potential through fiction, the metaverse carries with it a material basis of technology and economic networks. I thus draft the metaverse as an ambivalence between social empowerment and economic manifestations of powerful individuals.

– Nikola S.

I'm not particularly attracted by the idea that I should spend my biologically limited time inside a virtual environment. The metaverse, at least in its current form, feels like a more interactive version of *The Sims*, except this time *I'm* the one wandering around the neighborhood, dangerously close to the fireplace. Yes, there may be potential. Education, for instance – history classes that take place in ancient Rome, or biology lessons that let you walk through the chambers of the human heart. These are vivid, imaginative applications. Learning could become immersive in a way textbooks never allowed. However, these illusions may become seductive escapes from the real world – from its urgency, its problems, and its demands. Why protest the rising cost of housing if you own a gleaming villa in a semi-exotic

Jurassic jungle? Why care about climate change or war when you live in a post-apocalyptic techno-utopia where happiness is the default setting?

– Konstantinos T.

The metaverse is more than just a space of escapism. It is a rare opportunity to reimagine, or even reinvent, existing social structures to emulate a better version of our physical world, one where people thoughtfully engage with their liberty and social responsibilities. To achieve this, however, society must cultivate a clear understanding of the moral presence we have within the metaverse and the moral significance that our actions there carry, beyond the semi-fictional and gamified nature of these virtual environments.

– David T.

The Metaverse holds a peculiar opportunity for us – one rarely offered throughout the history of law. For perhaps the very first time, we are not confined to retrofitting justice systems onto existing social architectures, but are confronted with the possibility of building them from first principles. Here, legality may no longer take the form of courts, statutes, or punishments. It might instead be *felt* as friction in a user interface, as a grayed-out button, a system message, or the silent impossibility of expressing deviancy. The governance of the Metaverse is, in a word, *programmable.* And with that programmability comes a question so fundamental it feels almost naive to ask: *What should law and order look like in a world we can design from scratch?*

– Darius T.

What is virtual reality? Is it a parallel reality to our world? Or is it merely a new part of the real world powered by the technologies such as Artificial Intelligence and Blockchains created and developed within it?

– Narges K.

WHAT ARE YOUR VISIONS, EXPECTATIONS, AND CONCERNS ABOUT THE FUTURE OF VIRTUAL WORLDS AND THE METAVERSE?

Over the next decade or so, I anticipate the metaverse's trajectory becoming much clearer, though its ultimate destination remains dramatically uncertain. Technological advancements are the most crucial factor for the metaverse's success. This includes the hardware necessary to engage with the metaverse as well as its affordability on the market. Most notably this comprises headsets, motion tracking and movement devices, haptic features, and, in a distant future, potentially brain-wave or mind-control functionalities. Given current hardware limitations and the uncertain future applicability of Moore's law, software solutions (particularly advanced artificial intelligence) will be equally if not more important. (…) Public perception will also significantly shape the metaverse's success, though this will itself be heavily influenced by technological advancements.

– David T.

My vision is not for a perfect Metaverse, but for an intentional one, built with care, psychological insight, and ethical responsibility. A Metaverse that honors complexity, invites co-creation, and treats identity not as a product, but as a right. If we get it right, virtual worlds won't just reflect who we are, they'll help us imagine who we could become.

– Auxane B.

My hope is for a (multi-)metaverse that empowers individuals to shape inclusive virtual spaces democratically, ethically, and sustainably while preserving human dignity. Much like any technological evolution, the key is understanding the metaverse's technological and moral premise, without losing sight of existing human core values.

– David T.

Virtual worlds hold a huge potential of re-creating social spaces. In a world of rising inequality and conflict, the desire to flee into a separate space will grow. Nevertheless, as current forms of (social) media show, we as a society have not managed to create spaces that stand isolated from the power dynamics to which we have become accustomed. This is why I am convinced that we need to engage in some critical groundwork – to navigate the ambivalent fiction we call the metaverse.

– Nikola S.

(…) [O]ne should not get over-excited about it and disregard all legal, social, and cultural boundaries, considerations, and values it might encounter during its (metaverse) development path. While there is a strong chance that it (virtual realities) becomes a new normal, there is an equally real chance that it may be outrun or completely faded away by emerging technological newcomers. (…) [V]irtual reality and [the] metaverse still need legal scrutiny and governance while the phase of trial and error is still ongoing. However, there is no harm in benefit[ing] from its potential to model a more participatory, fair, and equitable justice system and dispute resolution mechanism, even if only temporarily, as a testing field rather than a formal legal jurisdiction.

- Narges K.

We quite literally stand at a crossroads: import the flawed logic of analog justice, or use this "reset" and deliberately architect new models of fairness, accountability, and repair. Yet even deliberate design carries inherent danger. In seeking to eliminate harm, we may be tempted to cross the threshold of eliminating agency itself. As such, every system we will embed reveals something about our deepest beliefs: how much uncertainty we are willing to tolerate, how we interpret harm, and where we locate trust. In virtual law, there are no natural constraints, only decisions. Terms like *justice*, *deviancy*, and *punishment* no longer are inherited truths of tradition but adjustable parameters for us to play with. We may never again encounter so clear a moment to transcend retribution and create systems that instead heal, educate, and evolve – But only if we *choose* to do so.

– Darius T.

The metaverse's future isn't just about technological advancement; it's fundamentally about holistic governance. I foresee not a singular, all-encompassing framework, but a dynamic, hybrid landscape. This will demand integrating diverse perspectives, from designing automated "code as law" for routine matters to engaging interdisciplinary thought on complex ethical dilemmas. My primary concern is the potential for regulatory fragmentation to undermine fundamental rights and effective enforcement, thereby creating untamed digital spaces. (...) Through collaborative, interdisciplinary efforts, we can build a future where fairness and accountability are woven into the very fabric of these virtual societies. This future demands professionals, who are not just reactive interpreters but proactive designers across all these fields, ensuring innovation flourishes under the vigilant guardianship of justice and human-centric values.

– Somya S.

Index